THE
CHINESE WAY
OF LOVE

Acknowledgements

The authors wish to acknowledge with thanks the help they have
received, either directly or indirectly, from the following:

Clarendon Press, Oxford, for permission to publish part
of C.Clementi's introduction to *Cantonese Love Songs*
Library of the University of Indiana, Indiana
Library of the University of Michigan
Metropolitan Museum of Art, New York
The Van Gulik Collection, Paris
The Wellcome Institute, London
Old Palace Museum, Peking
George C.Harrap & Co Ltd
Professor Liu Ta-Fa
Michel Beurdeley
Ralph Estling

Published by
CFW Publications Limited
130 Connaught Road Central, Hong Kong

Design:
Hon Bing-wah

ISBN: 963 7031 15 2
ISBN: 962 7031 15 1

Printed in Hong Kong

THE CHINESE WAY OF LOVE

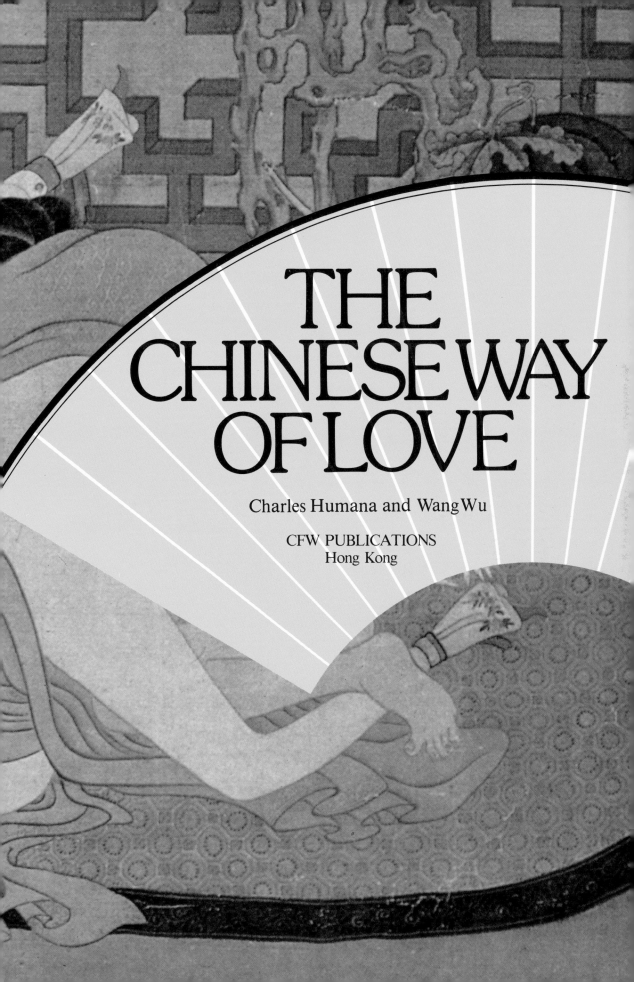

THE CHINESE WAY OF LOVE

Charles Humana and Wang Wu

CFW PUBLICATIONS
Hong Kong

Contents

Part 3

**From Fragrant Silhouettes to the Great
Leap Forward**

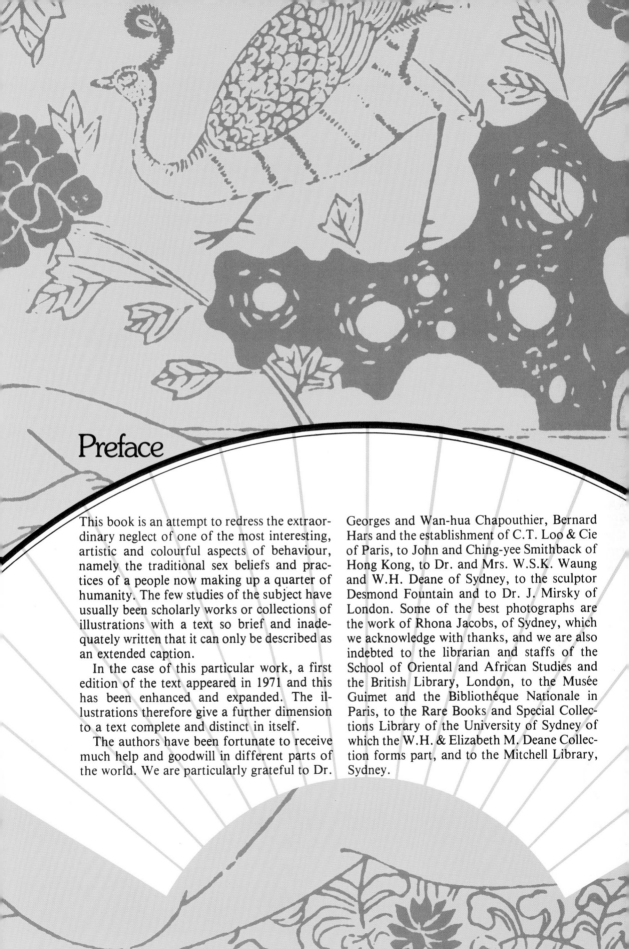

Preface

This book is an attempt to redress the extraordinary neglect of one of the most interesting, artistic and colourful aspects of behaviour, namely the traditional sex beliefs and practices of a people now making up a quarter of humanity. The few studies of the subject have usually been scholarly works or collections of illustrations with a text so brief and inadequately written that it can only be described as an extended caption.

In the case of this particular work, a first edition of the text appeared in 1971 and this has been enhanced and expanded. The illustrations therefore give a further dimension to a text complete and distinct in itself.

The authors have been fortunate to receive much help and goodwill in different parts of the world. We are particularly grateful to Dr.

Georges and Wan-hua Chapouthier, Bernard Hars and the establishment of C.T. Loo & Cie of Paris, to John and Ching-yee Smithback of Hong Kong, to Dr. and Mrs. W.S.K. Waung and W.H. Deane of Sydney, to the sculptor Desmond Fountain and to Dr. J. Mirsky of London. Some of the best photographs are the work of Rhona Jacobs, of Sydney, which we acknowledge with thanks, and we are also indebted to the librarian and staffs of the School of Oriental and African Studies and the British Library, London, to the Musée Guimet and the Bibliothéque Nationale in Paris, to the Rare Books and Special Collections Library of the University of Sydney of which the W.H. & Elizabeth M. Deane Collection forms part, and to the Mitchell Library, Sydney.

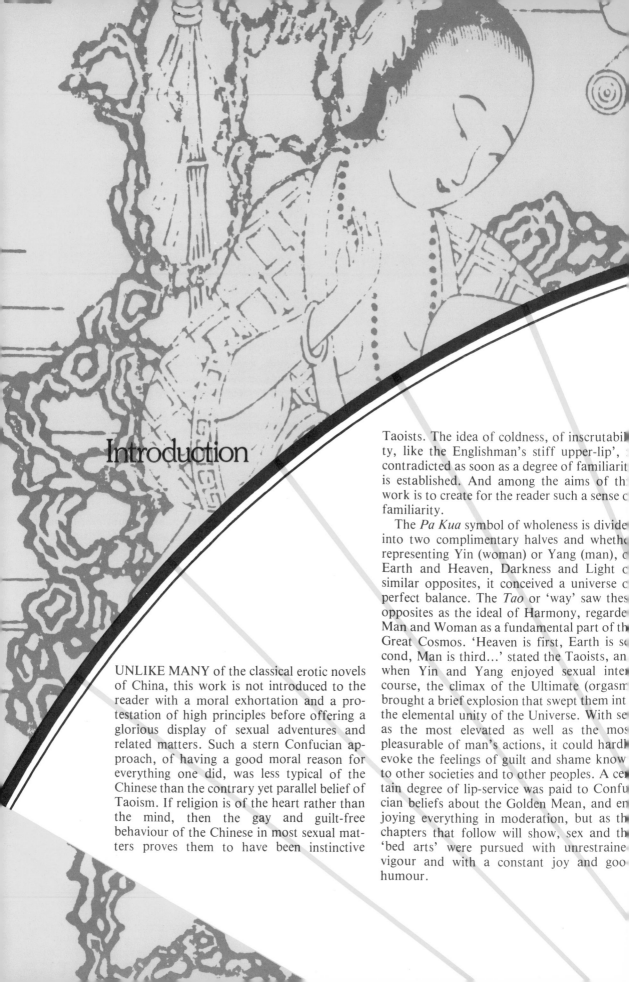

Introduction

UNLIKE MANY of the classical erotic novels of China, this work is not introduced to the reader with a moral exhortation and a protestation of high principles before offering a glorious display of sexual adventures and related matters. Such a stern Confucian approach, of having a good moral reason for everything one did, was less typical of the Chinese than the contrary yet parallel belief of Taoism. If religion is of the heart rather than the mind, then the gay and guilt-free behaviour of the Chinese in most sexual matters proves them to have been instinctive Taoists. The idea of coldness, of inscrutabil ty, like the Englishman's stiff upper-lip', contradicted as soon as a degree of familiarit is established. And among the aims of th work is to create for the reader such a sense c familiarity.

The *Pa Kua* symbol of wholeness is divide into two complimentary halves and wheth representing Yin (woman) or Yang (man), c Earth and Heaven, Darkness and Light c similar opposites, it conceived a universe c perfect balance. The *Tao* or 'way' saw thes opposites as the ideal of Harmony, regarde Man and Woman as a fundamental part of th Great Cosmos. 'Heaven is first, Earth is se cond, Man is third...' stated the Taoists, an when Yin and Yang enjoyed sexual inter course, the climax of the Ultimate (orgasm brought a brief explosion that swept them int the elemental unity of the Universe. With se as the most elevated as well as the mos pleasurable of man's actions, it could hardl evoke the feelings of guilt and shame know to other societies and to other peoples. A ce tain degree of lip-service was paid to Confu cian beliefs about the Golden Mean, and en joying everything in moderation, but as th chapters that follow will show, sex and th 'bed arts' were pursued with unrestraine vigour and with a constant joy and goo humour.

The dividing line between the factual and the fanciful in Chinese erotic novels, in the historical sex manuals and in the sociological aspects of the subject, must remain confused for a number of reasons. Some of the oldest sex handbooks are of obscure origin, or were first compiled as folklore and then suffered imaginative revision at the hands of Taoist and Buddhist monks. On the other hand the novel, apparently a work of fiction, which was regarded as an inferior art form and not subject to such a severe censorship as books claiming a higher status, could therefore deal more freely with 'forbidden' subjects. This should be borne in mind when reading the following chapters. The bizarre scenes from some of the novels were undoubtedly first-hand and perceptive accounts of domestic and bedchamber life of their various periods.

In its treatment of the sexual life of the Chinese, this work has followed a pattern of drawing on scholarly and historical sources in the first instance and then attempting to illustrate the material by turning to novels and other 'realistic' accounts. It can therefore be seen as a synthesis of the unadorned Confucian presentation of the facts and the more colorful flights of fancy of the Taoists. This has also influenced the translation of many of the extracts reproduced in the book. Where it has been necessary to keep to the original text, this has been done, but where it seems desirable to give a 'free translation', as is common practice with a language composed of ideographic symbols, interpretation rather than the exact terminology has been considered of more importance. This wish to communicate the spirit and the wider meaning has also been applied to the editing of certain material from archaic western sources.

The first section, 'The Bridge to the Bamboo Grove', offers a background of history and a 'panoramic' survey of the subject. The heart of the book, however, is the second section which, apart from the detailed study of the sex practices and customs of the Chinese, covers much that would be contained in the traditional pillow books of the bedchamber art. Whether one turns to the sex postures, however, or to a Rabelaisian extract from a Sung or Ming novel, one is enjoying an authentic glimpse of that part of the rich fabric of traditional life considered too intimate and too private for the curiosity of coarse barbarians and foreign devils.

The Chinese, as with many races and religions, saw their culture as the most advanced in the world and their country as its true and indisputable centre. Distant Europe, even in the eighteenth-century, was part of a dark periphery, beyond Africa, beyond Asia, its peoples uncivilized and predestined to servitude. As evidence of this one only has to quote the edict of Emperor Ch'ien Lung when welcoming Lord Macartney, envoy of King George III of England:

It is noted that your country lies across the oceans but that you humbly wish to acquaint yourself with Civilization and that your envoy has journeyed to this Court to kotow to the Celestial Emperor and to congratulate him on his Birthday. Such humility and respectful obedience meets with our approval …
In reply, your tribute envoy will convey to you our desire that your country over the seas will further demonstrate its loyalty to the Celestial Empire and that it will swear perpetual obedience …
Part of the 1793 Edict

A similar conviction of superiority extended to the theories and practices of their bedchamber arts. They were part of the Celestial Design and therefore to be enjoyed only by the Chinese.

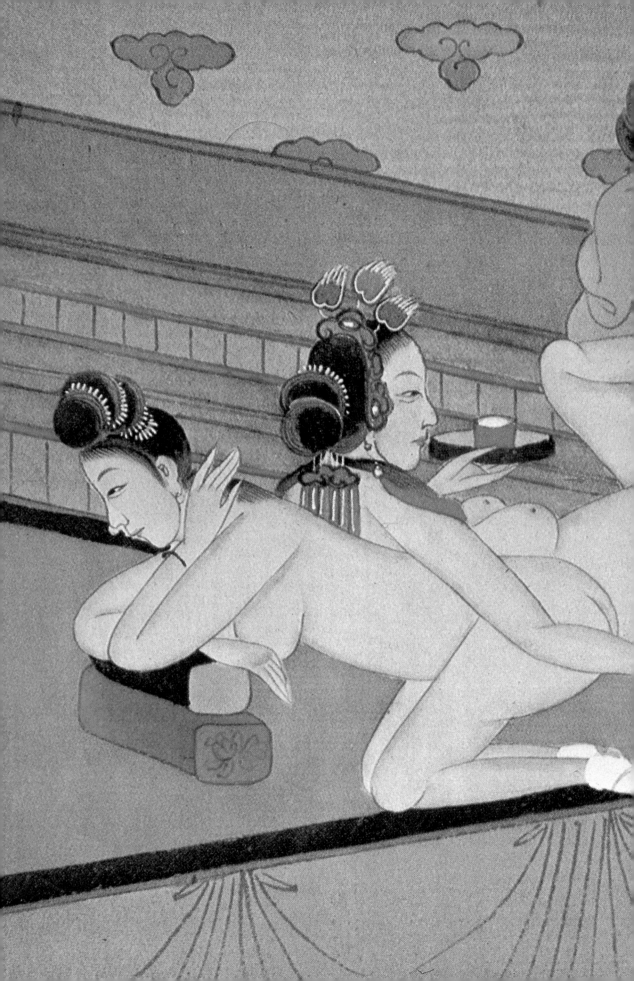

Part 1
The Bridge to The Bamboo Grove

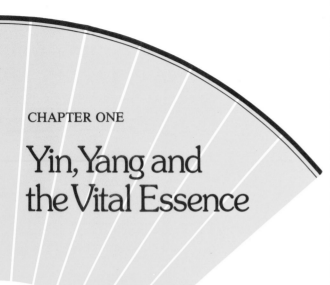

CHAPTER ONE

Yin, Yang and the Vital Essence

The clearest evidence of the continuity of Chinese sex beliefs and practices over nearly five thousand years can be seen in the unanimity of the writings of sages and scholars over that lengthy period. Three such figures will serve to illustrate this truth, Li Yü, seventeenth-century novelist and dramatist, the Most Noble Tung Hsüan Tzu, seventh-century medical authority, and the Yellow Emperor, Huang-Ti (2697-2598 B.C.), who is regarded as the father of Chinese civilisation and the author of *N'ei Ching Sü Wen,* the oldest extant treatise on sex. The opinions they shared, and which were accepted equally by the two contradictory philosophical faiths of Confucianists and Taoists, were the conviction that sexual intercourse raised men above his lowly place on earth, that at the moment of Harmony (orgasm) he and Yin transcended into an even wider union with the Cosmos, and that to assure the frequency of this happy state, he should learn as much as possible about the technique of love.

There may seem nothing remarkable in these self-evident truths but the Chinese took the positive step of adopting them as part of their way of life very much as other societies propagated a religion or a system of worship. The importance and wide acceptance of such a step may be judged from the fact that the sex manuals and writings on the subject were regarded as being worthy of mention in the Official History of the dynasties. This list, which was confined to the most distinguished of works, also included such manuals as *T'ang-Pan-Keng — Yin-Tao* (Sexual Advice from King T'ang and Pan Keng), *Yao-Shun-Yin-Tao* (The Bedchamber Books of Emperors Yao and Shun), *Hsüan Nü-Ching* (The Counsels of the Wise Maiden), and *Ch'ien-Chin-Fang* (Precious Concoctions). Although there were many faiths and religions in China, the theories and practices of sex were considered to be as basic to their heritage as were the calendar, the written characters of their language and the system of family names.

During the course of their long history, two conflicting faiths, Confucianism and Taoism, influenced the Chinese, but because of the flexible nature of the people and their society, there were few problems in reconciling and adopting contradictory teachings. Confucius and his practical and classical philosophy was an efficient instrument for ruling a country, organising society and establishing patriarchal family life. Taoism, on the other hand, was an

The master prepares to introduce the new bride to the pleasures of The Clouds and the Rain, helped by one of his other wives. The bodice — and her breasts remaining covered — indicate a young woman's modesty. 17th-century blockprint.

expression of the deep pagan romanticism of the Chinese, a protest against efficiency, of good-natured cynicism towards the notion that man governed the earth and could make nature conform to his designs. But whether the moral Confucian side was in the ascendant, or the easy-going Taoist feelings, the only difference in their approach to sex was in its degrees of importance. Was it the most significant part of existence or were matters of the mind or the spirit of more consequence? The contradiction was resolved with characteristic Chinese simplicity and wisdom. The head could follow one belief, the heart the other.

With so many traditional and spiritual beliefs related to the Yin-Yang battle, the moment of entry had great significance, as is evident from the faces of these lovers. K'ang-hsi (1662-1722). A painting on silk from the C.T. Loo collection, Paris.

In the writings of the three illustrious ancestors mentioned above, separated by four-and-a-half thousand years, and in the case of the Yellow Emperor living two thousand years before Confucius and Taoism, there is a remarkable consistency in the approach to sexual relations. This can be seen in their acceptance of the ancient beliefs of the Yin and Yang theory, of Harmony and the cosmic properties of the Vital Essence, and of the need to indulge in such relations with a certain moderation. However, it was not a moderation based on monogamy but on a household of many wives and concubines, and even a strict Confucian, obliged to nourish frequently the Yin-essence of all his womenfolk, would find that his sexual duties occupied part of most days and nights.

The father of Chinese civilisation, the Yellow Emperor or Huang-Ti, is regarded as the earliest chronicler, and perhaps the originator, of the traditional sex practices and beliefs. His *N'ei Ching Sü Wen,* inscribed on bamboo and tortoiseshell, is the oldest extant treatise on the subject, which forms part of a more extensive study of medicine and philosophy. The Yellow Emperor explained his preoccupation with sex in the following phrase: *To understand the head, investigate well the tail.* His treatise is written in the form of questions and answers, the Emperor seeking the wise counsel of his omniscient First Minister, and the quotation below shows how this investigation proceeded.

The Yellow Emperor: Today our men droop at the age of fifty yet in olden days they reached twice that age and produced the Vital Essence to the very end. Are we therefore, unknown to ourselves, disobeying the Laws of Nature?

First Minister: In olden times the people lived by the Principles of Yin and Yang; knowing Harmony because they were the two halves of the whole. Yin was the shady side of the hill, Yang the sunny side, and in the enjoyment of this wholeness they were tormented neither by restlessness nor dissatisfaction. Today the people turn to wine for intoxication, regard food as something with which to gorge themselves, are reluctant to work yet at all times are indulging in the *Clouds and the Rain.* But this only adds to their dissatisfaction because as the appetite grows it becomes more difficult to gratify, and as the rising and the retiring of the people is no longer according to the Natural Laws, their bodies are exhausted at half the hundred years.

The Yellow Emperor: You have stated well the problem. Let us begin our search for the solution by understanding the physical nature of Yin and Yang. How would you define the different Ages of Man?

First Minister: Let us first deal with Yin. When she is but seven years her teeth change, her hair grows longer and there is moisture in the vagina. At twice that age she begins to menstruate and so is able to bear children. If the Great Thoroughfare pulse is strong during intercourse, her children will be healthy. At three times seven her body is mature, its parts are eager, her hair has reached its full length and the last of her teeth have appeared. At four times seven her muscles and bones are strong and she gives birth with ease and her Sunlight Valley is at its brightest. At five times seven the pulsations of the Great Thoroughfare are less strong, her face begins to wrinkle and her hair to lose its lustre. At six times seven the pulses of the Three Regions (the chest, the stomach and the vagina) have deteriorated, wrinkles cover her whole face and her hair begins to whiten. At seven times seven menstruation has stopped, the vessel *(ch'ung)* no longer pulses and Yang receives no welcome at the Jade Gates.

The Yellow Emperor: Let us now turn to Yang.

First Minister: In the case of the boy Yang, his teeth begin to change at eight, his hair grows thicker and the first liquid pearl passes from the testes. At two times eight the emanations of Yang are copious and signal manhood. He is ready to unite with Yin in the attainment of Peace and Harmony. At three times eight his muscles and bones are hard and strong and the emanations of his testicles are powerful and frequent, and his last tooth has grown. At four times eight he is Yang of the Supreme Male Peak, his flesh is strong and the fires are constantly burning. At five times eight the testicles begin to dispel less semen, the hair begins to fall, the teeth to decay. At six times eight the powers of Yang are greatly diminished, his face shows wrinkles and his hair begins to whiten. At seven times eight his Days of the Vital Essence have passed, disease descends on him like a swarm of bees, his strength is near its end and the 'five viscera' are dry.

After this remorseless description of life, which seems to pass in a moment, the First Minister defines the Five Flavours of the Five Organs — acidity, sweetness, saltiness, bitterness and pungency. 'If acidity exceeds all others then the procreative juices will be diminished, if sweetness exceeds all others then the mind becomes depressed and in no mood for pleasure. If bitterness exceeds all others then the stomach becomes dense and the spleen

Fu Hsi, the third of the Heavenly Emperors, holding the 'Pa Kua,' the magic symbol representing the complementary halves of the Yang and Yin. Legends regard him as the originator of the symbol. 18th-century painting. By courtesy of the Wellcome Trustees.

dry, and if pungency exceeds all others then the face will appear drawn; and with Yin the female emanations will hang heavy in the air. Maintain well the Harmony of the Five Flavours.'

This preoccupation with learning the secrets of nature, and from this knowledge enjoying the fullest satisfaction in sexual relations was, in fact, a good example of how the strict Confucian side of the Chinese combined with his Taoist paganism. Once the head mastered the practical aspects of the matter, the heart could indulge to the limit its natural desires. And two thousand years after the Yellow Emperor, as is evident from the writings of the Most Noble Tung-Hsüan Tzu, this understanding of the contrary sides of man's nature, and the need to reconcile them, had become part of the traditional Chinese wisdom.

The one important development between the ancient writings on sex and those of such T'ang dynasty scholars as the Most Noble Tung was the addition of a detailed section on technique, usually defined as the *Art of the Bedchamber.* Many works which purport to relate the ancient Yellow Emperor's advice and instruction on sex techniques were, in fact, compiled by Taoist or Buddhist monks.

The sinologue, H. Maspero, author of *La Chine Antique,* suggests that the Most Noble Tung was Li Tung-Hsüan, head of the Department of Medicine in the Chinese capital in the seventh century A.D. His *Art of the Bedchamber* was divided into sixteen sections, and as an indication of its importance, it was revived at the beginning of the present century by Yeh Tê-hui (1864-1927) in his sex encyclopaedia *Shuang-mei-ching-an-ts'ung-shu.* In the introductory section of his work the Most Noble Tung wrote:

It is my belief that all things under Heaven are wondrous, but that Man is the most wondrous of all. This distinction is because of the unique nature of his sexual urge and its part in the harmony of Yin and Yang, and therefore of Heaven and Earth. If a man follows the Natural Laws, and understands them, he will nourish indefinitely his Vital Essence, prolong his life, and know gratification to the end of his days. If a man defies the Natural Laws, and abuses the Truths, his Essence will dry up before the end of his days and his life will be brief and sad.

The Rules and Methods of the Dark Maiden who advised the Yellow Emperor on Sex and Women are part of our heritage but they can hardly cover all aspects of the subject, and it has occurred to me that I should make my own humble contribution to this

This picture of Taoist freedom is not without its evidence of Taoist techniques. The peasants remember to use the bundles of bamboos to counter the steep slope. The size of the woman's unbound feet suggests wild spirits. 19th-century erotic album. By kind permission of the British Museum.

essential part of life. My purpose will be to add further details, to correct omissions and to make this a classic handbook for those seeking the fullest satisfaction.

This work will be quoted in more detail later but in this instance it serves to illustrate the continuity of Chinese sex lore. This is equally apparent in the novels and plays of Li Yü (seventeenth-century A.D.), a writer whose versatility bears comparison with William Shakespeare, and who, as the author of many erotic and pornographic works, could hardly be regarded as a classical traditionalist. In an introductory essay to a novel, he wrote:

In his brief sojourn between Heaven and Earth, man is plagued by hardship and worry, by responsibilities and the need to work. Other animals are spared all this as a condition of life, content to let nature take care of things and the world to revolve in its own way. Man's burden, however, is made tolerable by those brief moments when he again becomes an animal — that is during sexual intercourse. To those who refuse to accept this elementary truth, let them compare the lives of monks and eunuchs. The life-span of the monk is no different from that of ordinary men because though he is denied normal married life, he finds some satisfaction among the novices and the nuns. He may spend most of his days in a cell, but it is usually a space big enough for two. The eunuch, on the other hand, can neither enter the Jade Gate of the female nor Make Fire Behind the Mountain. When it is claimed by puritans that a completely chaste life enables one to reach a great age, remember those men without implements. If chastity is the answer, they should live to be a hundred. Yet what are the facts? The faces of eunuchs wrinkle at thirty, their hair turns grey and their backs stoop while they are still comparatively young. And when walking through a graveyard, who has ever seen a tablet to a eunuch who had lived his allotted span of a hundred years?

Taoist monks and sages were among the most prolific of writers on sexual matters, their rationalisation being that if the act between Yin and Yang was the wonderful moment when they transcended their miserable earthly existence, and briefly enjoyed consummation with the cosmos, then it must be both sacred and religious. The Taoists were therefore responsible for many of the colourful names and terms used for the sex act, the sex organs and other related details. The following selection illustrates the manner in which the poetic imagination regarded them.

Intercourse:
Yün-yu, the Clouds and the Rain
Fang-shih, Delight on the Couch
Wu-shan, The Mountain of Wu
Ou-yu, The Mists and Rain

The Male Organ:
Nan-ching, Male Stalk (or Root)
Yü-ching, Jade Stalk (or Stem)
Yang-feng, Male Peak
Kuei-Tou, Turtle Head
Yin-nang, Secret Pouch (testicles)

The Female Organ:
Yü-men, Jade Gate
Ch'iung-men, Coral Gate
Yü-tai, Jade Pavilion
Nü-Yin, The Secret and Feminine
Shen T'ien, Magic Field
Chieh-Shan-Chu, Pearl on the Jade
                 Step (clitoris)
Jui-t'ai, The Jewel Terrace (clitoris)
Pi-yung, Examination Hall (vagina — one
       'passes' or 'fails')
Chin-kou, Golden Gully (between the labia)

Lord Yang and Lady Yin prepare for a variation of Mule in the Springtime, one of the Thirty Heaven and Earth Postures. From a Ming dynasty print album.

The superiority and dominance of the male over the female was a traditional belief that was never questioned, though certain schools of Taoism saw Yin (woman) as an extension of the Earth-womb, and for that reason closer to the divine Life Force. The fundamental theory, stated briefly, asserted that the Earth turned to the left, Heaven to the right, and with the same inevitability, man *called* and woman *obeyed.* There was a fixed order to the Universe, of summer following spring, of things being high and low, first and last, strong and weak, and these immutable truths must apply to human relations. If, on the other hand, the Earth rose above Heaven, woman above man, or winter came before autumn, there could be little doubting that the Universe must be out of balance.

The need for Yin to accept and know her place was therefore an essential element to a happy society and the importance of correct behaviour ('*li*' — 'right thinking') for the inferior female was fully chronicled. The *Nü-chieh* (The Ideal Woman), an early Confucian work, began by asserting that Yin's subservience should be established at birth and that the female child, as a mark of the parents' contrition, should immediately be hidden under the bed. They should then fast for three days and offer prayers to the ancestral gods. The female child's early education and training should be devoted to fitting her to serve her menfolk, and for this modesty and obedience were the highest virtues. She should walk backwards from any room in which men were present, and the thought of complaining should never be allowed to pass through her head. The secret of acquiring such humility was to regard herself as always being wrong in any dispute, and to feel herself lucky if she avoided severe punishment.

If she lived up to this ideal, her reward would be to gain the respect of the family, to feel her reputation to be unblemished, to live without fear of insult, quarrels or degradation. And when she married, her virtuous character would make her the ideal partner of the Yin-Yang Harmony.

The *Nü-chieh* then stated:

The sexual union depends on Yang's ability to dominate and guide, and Yin's willingness to follow and obey. Man is wonderful for his strength, woman for her simple submissiveness. The truth of this is revealed in the old proverb: 'With the birth of a son the father prays he will have the spirit of a lion yet fears he will be like a mouse. With the birth of a daughter, he wishes her to be a mouse yet fears she will turn into a tigress.'

In the Bedchamber the woman must discourage excess by her restraint, not by opposing Yang but by transforming her own wish for '*fire inside the Jade Pavilion*' (orgasm) into transcendental thoughts. Excess of *Clouds and Rain* will induce physical deterioration, and this will lead to moral depravity and finally to the use of lewd words. Such a state can only result in the calamity of wifely disrespect for her master.

Further, this unhappy state will end in beatings for the wife, in screaming and anger, perhaps in the presence of others. How, then, can Harmony be restored? A woman must be chaste and respectful, choose her words carefully, never show distress, avoid laughter or jestful behaviour, refrain from peeping from windows and mixing with crowds. If she is at all times as discreet as a shadow or an echo, who can find fault with such a woman?

A further virtue of the Ideal Woman was her acceptance of other wives and concubines. 'She must bow to such other women as her master may take, but she herself can only marry once. A Husband is Heaven itself. There is only one Heaven. To seek more than one Heaven in this mortal life is to invite disaster.'

Confucius said: 'A woman should never be heard of outside her own home'. And in return for such self-effacement and sacrifice, the husband was expected to make his own contribution to marital accord. The *Li-chi* (The Book of Rites) stated: 'Neglect of one's wives and concubines is an offence against the Harmony of Heaven, Earth and Man. Until the age of fifty, a husband should enter the Pleasure Pavilion of his wives once every third day, of his concubines once every fifth day, of other maids of the household according to his wish. The principal wife may remain in the bed-chamber during intercourse with a lower concubine, and after the act she can order her back to her quarters and remain for the rest of the night with her husband. Thus her position is accorded respect.'

Although this may seem an inhuman document, and any society or relationship based on it a formal and joyless affair, people's feelings easily, and even gaily, survived such strictures. Women, like men, had desires and dreams of their own, and they also had a Taoist side to their nature. Whatever the discretions demanded by their status of inferiority, or the lip-service that had to be paid to 'right-thinking', the Chinese woman could hardly suppress her true emotions all the time. And perhaps, because of the irksome social conventions, when she was free to forget her inhibitions, her passions and her imagination were more than usually overwhelming. The following is an excerpt from one of Li Yü's erotic novels (*Chueh-hou-ch'an*), and the character of Madam True Heart should be regarded as that of the Taoist inside the skin of the humble and formal 'Ideal woman' of the *Nü-chieh:*

Soon after her marriage, True Heart's father, tiring of the quarrelsome ways of her young husband, had driven the impossible man from the home. For True Heart, however, her difficult husband had had certain redeeming qualities that her father would hardly appreciate, but being a dutiful daughter she had kept this information to herself. After five nights of sleeping alone, she had wondered why she spent so many hours twisting restlessly, then realised that like an addicted drinker or smoker, she had suddenly been deprived of what she needed most of all.

True Heart was no longer a single woman, and now this separation had lasted six months, the situation was becoming quite unbearable. In fact, the memory of the few weeks of her real married life, by being so brief that she could hardly believe they had happened, served only to agitate her imagination even more. A husband who did not spend his nights with his wife was as good as dead; and that was how she was coming to see it. Her first diversion, therefore — and she was driven to this after a few weeks — was to find his collection of erotic pictures and pillow albums, and study them for hour after hour. Instead of soothing her, however, they only further inflamed her desires.

She had then tried to distract herself by reading the books of her childhood, works of an uplifting and educational character such as the *Lieh Nü Chuan* (Stories of Noble and Illustrious Heroines) or the *Nü Hsiao Ching* (A Young Lady's Guide to Filial Piety). Soon, however, they gave way to the pornographic volumes her husband had read to her in bed, both before and after enjoying the delights of the *Clouds and the Rain*. Although they had disgusted her at the time, she now saw them in a very different way. She simply could not put them down. Her favourites were *Ch'i Po-tzu-Chuan* (Stories of Sex-crazed Women), *Hsiu-T'a Yeh Shih* (Memories of the Embroidered Couch) and *Jü-yi Ch'un Chuan* (Biography of a Man-about-town). These books were also illustrated, and in a way which not only stimulated her senses but had her comparing the equipment of the heroes with that of her dear, absent husband.

Over and over again she found herself studying the vivid pictures of male implements, reading of their dimensions and following every thrust of their continuous bedchamber battles. They were invariably described as of 'incredible length', 'bigger than a sea-cucumber' or 'too thick to be circled by a lady's fingers'. Its hardness when excited was at least that of an iron post, the strength of the erection able to support a bushel of wheat when hung from the end of it, its performance never less than a thousand thrusts without pause.

At first True Heart decided that all this was exaggerated for the purpose of the story, but as the weeks of frustration had turned to months, she was

The Jade Stem awaits the Flower Heart. K'ang-hsi (1662-1722). A painting on silk from the C.T. Loo collection, Paris.

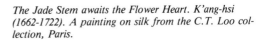

prepared to believe every word she read. In this way she began comparing her husband's equipment with that of the Great Prince Wang and the bandit leader Tiger-dragon Chiang. To the best of her memory her beloved's had been about four inches long, a couple of fingers thick, and he had never managed more than two hundred thrusts before experiencing the Ultimate. What should she believe?

Her answer did not really seem absurd. If there were millions of men in the world, and she had known only one, how could she compare her knowledge of such things with the authors of such stories? For all she knew it might be perfectly normal for a man's erection to be able to support a bushel of wheat, to thrust a thousand times without pause, to be at least twice the length of her husband's. Yet there was only one way of finding out, to enlarge her own experience on the matter. Yes, an absent husband should be regarded as a dead one, particularly since her father showed no sign of relenting and letting him return — so what was a young woman to do? To transform this lonely and despairing bedchamber required only one thing, and even if her husband's equipment hardly compared with that of Tiger-dragon Chiang, he would certainly receive the most passionate welcome any woman could give. But clearly he was not to be allowed back.

Old Chinese Proverb:
A wife can never be so desirable as a concubine,
a concubine never so exciting as an illicit love
    affair,
an illicit love affair never so maddening as the
    inaccessible woman.

The schematic symbol of Yin and Yang is a circle divided into two equal parts by a curving line. One side is the dark or female half, the other the light or male half. A study of the Chinese and their sex practices suggests, however, that the two principals of the act itself are hardly more than the actors in a play written and produced by a great ancestral god. If one had to contain within a circle the composite parts of the totality of the sexual experience of the Chinese, one would have to add two other elements. These would be the ancient theories and beliefs which influenced the relations of Yin and Yang until modern times, and the significant contribution of the art of the bedchamber which, to vulgarise the Sui dynasty writer, Hsü T'ai-shan, was 'to help men and women to do it well — and often'.

The remaining quarter of the composite circle, which needs to be mentioned in the brief survey of this introductory chapter, is therefore the important element of knowledge and expertise. The mystical significance given to the sex organs, as well as to the act itself, also contributed to the seriousness with which the art and technique of love was approached. The most beautiful piece of rough jade, to anyone but a skilled craftsman, would forever remain a lump of rock, and not even the right tools would make any difference if the person had no knowledge of their use. To learn the art of the bedchamber was therefore not only a means of increasing one's pleasure, it was a duty of almost religious significance to one's heritage.

The Confucianists and the Taoists were again in agreement on this. Yin and Yang must strive for Harmony, nourish each other with their vital essences, appreciate the cosmic nature of the act and therefore, by their proficiency, be worthy of it. As usual, however, these rival faiths adopted different poses and a different language in their approach to the art of the bedchamber. For the Confucianists it was part ritual, part discipline, and subject to the rules and regulations of the Master's teachings. For the Taoists it was a romantic, joyful and overwhelming moment of returning to the animal innocence of a lost and natural freedom.

The Most Noble Tung Hsüan Tzu's *Art of the Bedchamber* is an example of the formal Confucian presentation of a sex manual. But the deeper content and spirit of the text is essentially Taoist. 'This book will last for Ten Thousand generations because it concerns high and low alike, emperors and common people', claimed the Most Noble Tung. 'All men must know of the diverse ways of being with women, the ways of lying or sitting on top, of choosing to go behind or in front, of lying side by side, of thrusting deep or thrusting shallow. They must know the Principles of Sexual Harmony and the Doctrine of the Five Ways, and that these will decree whether they live happily or perish miserably.'

The elements of the two major faiths merge and complement each other throughout this treatise. The Confucian could relate it to the Golden Mean, consult it when calling for one of his wives or concubines, and find the ritualistic aspects compatible with a life governed by the Book of Rites (*Li-chi*). The Confucian classic stated: 'These beliefs are greatly dependent on a clear understanding of the roles of man and woman. The house should be divided into two, the inside area and the outside. The men should live in the outer apartments, the women in the inner, and all entrances to the women should be guarded by eunuchs. Men and women should not bathe

together, nor should the wife use the husband's clothes-rack nor place her possessions in the same boxes.' The aim of such severity, however, was to protect family life, which was a central tenet of Confucian faith, and provided the Most Noble Tung's guidance was diligently practiced with the women of the family, Taoist sexual permissiveness was allowed to prevail in the bedchamber.

The following is a selection from the text of the Most Noble Tung's teachings:

In the battle between Yin and Yang, Harmony is achieved when Man is double the age of Woman. When the woman is twice the age of the man, he will suffer during copulation. The following is a table of the most auspicious conditions for such intercourse:

In spring the head must point to the East, in summer to the South, in autumn to the West, in winter to the North.

The odd numbers of calendar dates, particularly the mornings, are beneficial. The even dates, particularly afternoons, can be harmful.

For effecting penetration, the following methods are recommended:

1. Plunge down on the Jade Threshold then use a sawing motion as if forcing open an oyster to obtain the pearl.

2. Thrust with an upward movement against the Golden Valley, splitting the rock to get at the precious stone inside.

3. Use the Yang Peak as a pestle, grinding into the mortar.

4. Move the Yang Peak slowly and steadily, as if refining one of the Five Elements.

5. Regard the Male Thruster as a plough in autumn, digging and turning over the soil, and move through the Precious Field towards the Far Valley.

6. When Yin is already fierce, the bodies should clash together like great rocks battering each other until they mix and bury one in the other.

For movement *after* penetration, the following methods are recommended:

1. Swing the Jade Thrusting Root to left and right as if a charging warrior were riding through the ranks of the enemy.

2. Make it resemble a horse leaping over a stream, first up, then down, then up again.

3. Float and sink in the same movement, like a duck on the ripples of a lake.

4. Peck like a sparrow with rice seeds, now deep, now shallow.

5. Plunge like a boulder into the sea, reaching the bottom.

6. A slow movement like a snake entering its hole to hibernate.

7. A swift movement like a frightened rat chased into its hole.

8. An eagle hovering before swooping on a rabbit.

9. Like a big sail in a gusty wind, sweeping along then pausing.

Once the Vermilion Door has given a moist welcome to the Jade Stem, the primary male fluid will add to that present in the upper stretches of the Far Field. This will help Yang to slant to the left and to the right, to move in a circular motion and to attack deep and shallow. The cries of Yin begging for her life should be ignored. A pause should be made periodically and a cloth used to wipe both his and the woman's organs, and if he instantly returns to the Upper Chamber he will know the pleasure of a huge boulder rolling into and blocking the bed of a river. After twenty-one such encounters desire will be satisfied and harmonised.

Most Noble Tung Hsüan Tzu's advice to men was not totally selfish. He advised them to hold the semen (tsing) until the woman was about to Burst the Cloud. If she was in advance of him, he should revert to shallow thrusts or play lightly, as if on the strings of a lute. If he was the more advanced, he should move the tongue round his own mouth, breathe through distended nostrils, raise the head and stiffen the shoulders. By perfecting such techniques he could be assured of bursting the Clouds only two or three times in every ten battles.

For anxious male lovers, Tung suggested that swift penetration had its advantages. *'In this way the Hundred Anxieties are scattered by the wind rather than forgotten one by one.'* He should strike immediately for the Upper Chamber, turning to both right and left, creating confusion by quick changes of movement so that the woman lost her sense of being while he remained dominant. Domination during love, however, was not enough. Withdrawal had to take place after the Cloudburst but before the Male Peak had gone limp. *'To retire from the field of battle in a state of miserable detumescence suggests that the Yin spirit has vanquished the Yang spirit.'*

Such advice on the art of the bedchamber was not confined to serious texts, and when it appeared in novels, which was a common and permissible practice, it was offered in the less formal manner of Taoism. The traditional Chinese respect for the teacher and the person of wisdom had to be acknowledged but provided the fictional characters acted out their roles in the approved way, the details of their colourful sexual behaviour were accepted as part of life. For example, in one of Li Yü's stories of the Ming period (1368-1644), the middle-aged prostitute is clearly derived from the mythical females of early history who knew all the mysteries of sex and who were consulted by none other than the great Yellow Emperor himself. Fairy Koo, like the Emperor's 'Plain Girl' or 'Forthright Female', sees herself as a teacher as well as a good Taoist woman, a cultivator of the Yin-Yang harmony as well as a possessor of *nü-tê* (the bewitching power of woman).

How Madam Fairy Koo Received Her Name

Madam Koo or Fairy Koo or Fairy Maid Koo was famous for three very special love techniques, and men travelled from the furthest districts of the land to experience them. And when they returned to their homes, their wives and concubines were quickly taught what they had learnt.

But what had the men learnt? They could hardly have fallen in love with the great woman's beauty because even in her youth she had been regarded as plain. She was also without the usual talents of a famous courtesan, neither playing musical instruments nor singing sweetly nor practising the social

An example of Confucian filial piety. The daughter feeds her father before her child. Children were breast-fed to a relatively late age. 19th-century ivory. By courtesy of the Wellcome Trustees.

23

Matchbox-size erotic ivories were carried as amulets to increase male virility. They could be concealed in pockets and bags. The idea of females praying to that which was imagined to give them most happiness was a favourite belief and stimulant of those seeking more yang power. 19th-century. Courtesy of the Mitchell Library, Sydney.

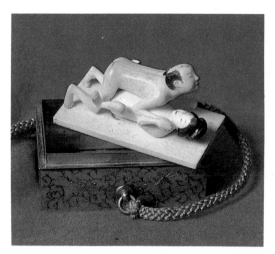

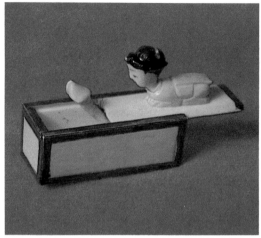

graces. Even though she was nearly fifty, however, her clientele were as eager as ever for her favours, wealthy landowners, mandarins, merchants and even princes continuing to place her above all others.

One may call her three special techniques her particular magic, or simply expertise, but they were made even more effective by her subtle understanding of every man who visited her, even when she had never before made his acquaintance. Her Number One technique she called 'Lowering the Recreation Chamber to greet the advancing Ambassador'. Her Number Two secret posture she styled 'Raising the Recreation Chamber to climb up to the Ambassador'. Her Number Three technique was related to the nourishing of the client's Yang-essence so that he never tired.

As we have said, Madam Koo understood men. The first thing she suggested to those who were a little past their youth was that they must be very tired from dealing with the important affairs of their lives, and that they should lie down and relax. She would then offer him special potions, not so much to arouse him as to increase his good humour, and at this point she would introduce her hand to his Jade Stem. When this showed signs of responding to her touch, she would sit astride the lower part of his body and welcome him to the Recreation Chamber with a minimum of preliminaries.

Once she was happy that the *turtle-head* was unlikely to slip out, she began to move her buttocks in a circular motion which she called 'Grinding the Corn.' She had given this position the name because so many men had declared that they felt they were being ground by a millstone. But she was too experienced to continue grinding away without variation, and

she would frequently spring up so that the *turtle-head* momentarily hung underneath her like an animal in the claws of a soaring eagle. Madam Koo, however, was so expert that not even the smallest instrument slipped from her grasp.

The strange thing about this grinding and bouncing technique was that instead of the participants tiring, they became livelier than ever. She seemed to have such an abundance of energy that this was as much a source of excitement as was the sex passion itself. When the moment of the *bursting of the clouds* came, it was also to allow them to proceed to her Number Two position.

For this, Madam Koo assumed the lower position but this must not be taken to mean that she left the initiative to her partner. She had very firm ideas about the desirability of what she called 'maximum participation.' When the woman was below, for instance, she must match him movement for movement. When he thrust down with the intention of spearing her to the bed, she would lift herself quickly yet gently to turn the fierce blow into a pleasantly cushioned collision. Or she would draw away in a weaving movement, which came from her skill in *Tai Chi* boxing, so that there would be a sensation of nothingness even though their organs were firmly together. This added to the man's excitement, which reminded him of a chase in a dream, and helped to prolong the enjoyable battle. When her friends told Madam Koo that she really went to too much trouble with her clients, she replied that their alternative would be no different from having available a wooden dummy with a hole between its legs, and pushing it into bed with the man.

Her Number Three technique, that of constantly nourishing each other's essences so that they never tired, had been perfected from her readings of the ancient manuals. When Yin and Yang enjoyed the orgasm of the Ultimate, she had been given to understand, too much of the vital juices flowed to waste. And this was what made a couple a little more tired after every encounter of the *Clouds and the Rain*. To be sure that every drop of their juices would flow into each other, and so nourish them for the next 'battle,' Madam Koo, at the crucial moment of the *bursting of the clouds* had learnt to seize the *turtle-head* and aim it with 'bull's-eye' accuracy at the 'fountain-spring,' of her Upper Chamber. She would then urge the man in her arms to keep completely still or to reduce his movements to a minimum. In this way the Yang-essence that throbbed from his 'little slit,' and her own Yin-essence, flowed past each other as they exchanged their respective vital fluids.

This technique was based on the Taoist principle of the 'return of the semen,' which prolonged both life and pleasure, and had been suggested to Madam Koo at the tender age of sixteen. The gentleman had been an itinerant poet who had never visited her again, but his theory had been perfected to such a degree that she had a distinct bodily sensation of rejuvenation whenever the spurting essences were exactly in line. And it was a fact that on the morning after a night spent in her company, the man would wake up refreshed and glowing in body and mind. This wonderful feeling invariably made them ask what could have caused such a miracle when such a night usually left them exhausted. Madam Koo's reply was always the same. She told them that in their sleep they had been visited by a fairy. To which they flatteringly replied that they had in fact spent the whole night with one. And in this way did she earn her title Madam Fairy Koo.

The position adopted by Madam Koo, which she called 'Grinding the Corn.' From Yanwo 5, in the Mitchell Library, Sydney.

CHAPTER TWO

Dragon Emperors and Queens

Noble Prince of Hai-nan
Seeking to extend his years
Mixes the Secret Elixir
With a jade spoon in a golden bowl.
He studies the Book of Wisdom
Masters his breathing
Chooses the correct diet
At last feels his Vital Essence stir.
He calls for his Most Precious
And soon is at the Jade Gate
She whispers loving words
But the years once more defeat him.

Pao Chao (Fifth Century A.D.)

Before The First Emperor of the Ch'in dynasty in 221 B.C. conquered the feudal states and formed the Celestial Empire, the origins of this civilisation were divided into six separate kingdoms. The Celestial Court itself was therefore the successor to six courts with their own traditions, customs, history and rulers. In giving a brief account of the lives of some of the more colourful emperors and kings, queens and concubines, only those rulers who lived after the unification of the states can rightfully claim to have occupied the Dragon Throne. Whether enjoying the status of king or emperor, however, court life was conducted with the magnificent extravagance of absolute rulers who expected total loyalty and obedience from their subjects.

The Lord of the Universe, one of the titles accorded the Celestial Emperor, ruled an area that stretched from Korea to Burma and Tibet, and an idea of the continuity of the dynasties may be gained from the fact that the Han dynasty, which effectively consolidated the Empire, lasted over four hundred years. But whether the dynasties survived for a long period or not, whether the court followed the beliefs of Confucius, Lao-Tze or Buddha, whether the rulers were benevolent or tyrannical, or indeed male or female, the sexual life of the occupant of the Dragon Throne was of paramount importance. Succeeding dynasties accepted that adherence to the principles of Yin and Yang was part of the totality of Universal Harmony. With sexual union man and woman came together as Heaven and Earth while the Emperor and his consorts were regarded as the highest expression of such a union.

The Dragon Ruler had therefore to become a symbol of potency to his people and he was expected to have a superhuman measure of *ch'i,* that is Life Force or Vital Essence. *Ch'i,* however, needed a constant flow of nourishment from the female Yin-essence, and for this the ruler maintained a large establishment of queens and concubines. In the case of the Yellow Emperor, legend claims that he had three thousand concubines and enjoyed Regal Coitus with twelve hundred of them during the course of every 'ten full moons.'

With so much importance, both social and religious, given to the sex act, particularly since the harmony of the whole of society was in-

Two of the Heavenly Emperors of the Golden Age of prehistory, Shen Nung and Huang-Ti (the Yellow Emperor). Carved ivory. By courtesy of the Wellcome Trustees.

creased by their ruler's sexual fulfilment, it was not surprising that this aspect of court life was not confined to the Royal Bedchamber. The palace, or indeed courts with many palaces, was the setting for orgies and sex carnivals, excesses and strange practices, which could usually be justified by their contribution to the total Yin-Yang harmony generated by the community.

The Emperor Hui-ti (second century B.C.), for example, ordered the palace eunuchs and the palace boys to make their contribution. They were dressed in women's robes, given jewellery and peacock feathers, had their faces powdered and rouged, and were turned over to the Palace Guard. The Emperor also decided that too many of his subjects were not participating in sex, and appointed special officials (*mei-shih*) to draw up a register of unattached men over the age of thirty, and women over twenty who were not married or part of a

harem. The names on the register were then given until the following spring to marry or consummate a union with one of the opposite sex. The punishment for defaulters was a hundred strokes of the lash, one of the rare instances where the sexes were treated equally, but it is recorded that even the most inhibited preferred an enforced introduction to the bedchamber to a flogging in the market square.

A thousand years earlier, before the establishment of the Empire, the life of a Yin dynasty king, Chou-hsin (1154-1122 B.C.), serves to illustrate the style of court life in the feudal states, and the precedent it set for later rulers. He is described by Ssu-ma Ts'ien, in *Tales from Early History,* as a man 'built like a bull yet with the lithe strength of a tiger.' Chou-hsin kept himself fit by a strenuous programme of exercises and combat which included contests with wild animals in a specially-built arena, and jousting with five or six of his

Love-on-the-Move, over a corrugated surface, was not only for Emperors such as Yang-Ti. His subjects, as this illustration from the 17th-century novel Su Wo P'ien *indicates, also favoured such love variations.*

knights at once. He also perfected certain techniques of Chinese and oriental boxing and wrestling, and could smash rocks and timber with his bare fists.

His manly feats, however, were not confined to physical combat, and his palace establishment included: I queen, 3 consorts, 9 second rank wives, 27 third rank wives, 81 concubines. Three thousand palace maids provided a permanent reserve for junketing, festivals and displays of exhibitionism. He would assemble his court to watch his sex feats in the same arena as he fought wild animals, and one of his exploits was to march round it with a naked woman supported on his erect member. In one hand he held a roast leg of venison, in the other a two-litre bronze vessel of wine, and as he ate

A Mongol invader with his prize. But his expression suggests that he is losing the Flowery Battle to the Chinese Yin. *Late 18th-century. Courtesy of the Library of Indiana, Indiana.*

and drank he urged the concubine, whose legs were round his waist, to raise and lower herself to complete his satisfaction.

After some years Chou-hsin became impotent, and not believing himself subject to normal human frailties, blamed his medical adviser, Fang-nei-pu. Fang had persuaded his master to live by the precept of the Yellow Emperor, which was 'to copulate each night with ten different women without losing the Vital Essence,' and this advice was also held to be responsible for the king's failure to father sons. Fang was decapitated, all women below the rank of consort were sent back to their families, and a fresh establishment built up. And the special court matrons (*t'ung kuan*) who recorded every instance of Regal Coitus as

a way of checking the legitimacy of any children, had their red writing brushes destroyed and replaced with new ones.

It was at the court of Chou-hsin that the role of the *t'ung kuan* was first regulated, duties that were later carried out by palace eunuchs. The matrons had the responsibility for arranging the emperor's sexual programme, choosing the girls for the night and occupying a special chair in the royal bedchamber to be sure that congress was actually completed. Regal Coitus was recorded with special calligraphy brushes, which in later periods created a genre of erotic literature known as 'Stories written with the Red Brush,' and the palace matron also enforced a strict individual timetable. The higher consorts were allowed to remain with the emperor so long as he wished, the concubines had to retire before the light of dawn, the lowly palace maids were sent away immediately after congress. Those who pleased the emperor were given a silver ring, and when they actually conceived, this was exchanged for a gold one.

No female, however, qualified for a gold ring from Chou-hsin, at least not for producing a male heir, and he exerted himself even more furiously against the wild beasts assembled in the arena and his knights lined up to suffer the strength of his blows. At this point in his life a girl 'more beautiful than peony and lotus' was introduced to his harem. She was called T'a Ki (Heavenly Beauty), and such were her special loveliness and talents that she succeeded in bringing to an end the Emperor's period of impotency. It is recorded that on her first night with Chou-hsin, her behaviour was so bold and wild that he could not believe her to be a virgin. It was only when the palace matron held a lamp over them, and blood was observed on his organ and on the silk sheet, that he was convinced of her purity.

T'a Ki quickly became Chou-hsin's favourite, being promoted to consort and causing him to neglect his other wives and maidens. Her hold over him, and her tireless response to the demands of the dragon-lover, although pleasing to the ruler, soon caused her to be regarded by the courtiers as a Fox Woman, the title given to nymphomaniacs and those believed to be the reincarnation of wicked spirits. The first of the many revolts that followed started among the neglected women of the harem, ten of them being flogged to death as an example to the others, but the reason for the concubines' fury was that they regarded a Fox Woman as unfair competition.

The basis of this early superstition is described in the *Huen-chung-ki,* which asserts: 'When a fox is five times ten years old it transforms itself into a lovely girl; at ten times ten it has become a beautiful woman and her body is wild with the spirit of *shen* (superhuman desire). Such women will know everything for a hundred miles, choosing their men from an instinctive knowledge of their weakness. And when a fox reaches the age of ten times ten times ten years it will be allowed through the Celestial Gates and will become a Celestial Fox because its *shen* can only be satisfied by the Dragon Gods and the Celestial Spirits.'

The fox is associated with other ancient rulers, and though not always reincarnated as a concubine, is invariably seen as an example of carnal wickedness. One story tells of King Ku of Wu who, while on a hunting expedition, heard the wind reading a list of women's names and was convinced he was eavesdropping on the Fox World. He despatched attendants to search the hillside and was soon called by one of them to the remains of an ancient tomb. He ordered his men to open it, and by the light that suddenly exposed the interior saw a 'hoary' fox sitting among the bones and reading from a scroll. The hounds were sent into the tomb to kill the fox but before they had reached it, it had added another name to those it was reciting. When the 'hoary' fox had been torn to pieces, the scroll was handed to the King. He found it to be a list of the hundred most lewd women in history, and added to it was a name circled in red, to denote a special entry. It was the name of his favourite consort.

Whether T'a Ki, Chou-hsin's favourite, was unjustly accused or not of being a Fox Woman, she soon proved too demanding even for her redoubtable husband. His virility, which had been restored by her, began to trouble him again, but before he had been driven to find scapegoats for his failure, she had persuaded him to spend vast sums of money on new diversions. Apart from orgies of unprecedented splendour, she helped create The Wine Lake and The Meat Forest. The lake was two hundred yards in diameter and filled with a most intoxicating liquor, and the forest was an area with joints of roast meat suspended from every branch, and the purpose of this pleasure garden was to restore a pagan simplicity to the orgies. In the company of three thousand naked Palace Guards and a similar number of maidens, the Dragon Ruler and his consort enjoyed days and nights in the magical surroundings, simply raising a hand to the trees or scooping wine from the lake when they needed sustenance.

Such extravagances, however, meant higher taxes and more oppressive land charges for the people, and a number of war lords inspired a revolt against Chou-hsin. It was easily suppressed and the leaders were captured and sentenced to be tortured then beheaded. T'a Ki again showed her inventiveness by devising a torture that was frequently used by later emperors. The victims were placed inside a copper cylinder ten feet long, the outside of which had been coated with fat. The cylinder was then hung horizontally over a long pit containing a blazing fire. When the cylinder became unbearably hot, the victim had the choice of being roasted inside or of jumping into the flames. They usually chose the latter.

In Ssu-ma Ts'ien's records of the life of Chou-hsin he also lists a number of aphrodisiacs favoured by the dragon-lover. They were:

1. *Three-Day Glory.* Red cock (soya), ox-penis (*niu-pien*), fresh root-ginseng and dried human placenta.
2. *Celestial Thunder.* Tongues of a hundred peacocks (*fung-huang* — fiery fowl), spiced with chillis from the Western Provinces and flavoured with the sperm of pubescent boys.
3. *Hunting Lion.* Long-simmered bears' paws flavoured with ground rhinoceros horn (*shi-ngiu-chiao*) and distilled urine (sex unspecified).

But neither the delights of his pleasure garden, nor the inspiration of T'a Ki or constant draughts of Three-Day Glory were enjoyed for long because at the age of thirty-two Chou-hsin was finally overthrown and beheaded.

The grand style of living of the early kings could not, however, be compared with the more ambitious of the later emperors, who also had had their superhuman representatives. The First Emperor of the unified country, who built the Great Wall in the third century B.C., a twenty-five foot high stone serpent that stretched nearly two thousand miles across north China, and who incorporated into his own harem the womenfolk of the six conquered feudal kingdoms, was renowned for his great plans and appetite, but even he seemed a modest ruler compared with the most ambitious occupants of the Dragon Throne.

One such ruler was the Sui emperor, Yang-Ti (A.D. 581-618). His rise to power gave some indication of the ruthlessness he was later to display. He killed his father, then his brothers, and made sure of his right to the throne by eliminating most of his remaining close relatives. Once his power was absolute, however, his frenzied energies turned to rather more constructive projects.

He began with the idea of building the greatest palace on earth, for which he conscripted two million labourers of both sexes. The finest marbles, of an infinite variety of shades, decorated the exterior, and it was furnished 'with a lavishness that taxed even the resources and riches of the most prosperous Empire in the universe.' The Dragon Palace was set in a walled park that covered a hundred square miles, in the centre of which was an artificial lake five *li* (two miles) wide. On the banks of the lake sixteen palaces were built for the concubines and the palace maids, and Yang-Ti's later taste for making love while afloat on water certainly began with moonlight excursions from the steps of these palaces. He took a special interest in defying the ravages of nature and the changing seasons, and an army of gardeners was employed to replace the falling leaves of trees and the withering petals of flowers with replacements of identical colours in satin and soft paper. The same attention was given to the lotus flowers blooming on the lake, so that they remained in full colour summer and winter.

On his outings through the palace grounds, whether riding on a horse or being carried in a sedan chair, Yang-Ti was followed by an entourage of a thousand palace maids. As he was subject to sudden and uncontrollable attacks of sexual desire, small pavilions surrounded by a spiked fence were scattered at two-*li* intervals. When he withdrew, in the company of the chosen girls, into one of the pavilions, the others assembled outside and sang and played the Emperor's favourite tunes. A painting of the period shows Yang-Ti, in the company of three girls, indulging in Regal Coitus in one of these pavilions. He is standing at the foot of a high couch on which lies a naked girl, her legs held high and apart by two other maids at either side of the Emperor. This requires only one of their hands, however. The maids' other hands are raising the loose robes of the Emperor and guiding his *Jade Stem* into the *Pleasure Chamber*.

When the palace suited to a Celestial Emperor had been completed, Yang-Ti then reinforced his two million labourers with a further two million and set them to work constructing the Grand Canal that would link the waterways of the north to those of the south. It was 2,000 *li* (700 miles) long, 2 *chang* (20 feet) deep and 6 *chang* (60 feet) wide. Willow trees were planted along both banks and forty palaces (*hing-kong*), to serve as resthouses, were built at intervals.

The completion of the Grand Canal not only encouraged travel from the north to the south, however, it demanded the construction of a fleet that would do justice to it. Again Yang-Ti spared neither money nor labour, and when the fleet at last began its pleasure cruises, it consisted of nearly two thousand junks. The most magnificent of these were the ten Dragon Junks, particularly the Imperial Dragon Junk itself, each 300 feet long and 50 feet high, and divided into four distinct decks with one hundred and twenty cabins decorated with jade panels and gold fittings; and furniture covered with tiger, bear and leopard skins added to the splendour. The Dragon Junks accommodated one thousand concubines and wives, musicians and entertainers, and carried part of the Royal Treasure. The five hundred 'second category' junks transported a supplementary supply of palace maids, servants and stores. Last in importance were a thousand 'third category' junks, following in the rear of the long convoy, and they carried ministers of the court and Taoist and Buddhist monks, foreign ambassadors and scholars, eunuchs and the military commanders. Yang-Ti had definite ideas on the relative importance of his subjects.

Historians of the period have left colourful accounts of such voyages, and a nineteenth-century work by H. Imbert, *La Sardanopale Chinois,* relates how the return journey was completed in two months. This study and others describe the beauty of the fleet being towed when there was neither wind nor current. Eighty thousand servants in magnificent silk uniforms formed a shimmering wall of colour on either bank, the silken ropes radiating from the junks seeming to create a glittering web along the extent of the canal. The willow trees planted at regular intervals added a cooling sense of shadow, and the air was intoxicating with the perfume from the concubines and palace maids. 'The fleet seemed to draw with it clouds of heavy scent, and when there was a mild breeze, villages seven miles distant knew that it was passing... On the throne specially built in the prow of the Royal Dragon Junk, Yang-Ti would drink wine from special four-litre cups and proudly survey his achievement before again retiring below decks for other pleasures.'

The forever-restless Emperor, seduced by love on the gentle currents of the Grand Canal, sought to enjoy the same sensuous delight on land. His first attempt was to construct a circular track one mile in circumference, the surface of which was corrugated in such a way that when a carriage was pulled round it, the jogging motion made it unnecessary for the copulating couple to make movements of their own. A more ambitious development of the same desire for 'love-on-wheels' was the construction of the Seven Glorious Chariots. These were not so magnificent as their name, or as some accounts describe, being simply coffin-like carriages in which lay a concubine waiting for her Emperor's presence. Yang-Ti's favourite diversion was to start a day's excursion early in the morning and, after a good meal in the Royal Coach, to move to the first of the Glorious Chariots. During the course of the day he would lie with each of the chosen concubines, and such was his virility, it is recorded, that 'he was usually back in the palace by nightfall.'

The most imaginative of his self-stimulating creations was the Maze Palace. In 'Record of the Maze Palace' (*Mi-lou-chi*), an anonymous T'ang author describes it as an erotic dream from which one need never be wakened. The palaces of the Ottoman and Mogul empires might have been more magnificent, and their rulers' exploits more violent and hot-blooded, but the Chinese emperors were unsurpassed in their sensuous diversions. The palace was a maze of chambers and passages, every wall covered with mirrors of polished bronze, the reflections so deceptive that touch rather than sight was necessary for moving about. There were no windows and the concealed lanterns were placed to give a regular yet subdued glow. The furnishings were simple. Mats and couches on which reclined the loveliest women of the harem, wine-fountains at frequent intervals, music played by groups of naked palace maidens.

In the musk and lotus-scented air, Yang-Ti regarded a visit to the Maze Palace as the ultimate test of the Dragon Emperor's potency. He was welcomed by his favourite eunuchs who immediately divested him of his worldly robes and wrapped him in a leopard skin. To the accompaniment of the clamour of gongs, bells and drums, and the concubines and palace maids chanting *Wang-Sui* (Ten Thousand Years — or Long Live the King), the Emperor first stimulated the Dragon Spirit with a drink or two from his four-litre gold cup, dismissed the eunuchs, then began his night's pursuit. As Yang-Ti was a man of considerable strength and lust, ten days were known to pass before the Royal Leopard withdrew from the palace and allowed dawn to break on the illusion of the Celestial Night.

In A.D. 607, briefly forsaking pleasure for matters of state, he undertook a journey with a less erotic purpose. The Mongolian Khan, Tou-Lu, was resisting the Middle Kingdom's demand that it become a tributary state, and rather than send an army to force him to submit, Yang-Ti decided to honour him with an Imperial visit. As this concession might involve some loss of prestige, Yang-Ti conceived a 'face-saving' way to move his whole capital with him. Every artist and painter in Lo-Yang was set to work on a circular painting. Two thousand yards of specially strengthened silk, erected to a circular plan, was covered with the views seen from the Celestial Palace, an exact copy of walls and roofs, temples and gates, outline of hills and colours of trees. When the convoy arrived outside the Mongolian capital, the Emperor set up camp within this panorama of Lo-Yang, and the subjects of the Khan were so impressed that they begged their ruler to make a suitable act of submission. And this, a little later, Khan Tou-Lu was happy to do.

Ten years after this visit, Yang-Ti's colourful reign came to an end. On a visit to Chiang-Tu, his palace maids were helping him. to dress when he caught sight of himself in a mirror. 'What a fine head I have,' he was heard to say reflectively. 'And what a splendid neck. Who, I wonder, will be the one to sever it?' It was a premonition not completely accurate. Hou-Sing-Ta, a rebel chief, swooped down on the city and rather than behead the Emperor, chose to strangle him with his own hands.

Yang-Ti bequeathed to history more than his reputation, and as a man of culture he expressed his less brutal thoughts in verse. The following suggests that he was not insensitive to the lives of others.

The Unwanted Concubine

Leaving the Inner Hall for the last time
She meets the new favourite.
Walking in the palace garden

She passes near the Emperor.
Should she bow or try to avoid him?

Her red-silk fan flutters
And covers her tears and sadness;
She loves him no less than before
Yet now in her own quarters
She must retire to oblivion.

Seven hundred years after the Mongol submission to Emperor Yang-Ti, China was invaded and conquered by the 'Mongol hordes' but such was their appreciation of the superior civilisation that it was quickly adopted as their own. And when Kublai Khan (Ho-Ba-Lieh) ruled the vast empire, he gained the support and respect of his cultured yet conquered subjects by encouraging and patronising artists and scholars. In his adherence to the magnificent style of earlier Dragon Rulers, he again showed his admiration of the traditional life of the Celestial Court, and this was nowhere more apparent than in his establishment of women.

As a departure from Chinese sources, one is able to give an impression of Kublai Khan and his court through the eyes of a Westerner. In the latter half of the thirteenth-century, Marco Polo was welcomed by the Great Lord of Lords, and in the account of his travels across the world, this redoubtable voyager offered his incredulous readers the following picture:

On being allowed into the presence of the Great Lord of Lords, one is instantly aware of the natural power of the ruler. His eyes are black and commanding, and though courteous to the visitor, he is clearly aware of the honour he is bestowing to an inferior. When he stands one is surprised to see that he is only of normal height, though his solid build and wide shoulders give an instant impression of physical strength. His mouth is wide and perhaps sensuous, and his nose distinctive without being prominent. The natural pinkness to his skin suggests his more northerly origins, and though he is a ruler of unparalleled riches and is surrounded by every luxury imaginable, he would be equally suited to wilder regions.

Marco Polo later turns to the subject of wives and concubines:

So far as I was able to enquire, he has four wives who are entitled to be regarded as queens, that is their sons can legitimately ascend the throne on the death of their illustrious father. Each of these ladies possesses a palace of her own, is served by no fewer than 300 palace maidens, 50 eunuchs, her own Palace Guard, ministers, physicians, robe-mistresses and attendants, numbering up to 10,000 souls.

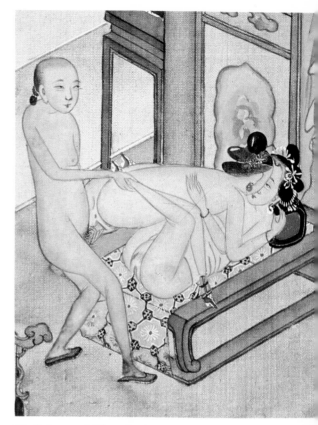

'Until the age of fifty, a husband should enter the pleasure Pavilion of his wives once every third day, of his concubines once every fifth day, of other maids of the household according to his wishes.' Confucius (551-479 B.C.), The Book of Rites. Ming dynasty blockprint.

When the Great Lord of Lords desires for one of his wives, she is escorted to his chamber. Apart from assuring male descendants with these wives, he has five hundred concubines, a number of whom are summoned each night. His favourite maidens come from a Tatar province called Kungurat, and every second year he despatches trusted eunuchs to select a fresh complement of girls. The selection takes the following form: On the arrival of the Royal Eunuchs all the maidens of the province are paraded before them. Those of passable beauty are then taken aside for detailed inspection. Every aspect and feature of face and body are examined, colour and texture of hair, colour and size of teeth and mouth, eyes, eyebrows and eyelashes, ears and neck and complexion. The body is similarly examined not only for shapeliness and to have proof of purity, but to be sure that the Great Khan will find those most private of parts free of the slightest blemish. The foremost beauties are then awarded a score of sixteen to twenty marks.

If the Great Khan has need for only the most beautiful, he will ask for those with the full twenty marks. If he is replacing more of his concubines, he will lower the acceptable number of marks. The chosen girls are then placed in the care of palace matrons and the wives of his courtiers, who observe them over a period of time. This is to be sure that

their personal habits are without fault, that their sleep is not marred by snoring or fitful movements, that their breath is sweet and that in the morning their bodies are without odour.

The chosen girls, when they are at last installed, are formed into groups of six, and when it is their turn to attend to the Royal needs, they pass three nights and three days in his chamber. When their duties are completed, six others take their place, and when the Great Khan indicates that he is stirred by Dragon Desires of unusual intensity, more girls are summoned to an ante-chamber where they remain available as he needs them.

Three centuries later a similar account of the 'restocking' was given by Matteo Ricci (1552-1610), the Italian Jesuit missionary and explorer. Ricci was even more qualified than Polo, having adopted Chinese dress and manners and gaining the confidences of his hosts by introducing them to advanced Western ideas on mathematics, astronomy and geography. Ricci stated that the Emperor and his sons chose their wives and concubines only for their beauty and that they were seldom concerned with the background or class of the women. The selection was by special magistrates chosen for the office, though not all the women, despite the honour, were happy with a life that separated them from their families and kept them confined to the palace.

The simple quality required by the Emperor was copied by his subjects, and Ricci states: 'All men are free to have concubines, and class or fortune means nothing in their selection as the only standard of preference is physical beauty. These concubines may be purchased for a hundred pieces of gold and at times for much less. Among the lower classes wives are bought and sold for silver and as often as a man may wish.'

The absolute power of the Dragon Rulers continued until the passing of the Manchu dynasty in 1912, and this method of selecting the most beautiful women of the Empire, in the absence of a better system, remained very much as it had been in the times of Polo and Ricci. When a father was asked why he did not object to his fair daughter being subjected to the indignities of being inspected for the honour of becoming a palace maid, he said: "If my daughter is chosen by the Khan then she has been born under a lucky planet. While he needs her, she will be provided with more than I could ever offer, and when he no longer needs her he will follow the usual custom of marrying her to one of his nobles. Could I do better?"

If the hen announces the dawn
Instead of the cock,
If the affairs of State
Are in the hands of women,
If the prince in bed
Is the one to be mounted,
Then will the Empire fall apart.
                    Yang Chen (A.D. 124)

The warning of the poem was not without reason, and there were moments when the Celestial Empire was 'in the hands of women'. This was usually when a queen had too much influence on the emperor, but occasionally a woman, by accident, by cunning or by ruthless wickedness, succeeded to the Dragon Throne. Such empresses were quick to protect themselves when fate gave them power over men, and the usual method was to promote other women and eunuchs to ruling positions. It must be recorded, however, that in at least one instance the Empire benefited rather than fell apart when the affairs of State got into 'the hands of women'.

The formidable empress who influenced or governed for over half a century was Wu Tse-tien (Wu Chao), a life that ended in A.D. 705 when she was eighty-one. Her rise to power had begun in the most modest manner possible, as a Fifth Grade concubine (*ts'ai jen*) at the court of Emperor T'ai Tsung. Although only fourteen when sent to the royal harem, she had shown her innate maturity when saying farewell to her weeping mother. 'Why should you cry when I may be chosen to bear the children of the Son of Heaven?' the daughter had asked. This naive hope failed to comfort the mother, who knew that only a limited number of the Emperor's concubines were allowed to bear his children (the eunuchs being very busy in their role as abortionists).

On entering the harem, Wu Chao had been given the name Most Beautiful Wu, and at the age of sixteen she was appointed one of the palace maids to the Royal Toilet. Her job was to stand by the Emperor's side while he urinated, holding a bowl of water so that he could immediately rinse his fingers. The *Chao-hou-l-shih* (Sung dynasty) relates that on this occasion, however, he carelessly urinated over the hem of his gown and Most Beautiful Wu instantly offered to fetch him a change of clothing. Her sweetness caused him to ask her to raise her face, which she had modestly kept lowered, and noticing her fresh beauty, he said: 'No. This stained robe will remind me of this meeting.' He was so impressed that he then flicked at the basin she was holding. 'I splash water on your powdered cheeks,' he whispered. This was one of the traditional phrases for indicating desire, and the virgin immediately gave the appropriate reply: 'I will welcome the Celestial Rain and Mist.'

She received the Rain and Mist on the couch in the toilet, and the Emperor then promoted her to Third Grade concubine, which gave her the new title of Most Elegant Beauty Wu. This soon brought Wu Chao promotion from the Royal Toilet to service in the palace itself, not as one of the favourites for the Emperor's bedchamber but as someone who had a pleasing disposition for functions of less importance. As a Third Grade concubine her chances of further promotion were limited, the competition being greater in the higher grades, and despite the Emperor's virility, the years of her youth could have passed without her again participating in Regal Coitus. The incident that changed her destiny came when the Emperor fell ill. With the other concubines she was hidden from the eyes of all men except the palace eunuchs, but so serious was the Emperor's illness that the Crown Prince, his son Li Chih, was hurriedly called to his bedside. When he eventually withdrew from his father's presence, Most Elegant Beauty Wu was waiting outside the bedchamber, and despite his filial anxiety, she instantly impressed him. He paused to ask her name, then returned to his own quarters.

There followed secret meetings between the Third Grade concubine and the Crown Prince, and Wu Chao, realising that the Emperor had not long to live, decided that her future lay with the younger man. The Emperor died soon after, and the Crown Prince was duly elevated to the Dragon Throne, but Most Elegant Beauty Wu had overlooked an important custom of the court. A new emperor was forbidden to take over his predecessor's harem and wives. Instead, therefore, of being installed as one of the royal favourites, Wu Chao, with T'ai Tsung's other women, had her head shaved and was confined to the Buddhist convent of Kan Yen. She was then twenty-four, and was expected to spend the rest of her days as a nun.

The new Emperor had taken the name of Kao Tsung, and the beginning of his reign was threatened by the vicious squabbling of his wives. Two in particular were constantly intriguing for the rank of Empress, and the Emperor, remembering the uncomplicated delights offered by the cloistered Wu Chao, forced his ministers to revoke the old customs and to have her released. Once Most Elegant Beauty Wu was again in the palace, this time with the high rank of consort, she deliberately set out to supersede the two powerful wives. This she did soon after giving birth to a male child. The baby was one day found dead and the apparently distraught Wu Chao charged that it had been killed by the two jealous women who had failed to bear sons. She convinced the Emperor of their guilt, and demanded that they be delivered to her for punishment, and such was her persuasiveness that he agreed.

The wives were punished in a manner appropriate to the period. They suffered one hundred blows each with a cudgel, then had their hands and feet chopped off. They were then dropped into large wine vats and left to die. One of the queens, Pure Favourite, survived for two days and was frequently visited in her agony by Wu Chao. With almost her last gasp, Pure Favourite cried that she would return from the next world as a cat, and would have her revenge. It was a threat that Wu Chao remembered all her life because after that she refused to have cats in any of her palaces.

Soon after she was installed as Empress, her master Kao Tsung suffered a stroke and, having alienated most of his ministers because of his attachment to her, he was forced to entrust her with high matters of state. She was quick to take advantage of her new power, her intuition again preparing her for a dramatic change in her fortunes. To this end she began to intrigue against possible rivals, accusing them of crimes against the ailing Emperor and having them either decapitated or banished. She did not spare even her own son, whom she had poisoned, or the sons of other consorts who might qualify to the rank of crown Prince.

The liquidation of all possible rivals for power had not been quite completed before Kao Tsung died, but her power was such that a weakling prince, Chung Tsung, was nominated for the throne. She was not deterred, however, from pursuing her ambitions. As Empress Dowager her authority, together with her reputation for ruthlessness, was enough to prevail on the ministers to have the young man deposed on the grounds of his immaturity, and once he had been banished to a distant province, she took the opportunity to kill off those of her rivals who had survived her first onslaught. Anyone with the slightest claim to the throne, not only the relatives of her late husband but her own brothers and nephews, were exterminated. At last there was only one

A painting based on stories of the untiring Emperor Yang-Ti. The maids hold apart his robe 'and guide the Jade Stem into the Pleasure Chamber.' 19th-century painting. Courtesy of the Library of the University of Indiana, Indiana.

possible claimant to the Dragon Throne. When she became Empress Wu Tse-tien, she was the first woman to rise to this exalted rank.

Confucius on Women:
She who lacks great talents and remarkable qualities is more likely to please as a woman.

Empress Wu's ascendancy had been achieved by cunning and cruelty. It also owed much to the use of her sexual charms. She had an unerring instinct for men's weaknesses, and having been the mistress of two rulers, as well as having been involved in many unrecorded liaisons, she was uniquely suited to dominate the stronger sex. She further established this dominance by promoting women to places of power. This was not limited to affairs of state, however, and one of her more remarkable appointments was that of Celestial Sex-Selector. Shang Kuan Wan-er was promoted from concubine to this arduous post, and her duty was to select from intimate knowledge those men most likely to please the Empress. The Celestial Sex-Selector was ordered to start with the three thousand men of the Palace Guard, and after a month of continuous trials she petitioned the Dragon Ruler with the following plea: 'Your humble subject, without the dragon Yin spirit and fire of Your Majesty, is unlikely to survive much longer these duties. My parts are so tender that I am unable to sit, my mouth is so sore that it is impossible to eat, and my body aches so much that I am denied even sleep.'

Empress Wu, now in her late forties, was sympathetic to the plea and decided on another method for selecting the most formidable males in the Empire. This variation of the traditional 'beauty contests' by which concubines had been chosen for the emperors was entrusted to General Liu Jen-Kuei (601-685). When the Empress had been a young concubine she had witnessed the humiliation of her first husband by the general, and now proposed to return the insult. In the earlier incident, the Emperor T'ai Tsung had been sporting with her in an enclosure of mirrors, a favourite diversion enabling him to see himself from many angles. Suddenly General Liu demanded an urgent audience, and without the Emperor pausing in his pleasures, he gave his permission to enter. The general, a stern Confucian, stared disapprovingly round the box of mirrors and said: 'There is only one Sun in the Heavens and only one Ruler on this Earth. Yet in these mirrors your humble servant sees before him many Celestial Rulers. Surely this cannot please your illustrious ancestors?'

Twenty years later the Empress, with some delight, despatched the victor of many military campaigns on a less heroic mission. He was ordered to exchange his uniform for civilian dress, and in the company of a detachment of officers similarly attired, he was to search the country district by district for men of unique virility and physique. The Confucian general accepted the order, though knowing that the commission required enquiries to be made in the brothels of each town. And it was in such an establishment that the great Hsüeh Huai-i was discovered.

The general and his men had just called at a brothel to make their enquiries when they heard two of the girls screaming at each other. One of them cried: 'May the Jade-Thruster of the Great Hsüeh rip through the walls of your Flowery Path!' A visit to the man's home proved that his reputation was deserved, and he was informed of the honour that now awaited him. In his native town of Lo-yang the Great Hsüeh had been a drug-pedlar and a trader in aphrodisiacs, and this expertise, together with his formidable equipment, soon ensured that he was the most favoured of all the Empress's male concubines. This he confirmed in a series of sex competitions and his mistress, in publicly acknowledging his triumph, is recorded to have said: 'This that I hold in my hand gives me more delight than my whole Empire' (*Ta-yeh-shih-i-chich* by Li Ta-t'ien, 631-725). And despite her obsession with humiliating the male sex, the Empress was known to bathe lovingly the Great Hsüeh's remarkable Jade-stem in lotus-blossom water.

Within two years the indefatigable Empress Wu had exhausted this formidable male concubine, and so deep was her sorrow following his death that she moved to the San Yang Palace at Ch'in. Among the high mountains her spirits revived, and her tireless preoccupation with sex was soon pursuing new diversions. She filled the San Yang Palace with four hundred men each reputed to be seven feet tall and similarly proportioned, and placed them in the charge of thirty physicians. The medical men were ordered to perfect the elusive Elixir of Eternal Youth. From ancient times the basis of this had been considered to be male sperm and tiger blood, and the results of their experiments were claimed to be so successful that she used the elixir to the end of her days.

When she was nearly eighty she began a close relationship with the Chang brothers, and though they were regarded as homosexuals, they remained with the Empress day and night. Her downfall came when they were together in her bedchamber. Five hundred men of the powerful Left and Right bodyguard revolted, invaded the palace and seized her two favourites. They were dismembered over a period of twelve hours and their heads and genitals exhibited on the stonework of the Bridge Leading to Heaven. The Empress was spared such a gruesome fate. Out of respect for her great age, she was quietly retired, and her place taken by the weakling Chung Tsung, whom she had deposed thirty years earlier.

Old Chinese Saying:
The Dragon Woman has eyebrows the shape of an eight [Chinese character], eyes with double pupils, ears with three holes. Her breasts have double nipples, her ribs are of one piece, and her clitoris is one inch long.

Dragon Woman would hardly have been an exaggerated description of Princess Shan-yin, the unmarried sister of Emperor Ts'ang Wu. She was in her late twenties when she petitioned her brother about the unfairness of their respective situations. They were both of royal blood, she reminded him, of the same parents, yet he had thousands of concubines to nourish his Yang-essence while she, because of her inferior sex, was denied a harem of men to nourish her own Yin-essence. The Emperor, conceding the justice of her argument, invited her to take her pick of his finest warriors.

Her first request, by the standards of the time, was distinctly modest. She would be satisfied with thirty male concubines, one for every night of the Chinese calendar month. Her freedom at that time (T'ang dynasty 618-916) was shared only by prostitutes, but because of the immense power and prestige of the Emperor, her departure from Confucian ideas of the place of women was accepted by his subjects.

Soon, however, the Princess Shan-yin wished to have all her thirty male concubines with her every night, and for this purpose she had constructed a 'Bed of a Hundred Legs.' Once the novelty of this passed, she complained to her brother that her complement of men failed to satisfy her and that she suffered from a surfeit of Yin-essence. The Emperor was so impressed by her formidable 'dragon-desire' that he built for her the Palace of the Mysterious Gate Desire. This was located in the most remote corner of the vast grounds of the Chang-an palace and was guarded by a special detachment of eunuchs named Glorious Heads and Shoulders.

A feature of court life among concubines and palace maids was the jealousy between some of the royal favourites. Although most of the thousands of neglected women of the harem accepted that they were hardly likely to be promoted to consort or queen, once they were elevated to a status where they might be part of their ruler's daily life, they were quick to seize every opportunity to rise above their closest rivals. There are many accounts of the cruelties inflicted by concubines and consorts on each other, and Hsu Ying-Ch'iu (fourteenth century), an historian, recounts the story of Prince Ch'ü's favourite, Kao-hsin. She was with Prince Ch'ü when two jealous concubines, Ch'ao p'ing and Ti-yü, rushed into the bed-chamber and tried to kill her. They were seized by eunuchs and to show his regret that Kao-hsin should have come so close to death, Prince Ch'ü allowed her to decide on their punishment.

Hsu Ying-Ch'iu states: 'Ti-uü and Ch'ao-p'ing were taken to the public square, stripped of their robes and staked to the ground in a kneeling position. Rams, goats and even dogs were encouraged to mount them, the efforts of which greatly pleased the watching Kao-hsin.' The torment of the two concubines came to an end when, instead of suffering the traditional decapitation, their bodies were severed at the waist.

From this taste of power and sadism, Kao-hsin proceeded to watch vigilantly for opportunities to prove her love and loyalty to Prince Ch'ü, and the cruel streak in her soon found another victim. She was particularly jealous of a half-Persian concubine called Wang ch'ing, and hearing that she was having her portrait painted, informed the prince that she was posing in the nude. This was a charge graver than infidelity, which the prince chose to believe, and when Kao-hsin requested to be allowed to administer an appropriate punishment, the wish was granted.

To quote Hsu Ying-Ch'iu, Wang ch'ing was first whipped and tortured with red-hot needles, then had her hair ripped out. At this point she managed to tear herself free and rushed towards a well with the intention of jumping into it. The attempt failed, she was seized and brought back to Kao-hsin who ordered that 'she be staked to the ground and red-hot irons inserted into the Jade Pavilion.' When Wang ch'ing lost consciousness, 'she was then cut to pieces, beginning with the facial flesh, and the remains at last thrown down the well she had been so determined to reach.'

Kao-hsin carried her sense of loyalty to Prince Ch'ü even further, setting herself to improve the behaviour of the girls in the harem. When Yung-ai, a concubine, was caught in the arms of a eunuch who was wearing a 'dragon instrument,' she was reported to the prince not only for the infidelity but because of the insulting reflection on his virility. Yung-ai, like others before her, was handed over for the appropriate punishment. This took the form of being bound to a pillar, having her arms and legs torn from their sockets, her eyes gouged out, and liquid lead poured into the open wounds as well as into the two lower bodily orifices.

In the course of her career, Kao-hsin had fourteen women tortured to death, and her influence on the prince caused him to exceed even his own cruel excesses. He had every wall in the palace decorated from ceiling to floor with murals of colourful sexual scenes, and every day he paraded his palace maids and guards, his adult children and other relatives, even aged aunts and uncles, and forced them to imitate the scenes on the walls. Prince Ch'ü also possessed a remarkable collection of erotic illustrations painted on the skins of stillborn babies, such skins possessing the advantage for a painter of having the smoothest surface known at that time.

The devotion of concubines did not always, however, express itself in such a gruesome manner, and there are many stories of beauty and self-sacrifice which reveal these women to have been courageous as well as of high principles. Li-shih was a concubine in the harem of Prince Wang Ping-shüh, and soon after her induction, his first wife, Princess Nan-nang, overcome by jealousy, entered the new concubine's quarters with the intention of stabbing her.

Li-shih was standing by the window combing her long hair when the princess, swinging a sword, ran towards her.

'Why do you stay so calm in the face of death!' she cried.

'When your husband conquered my provinces,' replied Li-shih, 'he killed all my family except for the young women, and because I was one of the most beautiful, I have been added to this harem. Why should I wish to avoid joining my illustrious ancestors?'

Her serenity was so moving that the princess threw away the sword, embraced her, and said, 'From this moment I shall regard you as a younger sister. In this way shall I try to make good my husband's crime.'

It is recorded that they remained as sisters for the rest of their lives.

A subtle story of a loving concubine is that of Fairy Consort (First Category) Fan Chi. One day after the King of Ch'u had stayed in audience with his ministers for an unusually long time, he was met in the palace corridors by the concubine.

'Your majesty, how tired and hungry you look,' said Fan Chi. 'What comfort can I offer you?'

'Fairy Consort,' said the king. 'when I listen to the loyal and thoughtful words of my First Minister, I forget such things as hunger and fatigue.'

'Then you regard loyalty and thoughtfulness as the highest of virtues for a first minister?'

'Undoubtedly,' said the king.

Fan Chi reflected for a moment, then said: 'For eleven years I have attended your person. I have bathed you daily, I have washed your hair, held your towel and helped you into your robes. When you rest on your couch, I draw up your coverlet. When you are tired of my sexual attractions I send my servants into the country to find you new girls. In your household there are ten women of my rank and your two wives who are my superiors. Have I ever shown jealousy towards them? In what way, then, is First Minister Shen's loyalty greater than mine and when has he thoughtfully advanced others who might please your majesty more?'

The king bowed his head in agreement.

The Derelict Palace

Whose abandoned domain is this,
Grey mice in the dust
The wind sighing through empty windows...

Who was the prince who owned it,
Palace of a thousand voices,
Singing and feasting until dawn...
His virgins are now laid in graves,
The prince with his Ancestors —
The long grass leans in sorrow
And the branches bow with lament.
Who can ever know eternity?

Tu Fu (713-770)

Under the Silken Canopy. K'ang-hsi (1662-1722). A painting on silk from the C.T. Loo collection, Paris.

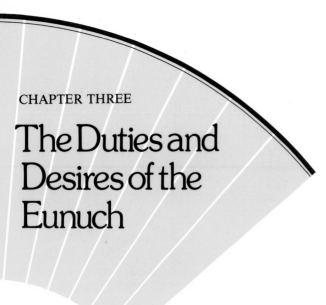

CHAPTER THREE

The Duties and Desires of the Eunuch

In The Celestial Kingdom it was said that the only misfortune greater than that of being a female was to become a eunuch (though this would not necessarily apply to those who were honoured by a high position at Court). The most renowned Chinese eunuch was Admiral Cheng Ho, who led an expedition to the African coast in 1405, the longest voyage of discovery to that date, but most of the court castrati — 'court-rats' or 'flapping crows' — were equated with women. The ancient Book of Odes says:

Not Heaven but Women and Eunuchs
Bring Misfortunes to Mankind.
Wives and those without balls
Bleat with similar voices.

The facts of Chinese history lend some support to this prejudice. The status of the eunuch, because of the part he played in the most intimate affairs of men and women, gave him influence where emperors and princes were most vulnerable. He was considered to have much in common with both sexes, to be suited to his tasks because he had — or at least could appreciate — the rational outlook of men yet, by the nature of his neutered condition, to be able to understand female psychology. His power in the courts was achieved by the single-minded personal ambition of one suffering a deep bitterness from his deprivation, and because eunuchs realised that they had to be united to defend themselves. They therefore formed a very powerful and ruthless clique.

Their fortunes, and their place at the Celestial Court, varied with the temperament and the authority of the emperor, some rulers making greater or lesser use of their establishment of *castrati*. Certain unpopular emperors, or those who could not be sure of the loyalty of their ministers, promoted eunuchs to positions of great authority, a role in which they served as administrators, military commanders, financial advisers and comptrollers of taxes. Their traditional role, however, was to manage the affairs of the harem.

Young and strong eunuchs formed the seraglio guard, capable and businesslike eunuchs supervised the internal arrangements, the older ones and those trusted by the emperor managed his sexual programme and were therefore in a position to favour certain of the women. This was a remunerative source of extra income, and since the eunuch had clear ideas about the power of money, every opportunity to add to his wealth was seized. The promotion of concubines to higher grades, perferential treatment for the honour of Regal Coitus, helping their families to gain certain court privileges, even being allowed illicit affairs with other men — these and other aspects of harem life brought the eunuch his reward. In the court itself they were often the power behind the throne, and the knowledge of enjoying the emperor's protection, in a society that hated eunuchs, assured their loyalty to him.

The eunuch was often compared with gelded animals. Castrate the horse, it was said, and it stops prancing about but can still be put to work. Castrate the bull and it loses its fury but remains as strong as ever. And a dog who is castrated never roams but stays obediently at its master's heel. The castrated servant (*hsing-ch'en*), however, might have lost his virility and many of his male characteristics, but as a human being he acquired different and infinitely more complex feelings. His nature usually became more arrogant, cruel and suspicious, and he was hypersensitive about his physical handicap. His loss of identity with his fellow men made him the outsider of society and gave him an obsession with power and wealth. His constant association with the harem, however, and his closeness to the womenfolk, inevitably identified him with a female world even when he was a towering bodyguard in a military uniform.

To understand the unique character of the eunuch, the traumatic nature of the operation itself and the different degrees of castration, the following description is of great relevance. It was written by Carter Stent, an authority on Chinese court life, and appeared in the *Journal of the Royal Asiatic Society (North China Branch 1877).*

The operation is performed in this manner. White ligatures or bandages are bound tightly round the lower part of the belly and the upper parts of the thigh, to prevent too much haemorrhage. The parts about to be operated on are then bathed three times with hot pepper-water, the intended eunuch being in a reclining position. When the parts have been sufficiently bathed they are cut off as closely as possible with a small curved knife, something in the shape of a sickle. The emasculation being effected, the wound is then covered with paper saturated in cold water and is carefully bound up. After the wound is dressed the patient is made to walk about the room, supported by two 'knifers,' for two or three hours, when he is allowed to lie down. The patient is not allowed to drink anything for three days, during which time he often suffers great agony, not only from thirst but from intense pain and from the impossibility of relieving nature during that period. At the end of three days the bandage is taken off and the sufferer obtains relief. If this takes place satisfactorily, the patient is considered out of danger and congratulated upon it. But if the unfortunate wretch cannot make water, he is doomed to a death of agony, for the passages have become swollen and nothing can save him.

There were three kinds of castration, total loss, the removal of the penis only, the severing of the testicles. With total loss (*hsing ch'en*), once the wound had healed a metal, bamboo or straw tube was inserted to permit urination. The 'tube' was also needed by those in the second category, eunuchs retaining their testicles, and since they frequently experienced sexual desire, it permitted the draining away of semen. In more modern times, with the use of rubber sexaids, the semen was directed through an artificial penis, a device that helped those eunuchs who had married to pretend to lead a family life. The third category of *castrati,* men deprived only of the testicles, included those suffering the operation as punishment or because they were prisoners of war. In this latter case emasculation was effected by crushing, searing with red-hot irons, tearing from the

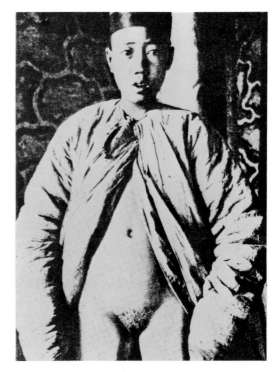

Chinese Eunuch, Peking, 1890. Total castration ('swept clean') was frequently favoured. By courtesy of the British Museum.

body, or binding with a tight cord that stopped the blood-flow. This was followed by total withering.

Castration usually took place before puberty, at least for young boys chosen to serve the emperor, and many fathers, anxious to see their sons rise in the world, had them neutered in the hope that the palace would accept them for service. Such paternal ambitions were not always from the highest motives. Once in a high position, the *castrato* was under an obligation to help every member of his family and clan. For those submitting to castration after puberty, the risks were much greater. The operation resulted in a mortality rate of one-in-three, and since the eunuch had previously known sexual longings, if not experience, he was usually tormented by very real frustrations. These are described by a chief eunuch in a work by Baron Montesquieu (*Lettres persanes,* 1721):

In the harem the women and the surroundings constantly excite me. In their company, seeing them naked, I wonder why I must forever be deprived of this pleasure; how long can this despair be borne? I never lead a woman to my master's bed without suffering the wildest rage in my heart, the blackest helplessness in my soul. Once, to my cost, I lost my self-control. I had been attending to one of my master's ladies in her bath and I dared to grasp her between the legs. For a moment, from her expression, I thought my last day had come, but thankfully I escaped the dreadful death that reporting this would have meant.

The fair one, however, extorted a heavy price for her silence. I entirely lost command of her and on a thousand occassions I was pressed to do favours disloyal to my master and which could have cost me my life.

The origin of eunuchs in the service of the Celestial Emperor is obscure and the earliest records relate to Cjou-Kung, brother of the first monarch of the Chou dynasty (1050 B.C.), who was ordered to frame a code of laws for China. There were five forms of punishment, and castration was one of them. The term *kung-hsing,* or palace punishment, was commonly used for castration while *lao-kung-yen* (royal palace victim) referred to a eunuch. It may be imagined that the society of those days would have yielded a good supply of criminals and captured enemy soldiers for *kung-hsing,* but in fact there were still not enough for the many palaces of royalty and noblemen, and fathers of lower class families were pressed to offer their sons. The sacrifice was well-rewarded and from about 250 B.C., when the harems became one of the special duties of eunuchs, there was an even greater demand for these supplementary boys.

It was one of the few ways in which the lowborn could rise to positions of power, and as trusted servants or even ministers, they frequently had to administer unpopular assignments. In the Chou period, for example, a eunuch was appointed Minister of Death and another given the title of Execution Minister. Palace life, with its rivalries and ambitions, was an ideal place for scheming eunuchs and there are many instances of emperors and princes being among their victims. On the other hand, when their schemes failed, retribution was merciless. When Emperor Ling (A.D.170) died, his ten principal eunuchs decided to prevent his son Ho Chin from mounting the throne. They were powerful enough to summon him to a conference while insisting that his five hundred followers remained outside the palace. After waiting some hours, the followers began

Ivory miniature of a woman worshipping the Jade Stem, which rises as the lid of the box slides open. Eunuchs tried many concoctions to restore the object of her worship. 19th-century. Courtesy of the Mitchell Library, Sydney.

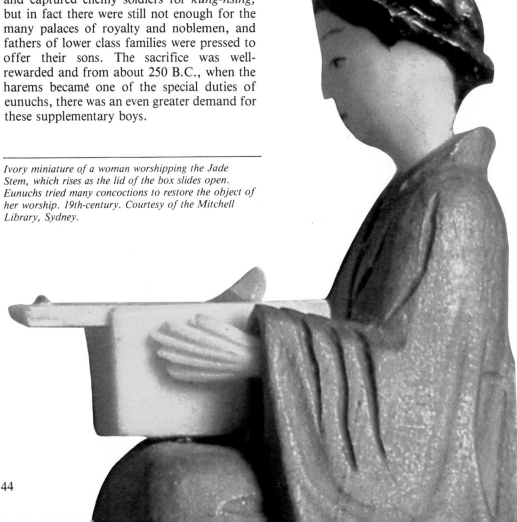

demonstrating. However, they quickly received the reply of the eunuchs. The head of Ho Chin was thrown over the wall and into their midst. It is recorded that the followers immediately broke down the gates, dismembered and killed the eunuchs and set fire to the palace.

The powers and numbers of the eunuchs did not diminish with succeeding centuries and from the reign of Ch'ien Lung (1736-96) until the downfall of the Court in 1911, they enjoyed a period of unparalleled influence. Emperor Ch'ien Lung was a ruler preoccupied by artistic and literary pleasures, and was eventually persuaded to leave the running of his affairs — and indeed the state — to his eunuchs. This transfer of responsibility was helped by the fact that the Emperor was too exalted to have ordinary mortals as personal friends, which meant that the eunuchs, who were not considered to be men, were at liberty to get closer to the Emperor than would normally have been court practice.

Ch'ien Lung's indulgence allowed the eunuchs to consolidate their postion. It also permitted them to live in the style of the most debauched of their masters. Once the old office-holders and ministers had lost their powers to the eunuchs, with the Emperor left in peace to enjoy his aesthetic life, the new masters were free to give expression to their ambitions. The palaces that were taken over continued to have their establishments of concubines but they were now in the service of eunuchs. An era began which gave them both the opportunities and the powers to dedicate themselves to the ancient beliefs in restoring their lost manhood.

With their private harems they at last had the resources for practicing the unremitting sexual activities they hoped would cause the organs to renew themselves. The first stage of the 'rebirth' was to have a constant relay of women saturating the scar area with 'fertilizing' Yin-essence. The prolonged excitment was then supposed to revive the Yang urge which, in turn, would force the body to complete the regrowth. The palaces became not only playgrounds but battlegrounds, however, with both the women and the eunuchs in a state of tormented frustration.

A thirteenth-century record states: 'The area of the healed scar burns with maddening erotic sensations. The blood vessels feel they are about to burst yet one knows there cannot be relief.' The women were therefore subjected to a series of sadistic and exhausting outrages, including endless manipulation by palace boys and girls to encourage the flow of Yin-essence.

Sir Richard Burton (1821-90) met a eunuch's wife in his travels and she described the tormented fury of her husband. As the eunuch struggled to reach an orgasm (which was probably a secondary urethral discharge), she had to hold up a pillow into which he could bite, otherwise her shoulders, cheeks and breasts would have been torn to shreds. The efforts of eunuchs to regenerate their lost sexuality are recorded in detail but there is no evidence of the successful growth of a second penis. There was always a fear, however, among their emperors and masters, that this miracle could occur, and there are instances of an over-zealous ruler ordering a precautionary trimming of that already emaciated area.

One such story features Chief Eunuch Wei. He was so sure of his powers under the Emperor Ch'ien Lung that he defied the Chief Minister. The minister was helpless for a time, then conceived a plan that would upset even that indulgent ruler. He informed the Emperor that the organs of his eunuchs were growing again and that they had designs on the royal concubines. Ch'ien Lung was sufficiently alarmed to order an inspection, placing the Chief Minister in charge of the investigation. The minister, primarily concerned with his own authority, reported that there was substance to the rumour and that the eunuchs had developed a second growth. The Emperor consented to his Chief Minister taking the necessary measures, and among those who succumbed to further surgery in that area was Chief Eunuch Wei.

Apart from aphrodisiacs and herbal concoctions, constant massage with Yin-essence and quasi-sexual gymnastics, a favourite regenerative remedy was fresh human brains. The senior eunuchs had the authority to order the decapitation of many of the emperor's enemies and certain categories of common criminals, and those eunuchs seeking regeneration had the heads immediately split open and their contents brought to them while still warm. In the circumstances it was only natural-or unnatural-that the eunuchs should explore the occult arts in their efforts to revive their lost sexuality, and in a society normally dominated by superstition and various forms of magical beliefs, this produced a remarkable range of potions, philtres and remedies.

The most favoured potions were derived from human sources, and the constituents

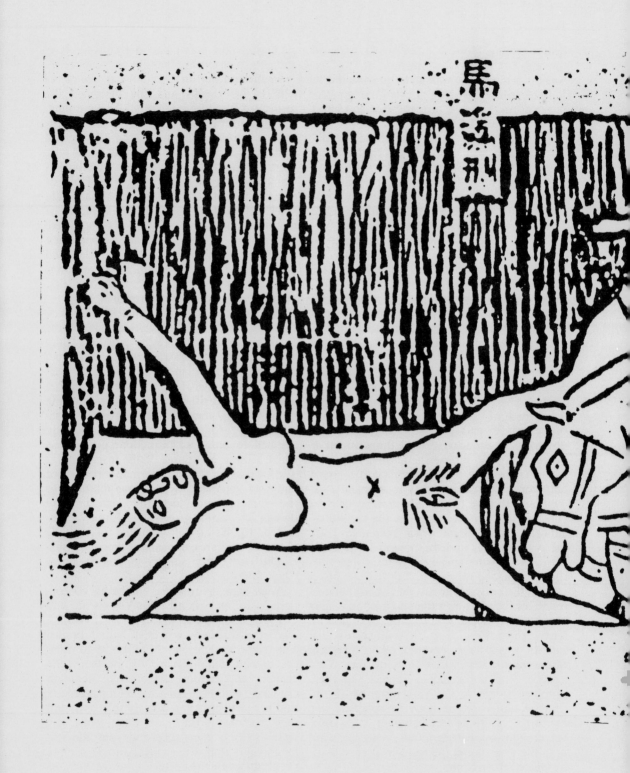

Eunuchs usually carried out the punishment of the Emperor's unfaithful wives and concubines. This early stone-rubbing, possibly Later Han dynasty (25-220 A.D.), depicts death by 'horse weapon punishment'.

Punishment with the 'long stick' was inflicted on men and women alike. Eunuchs frequently made it a 'market square' spectacle. A disobedient wife or concubine could receive eighty strokes, leaving the flesh torn and the victim lying in blood. From a 19th-century album. Courtesy the Rare Books and Special Collections Library, University of Sydney Library.

'Senior eunuchs had the authority to order the decapitation of many of the Emperor's enemies and certain categories of common criminals.' From a 19th-century album. Courtesy the Rare Books and Special Collections Library, University of Sydney Library.

believed to have the most powerful properties were the liver, placenta, semen and menstrual blood. They were claimed to be good for 'strengthening the *tsing* (semen),' for 'restoring the Male Peak' and for curing convulsions. In his *Collection of Fine Cures* (twelfth century), Wu Khiu emphasises the remarkable restorative powers of human placenta. His method of preparing the medicine is as follows:

No distinction need be made between the Purple Riverboat (placenta) of male or female children, though that of the first child is particularly beneficial. Once the Purple Riverboat has been expelled by the mother it should be washed in a bowl of rice water then carried for further cleansing to a stream of running water. It should stay immersed until it has been washed of surface slime and loose fibres, then for a final cleansing of evil spirits it should be dipped in a bowl of mother's milk. After this it should be dried in the sun until it is brittle, then finally pulverised. The powder should then be roasted on porcelain.

Tung P'in, another physician of the twelfth century, recommended cooking the placenta in alcohol, then kneading it, and with certain herbs and powders serving it as 'dumplings.' Li Shi-Chen, in his *Medical Treatise* (fourteenth century), described the *tsing* as the Flame and Fire of the Soul, and asserted that the devilishness of eunuchs was because the Vital Essence never found release. This did not deter Li, however, from recommending a potion for the hated eunuchs. 'The semen of virile young men should be mixed with the excrement of hawks or eagles and taken in pellet form.'

The coveting of elixirs containing menstrual blood was an approach from the opposite direction, that of exciting the eunuch's Yang-spirit with the fluids of the female sex. Virgins' menses were preferred, particularly that of the 'first flow,' and it was mixed into an ointment, in the case of eunuchs, for rubbing on the scar tissue. A variation of this, quoted by Li Shi-Chen, was the use of the mother's 'first flow' after the birth of a male child, though in this instance it was taken orally.

The consumption of human flesh was also favoured at certain periods and in certain districts as a way of restoring or reviving the lost sexuality of the eunuch. It was described by Chief Eunuch Li Kwoh (second century A.D.) as 'sweet and of delicate flavour, comparable to young venison, particularly the liver...' Li Kwoh relied for his gruesome diet on the pit into which the severed hands of thieves were thrown, and had one of his slaves collect them every morning. The liver and the gall bladder, being regarded as the probable seats of life and the Vital Force, were recommended for their generative powers. The human 'blood flow' was also credited with making Li Kwoh invisible 'once darkness had descended.' This led to his being accused of circulating unseen among the concubines while they slept. The evidence of his guilt was the lovebites and bruises on the bodies of women who had not received Regal Coitus for months, and since it was necessary to find a culprit for the reputations of all concerned, Li Kwoh paid the penalty for his claims of supernatural powers. He suffered execution by 'Cutting into Small Pieces.'

One of the traditional forms of capital punishment was called 'Cutting into Small Pieces'. Discrimination between the sexes, in this instance, was not practiced and the adulteress was a common victim. From a 19th-century album. Courtesy of the Rare Books and Special Collections Library, University of Sydney Library.

I awoke from a dream of Paradise
In which I was like other men
And knew the delights of Yin.
Now, again myself, I find she was a rainbow,
A beauty seen but never touched.
I know life only in my dreams
And perhaps in that longer sleep
That promises so much with Death.

Hu Yung-hsi (Ming dynasty eunuch)

The practice of eunuchs taking wives had been encouraged by the earlier and redoubtable Empress Wu (Wu Chao), who had been determined to reduce the power of men who she knew objected to being ruled by a female. Her eunuchs, responding to her efforts to give them social respectability and increase their popularity, attempted to lead family lives of unexceptional normality. They frequently adopted children and brought them up to the highest Confucian standards, and to add to the impression of a conventional way of life they kept an establishment of secondary wives and concubines. Under the Empress they were given the further task of supervising the education and the cultural instruction of the thousands of harem women retained for her male relatives, and this also helped to restore the eunuch's self-esteem.

Not all rulers who favoured their eunuchs sought to employ them in the more administrative offices of court life, and the Emperor Hsüan Tsung made use of their belligerent sense of inferiority by giving them command of the security forces. Kao Li-Shih,

regarded as a 'dragon eunuch,' was promoted to commander of the *corps d'elite* of Palace Guards, and ordered to punish the hundreds of Buddhist monks and nuns who had incurred the fury of their ruler. At this time Buddhism was in favour at the Celestial Court, and the Emperor placed great reliance on their prophecies and advice, but in 695, when the Ming Tang temple was burned to the ground, he regarded this as a sign of Celestial displeasure. He felt that his monks should have helped him avoid such calamities, and encouraged by the Confucians who were temporarily out of favour, Hsüan Tsung ordered Kao Li-Shih to torture and decapitate the whole establishment of Buddhists.

Commander Kao first ordered the monks to be castrated, then had their genitals cooked and fed to the nuns. In turn, according to *Early Tang Anecdotes* by Hsun-fu, nuns with large breasts had them removed and cooked for those monks who had survived castration. They then suffered a torture known as Bright Eyes (bags of unslaked lime placed on their eyes), Finger Crushing (sticks placed between the fingers and bound by tight cords), and Hot-water Snake (their naked bodies having soft metal tubes designed as snakes wound round them, and boiling water poured into the open mouths of the snakes). Commander Kao finally gave the order to transport the surviving Buddhists to a narrow ravine, where they were released, and the command given to his horse guards to trample them to death. At the time of his own demise, Kao's harem contained five hundred concubines, and his collection of sex-aids and instruments, even in those days, was considered remarkable.

Another 'dragon eunuch' of Hsüan Tsung's reign was Wang Fei-Sheng. He was persuaded by the First Minister, Shang Kuan-I, to join in a plot to dispose of the Empress, whom they both hated. Wang had been approached by the minister because of the esteem with which the Emperor regarded him. The eunuch had gained favour when his master, bored by beautiful concubines, demanded the company of the ugliest and the most deformed women in the Empire. Wang dutifully obeyed the order, built a palace (Palace of the Desirable Monsters) and accommodated in it the ugly and the disfigured, dwarfs and freaks, and even a woman reputed to have had two heads which, during the Emperor's love-making, simultaneously returned his passion.

As Wang was therefore a favoured servant

of the Emperor. Shang Kuan-I confided in him that the Empress was practising witchcraft and had been converted to a Taoist cult of black magic. The neglected Empress, he added, was casting spells to afflict the Son of Heaven with impotency. When the eunuch passed on the information to the Emperor, the ruler called for his First Minister and asked for his advice. Shang Kuan-I suggested that the Empress should be dismissed before she could harm him but the Emperor, who loved his wife, asked the eunuch to first bring him more evidence.

Eunuch Wang then promoted a number of concubines who swore on oath to give evidence that they had witnessed the Empress practising the black arts, and bribed a number of Taoist monks (with visits to the harem) to make similar statements. Unfortunately for Wang, an incorruptible monk informed the Empress of the plot against her, and before the evidence had been assembled for the Emperor, she had successfully convinced her husband of her innocence. She had a very forceful personality and prevailed on him to allow her to punish the wicked plotters.

She adhered to the constitutional procedures by first making Wang and Shang sign confessions, though the correctness of this was accompanied by tortures that lasted two days. They were then beheaded, their estates confiscated and their families enslaved.

Chinese torture was based upon the principle of a punishment appropriate to the crime, and apart from the summary penalties of thieves having their hands chopped off, or those escaping from the authorities having their hamstrings sliced through with a sword, torture was meant to impress on the victim the error of his ways as well as being physically punitive. Public degradation was also part of the total punishment, and in a society where status and 'face' were particularly important, this was not the least of the victims' sufferings. The thought given to tortures that pained the culprit both physically and psychologically is exemplified by the punishment of 'Wearing the Cangue', which was administered to embezzlers, compulsive gamblers and insolvent debtors. The Cangue was a heavy wooden board three feet square, with a hole in the centre, and this was locked round the culprit's neck. He was not imprisoned but allowed to return to his normal life or made to stand for so many hours a day in public. The Cangue weighed a hundred pounds and the usual sentence was between one and three months, but as the culprit was unable

to feed himself or attend to other necessary functions he relied completely on the help of others.

The eunuch was actively involved in the whole field of torture, in positions of power having the authority to impose it, and at the lower level of jailer, servant or harem guard, being called on to administer it. Because of the inherent grievance he felt towards society, it was a task to which he applied himself with demoniacal vigour. This was particularly the case with flogging and beating, which were among the more popular public spectacles. The law stated that public beatings should only be inflicted after sentence by a Mandarin of Justice, but court eunuchs, as well as jailers and petty officials, often held such 'market square' spectacles without much fear of retribution.

The legal court procedure was for the magistrate to be seated at a table on which lay a box of pencil-like sticks. The accused knelt in front of the table and sentence took the form of a number of the sticks being thrown on to the floor by the magistrate. Each stick denoted five blows with the *pan-tsee* or bamboo rod. There were two kinds of rod, one five feet long and two inches wide, the other three feet long and an inch wide. The legal maximum was one hundred strokes, male prisoners being stripped of clothing, females simply having their outer garments removed. The officer administering the punishment was not only skilled in making it as painful as possible, he also accepted bribes from the prisoner or his family to wield the rod lightly, his adeptness in this instance being in appearing to strike with all his strength.

Another form of beating seen as appropriate to the crime was that inflicted on boatmen or seamen. Instead of a rod, a leather-covered bat the shape of a canoe-paddle or oar was used, and the blows were applied to the cheeks of the face. This was often supplemented by 'ear-twisting', a method of twisting 'the cartileges reaching into the brain'. These punishments to the head or face were considered to be a direct way of reaching impure or evil thoughts.

There were four traditional methods of capital punishment in China, and the role of executioner was one often performed by the eunuchs. The most protracted and gruesome method of killing was called *Cutting into Small Pieces*. This started at the top of the head, descended to the eye-brows, the cheeks, neck, arms and chest, the technique being for the cuts to leave strips of flesh hanging downwards.

When the prisoner was on the point of losing consciousness, the executioner plunged his sword into the stomach, seized him by the hair and decapitated him. This method was also the one recommended for women 'guilty of defiling their bodies in adultery'. The most merciful was simple beheading with a two-handed sword, but this punishment was considered equally disgraceful because it meant consigning the body to the grave without the head (this was usually displayed in public), or of having it separate in the coffin. This would deny the victim the blessing of the usual burial rites, which would prevent his reunion with his Illustrious Ancestors, becuase 'the body would not reach the Next World as it had arrived in this one'. The least reprehensible variation of the public death penalty was strangulation, which was effected by tying the prisoner crucifix-fashion and passing a cord through a hole in the insterstice of the cross. This was then looped round the victim's throat and tugged downwards by someone standing behind the cross. The fourth method, often a sign of favour or even of honour, was to receive a silken cord from the Emperor. With it was a request that the recipient should be his own executioner.

The emperor of China seldom orders a subject to be executed until he has consulted with his law officers whether he can avoid it without infringing the constitution of his realm. He fasts for a certain period previous to signing the Execution Order; and his Imperial Majesty esteems those years of his reign the most illustrious and the most fortunate in which he has had the least occasion to let fall upon his subjects the rigorous sword of justice.
The Punishments of China (1801)

G.H. Mason

The most powerful eunuchs of modern times were An Te-hai and Li Lien-ying, both of whom were favourites of the Empress Dowager Tzu Hsi (1835-1908). On the death of her husband she was installed as regent until the Crown Prince was of age, but to the end of her life this formidable woman never relinquished real power. In a society still adhering to Confucian and traditional ideas of male superiority, she turned to her eunuchs for support, a mutually advantageous arrangement and one which she was not to regret.

One of Chief Eunuch An's first duties for the Empress Dowager was to ensure that the adolescent Crown Prince left the means of effective rule in her hands. This was not done by force or threats. The prince was introduced to the pleasures of the harem at an early age, and once it was apparent that the experience was to his taste, An made sure that the concubines allowed him no respite. With both the chief eunuch and the women urging the young prince to prove that he shared the dragon spirit of his ancestors, the youth was quickly reduced to chronic weakness and eventually to a degree of insanity.

For the Dowager-Empress, however, palace orgies were organised in a more sophisticated way. Her deep interest in the theatre added to the sympathy she felt towards An, because the eunuch was a talented actor himself. The court debauches were turned into spectacular pageants, with the whole palace a stage, costumes and fancy dress at all times encouraged, and though her chief eunuch could hardly have satisfied all the desires of such a formidable woman, he was adept at finding men of outstanding virility. Among these was the guardsman Jung Lu, who was quickly promoted to the rank of military commander.

An Te-hai, as well as Chief Eunuch Li, who was to follow him, was also a genius in operating the system of 'squeeze'. As Court Chamberlain and confidant of the Empress, every favour or transaction in which he was involved added to his wealth. Audiences with the Empress, appointments to the many palace and government posts, even a military commander's request for ammunition or reinforcements, fell within the area of 'squeeze'. Tributes and taxes were paid on bullion, silver, silks and other precious commodities, and these were divided as to one half for the Empress, one quarter for Jung Lu and the military budget, and the remaining quarter for the chief eunuch. The Empress's share of the Imperial intake, however, had to cover all her personal expenses, and as An was in control of the palace accounts, she made a further contribution to his fortune. She was charged — though unknown to herself — a hundred times the market price of meat, two pounds (sterling) for each egg, and for such items as entertainment she apparently rewarded actors and artists with the highest fees they had ever received.

The Chief Eunuch, however, made the mistake of venturing outside the palace and therefore beyond the Empress's formidable protection. He left to attend to certain affairs in Shantung province and the Governor, Ting Pao-chen, found a pretext for charging the court favourite with 'disturbing the peace' and daring to pose as the Empress's representative.

Unlike the phoenix, there was no miraculous regeneration of the eunuch's lost parts. A hinged cover conceals an ivory miniature of lovers in this pair of phoenixes. Porcelain decorated with enamels on biscuit. K'ang-hsi (1662-1722). By kind permission of the British Museum.

An Te-hai was summarily beheaded before the court could intervene, and his eunuch companions were strangled and thrown in the river. Governor Ting then sent off a dispatch of loyalty to the Empress.

An was followed by Li Lien-ying, who remained at her side for the next forty years, and with the Empress now all-powerful and without rivals for the throne, they formed an able combination. Chief Eunuch Li proved himself an efficient administrator, a hawk for swooping on conspirators and trouble-makers, and even more avaricious than his predecessor in manipulating the 'squeeze' system. He also made sure that the male claimants to the throne never reached their majority. He imitated An in keeping the youths busy with 'night and day pleasures', and those who did not succumb to this were killed by less entertaining methods. One of the princes, who later became Emperor Kuang Hsü, was allowed to survive in the knowledge that when he became ruler, he must be obedient to the Empress's orders. His total subservience was shown when his favourite wife, Pearl Concubine, was charged with insubordination towards the Empress, and he was without sufficient authority to save her

Empress Tzu Hsi in later life. She had begun harem life in the third rank (of four) of The Imperial Concubines. In the photo her chief eunuch Li Lien-Ying stands on the right. Circa 1900.

當國今聖母皇太后萬歲萬歲萬萬歲

life. Chief Eunuch Li and a servant called Sung showed their contempt for the young emperor by wrapping Pearl Concubine in a carpet and dropping her into the well at Ning Shou Palace.

The personal relationship between Empress Tzu Hsi and Chief Eunuch Li has produced many stories, some factual, some fanciful, but all imply that despite his emasculation he was able to delight his mistress in a way that was seldom equalled by sexually complete men. In *Summer Palace Tales* (Shanghai 1915), an anonymous writer described a method by which Li strapped himself to young men so that the lower part of their body substituted for his own while the rest of him was 'involved with the full fury of a raging lion'. The writer adds that both the dragon empress and the dragon eunuch were so insatiable that a line of men stood in readiness to have the leather harness strapped to them. Li's reputation became almost that of a ruler and he was referred to as Lord of Nine Thousand Years (respectfully as well as bitterly) after the usual Imperial title of Lord of Ten Thousand Years.

In 1908, at the end of her long reign, the Empress succumbed to a recurring sickness. Before she died she made a statement in the traditional manner to those at the bedside: 'The Dragon Throne must never again be under the power and influence of a woman. The Laws of our Dynasty are against it and it must be enforced more strictly than in my time. But worse than giving power to women is giving it to eunuchs. The Ming Dynasty met its disastrous fate because of the meddling and the ambitions of eunuchs, and many of our own misfortunes today are their responsibility.'

Despite her dying denunciation, Chief Eunuch Li, now seventy, was conspicuously present at her funeral; and it is recorded that he was the only mourner to seem sincerely overwhelmed by grief.

The Empress Dowager Tzu Hsi with court attendants and, on the extreme right, her niece. Her court was dominated by eunuchs and she died in 1908.

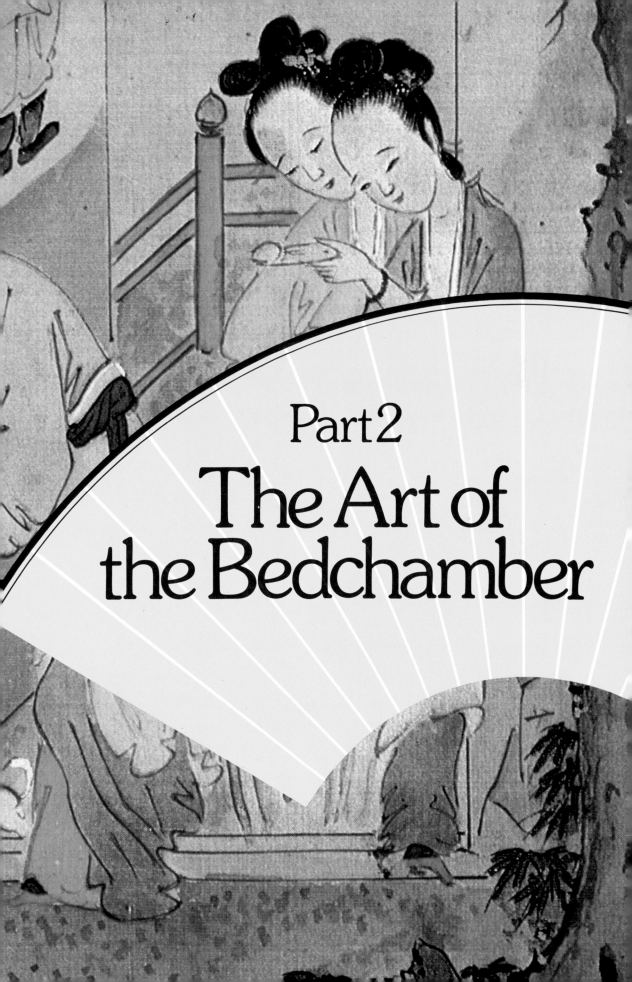

Part 2
The Art of
the Bedchamber

The problems of an indulgent man with many wives. An unusually boisterous scene in an erotic album. 19th-century gouache. Private collection, Paris.

CHAPTER FOUR

Celestial Stems for Precious Flowers

I toss aside my painter's brush
She puts away her embroidery
We face each other on the bed
Then reach forward wildly.

The night to the furthest corner
Is filled with our embrace,
Why should I call for lotus wine
When I am drinking her fiery breath.
Fann Fann Chan

As Yang and Yin represent the opposite yet complementary forces of life (man and woman locked in eternal battle yet seeking to resolve this in the Ultimate Harmony), so the beliefs of Confucianists and Taoists can be seen as the contradictory male and female elements of the moral and the social aspects of life. Confucianism favoured a partriarchal society, classical and authoritarian, while Taoism, with its romantic ideals, permitted expression of the more naturalistic side of the Chinese spirit.

For the followers of Confucius the function of woman was to serve her master, to perpetuate his name by having male children, to leave important decisions to him, and to accept with grace and humility her inferiority. She had also to be chaste, without passion and personality. Believers in Lao Tse, however, accepted that there was a more intimate side to human relations, that ability to manage public affairs and practical matters was simply one side of a very complex whole, and certain Taoist schools even asserted that woman was the more important of the two partners. Her womb nourished humanity, they reasoned, she was the object of man's greatest pleasure and inspiration, and if there was such a secret element as the Life Force, it was more likely to be in her blood than in the male's.

Against the classical severity and the insistence on 'right-thinking' and correct attitudes of the Confucianists, the Taoists placed their trust in the capricious yet ultimately harmonious world of nature. The simple regenerative pattern of life covered all species, all time and evolution, and Man's object should be to submit to his modest place in The Great Design. His problems came with defying the natural destiny, with allowing intelligence and purpose to confuse his mind with higher schemes, with ambition, materialism and a perverse desire to impose his will on the universe. The 'Be Wise' exhortations of Confucius were answered by 'Be Stupid', the ideal of developing 'character' by the observation that 'character' killed benevolence and created in man one of his most insufferable faults — self-righteousness.

Such faith in the 'natural animal' rather than in the 'intellectual' was one of the reasons why sex dominated much Taoist thinking and behaviour, as with Buddhism when it was later introduced into China, and why most books and writings on the subject have come from such sources. This inclination to treat sex as a natural part of life, without guilt or shame, was and is a fundamental Chinese attitude. Periods of puritanism, usually associated with Confucianism, though briefly fashionable, invariably failed to change this, partly because of the traditional Chinese ability to serve many masters and to worship many gods at once, and partly because the social pattern had been created for the convenience of the male. The dominant Yang would hardly agree to give up voluntarily what was essential to his happiness.

The ability of the Chinese to embrace two contradictory ways of life must be regarded as a praiseworthy reflection on his sophistication and his will to survive. The traditional Chinese found it possible to adhere to the severe Confucian beliefs in family and social matters and yet at the same time, with concubines and prostitutes, to indulge in pagan delights with a guilt-free spontaneity. This duality was helped, however, by the fact that neither of the two major beliefs of China was religious in the western sense of the word. His pleasure was never inhibited by the real or imagined presence of a punitive God waiting to consign him to Hell for his misdeeds — or to Heaven if he remained chaste.

The status of wives and concubines serves to illustrate this essential pragmatism. In a middle-class Confucian home the wife would hold the highest rank of all the womenfolk, she would be in charge of the domestic arrangements, bear the master's children, be appropriately honoured — yet be hidden from strangers and seldom enjoy any social life. The concubine, on the other hand, would be chosen to satisfy the Taoist side of his nature, a sweetheart who would please him in bed, entertain his friends, a creature of beauty and accomplishment.

This regard for the talented woman goes back to the time of the legendary Yellow Emperor (Huang-ti) and in the *Handbooks of Sex,* reputed to have been compiled almost five thousand years ago, his detailed dialogues are with three mysterious goddesses called The

A rare illustration of 'plucking the fragrant buds simultaneously.' The breast is also uncharacteristically voluptuous. 19th-century gouache. Private collection, Paris.

Chosen Maiden. The Wise Maiden, and The Forthright Female (frequently known as 'Elected Girl', 'Dark Girl' and 'Plain Girl'). His readiness to search for light and knowledge in the company of women clearly revealed his Taoist sympathies, and this regard for the 'instinctive' wisdom of the apparently inferior sex was a feature not only of 'pillow books' but of her status as a worthy adversary in the Flowery Battle.

The versatility of the Chinese male in living with two contradictory beliefs fitted him for the equally confusing task of fulfilling his distinct and differing roles. As the romantic Yang intent on winning the traditional 'sex-battle,' he had to be the merciless invader of the Jade Pavilion (the Flowery Field, Precious Estate et cetera), yet as the practical Confucian he would frequently pause in his wild passion and consult, with an intellectual regard for correct positions and techniques, his pillow books. The dual role and preoccupation also applied to the sexual climax. As Yang the Taoist he would be striving to sweep Yin towards a mutual enjoyment of the Ultimate, as Yang the Confucianist he would be drawn to the method of *coitus interruptus.* The attraction to the Chinese of this method was the belief that it caused the *tsing* (semen) to return to the head, thereby renewing desire, encouraging fine thoughts and, most important of all, prolonging virility.

The combative nature of this sex 'War and Peace' inevitably placed the greatest emphasis on the weapons of battle, and most traditional books on the bedchamber art included a detailed study of the penis and vulva. If a craftsman is identified with his hands and a singer with her voice, the traditional Yang and Yin were regarded as the personification of their sex organs. Penis and vulva had character, beauty and ability. The female 'parts', however, did not include the breasts. It was customary for these to be bound and flattened, and such was Yang's concentration on the vulva that it was rather summarily called 'the one square inch'.

The inability of the male to appreciate — or get excited by — that part of the woman's body that lay outside 'the one square inch' explains the failure of Chinese artists and painters to draw inspiration from it. The nude body as a subject for art was almost totally ignored, apart from 'pillow books' which featured bedchamber seenes for practical demonstrations of the sex-act. Poets were more lyrical about physical beauty, but as the sources of inspiration were usually concubines or prostitutes, or the stolen moments of an illicit affair, such heroines could hardly be seen as reflecting a more general appreciation. Lin Yutang in *My Country and My People* (1936) makes the pertinent observation: 'For woman's body, as body, the Chinese have no appreciation. We see very little of it in art. Chinese artists fail dismally in the portrayal of the human form, and even an artist like Ch'iu Shihchou (Ming Period), famous for his paintings of female life, shows the upper part of the female nude form very much like a potato. Few Chinese, unversed in Western art, can tell the beauty of a woman's neck or of a woman's back.'

Such an attitude towards the body led to a very practical approach to the choice of sex partners. If pillow books were the source of instruction, the sex handbooks were regarded as a sound guide to the necessary physical attributes of a desirable consort. The primary sex organs, the suppleness of limbs and joints, the texture and variations of pubic hair, the position of the vulva — these and many other features were the subject of the closest scrutiny and classification.

One of the oldest examples of such classification is in the form of a dialogue between the Yellow Emperor and the goddess-instructress, The Forthright Female (Su Nü). It forms part of the *I-hsing Fang,* a collection of such writings and books compiled by the modern

Chinese authority Yeh Tê-hui (1864-1927). The Yellow Emperor, seeking advice on the choice of women for coitus, asks:

Let us first dispose of those who cannot bring man happiness — which women should be avoided?

The Forthright Female: Before one even examines her vulva, there are many signs that reveal her unsuitability. If she neglects her hair so that it resembles an overgrown bush, if her face is surly and her eyes glare or are surrounded by dried secretions, then she should be avoided. If her voice is masculine and loud and her teeth are grain-coloured slabs, if she has hair on cheeks and chin, then she should be avoided. If her body is miserably lean and frail, she will prefer the top position, and if she is over forty her heart and stomach will be in constant disharmony; these, too, should be avoided.

The Yellow Emperor: And what of the vulva?

The Forthright Female: If the pubic hair is coarse and stiff, like bristles, or if it sprouts wildly and in different directions, this woman is unsuited. If the lips of the vagina do not cover the Jade Gate, and it hangs below, if the secretions are pungent, then such women are harmful. To have intercourse once with such creatures can bring a withering to the Jade Stem equal to that of one hundred battles with a good woman.

The Yellow Emperor: Now let us turn to such good women — which are the most suited to coitus?

The Forthright Female: Women should not be appreciated just for their beauty but should be regarded as the means to good health and of living to a great age. A young woman is the best choice for such a partner, and she should be a virgin with the Flowery Field as yet unseeded. Her breasts will then be high and not yet milked, and her Yin-essence unspilt. Her flesh should be firm, her skin well-oiled and silky to the touch, and her 'hundred joints' should be well-hinged and smooth in their movements. She should neither be too tall nor too short, and her disposition should be tender and affectionate.

The Yellow Emperor: Tell me more about the Flowery Field.

The Forthright Female: The outer lips should be high and not hanging, they should be firm without being too fleshy, and the Jade Gate should be so placed that penetration is easy. If it is too near to either the front or the back, it will cause strain or cramp for the man. The pubic hair should be smooth and silky, but not profuse. To be without such hair is better than too much, and her Vital Essence should flow at a touch and be sweet-smelling. Such a woman will soon move in unison and attain harmony with the man. Her body will convulse passionately, she will perspire freely, and even if all is not conducted by the Code of Rules and Principles, you will come to no harm.

The classification of suitable partners at a social level lower than the Royal Court was concerned more with general virtues than with the exact physical peculiarities of the sex organs. Modesty, obedience and virginity were the requirements of girls and brides, and Marco Polo, in the thirteenth-century, describes how they excelled 'in modesty and the strict observation of decorum. They do not frisk and frolic and dance ... or expose themselves to the gaze of passers-by.' He went on to praise them for not listening to lewd stories and for avoiding parties and entertainments, having their mothers for company when they walked outside and keeping their gaze to the ground rather than staring at others.

Such girls were ultimately reared and prepared for what was regarded as their purpose in life, marriage and motherhood. Marriage was usually preceded by the drawing up of a contract between the families of bridegroom and bride, and when both parties were satisfied, it remained only for the girl to offer proof of chastity. For this she was taken to the bath-house where experienced matrons sought to confirm her virginity by trying to insert a pigeon's egg. The failure to penetrate, in this test, did not always satisfy the bridegroom's family because certain medicaments were known to contract the vagina. If this was suspected then one of the matrons wrapped a finger in soft white linen and slightly ruptured the *vena virginalis*. The reason for this was the belief that the blood of the hymen had an enduring quality and could not be washed from the linen.

Marco Polo writes: 'If the blood is washed out, the girl is not an undefiled virgin and the bride's father must therefore pay the indemnity stated in the contract.' He then describes one of the ways in which girls protect themselves against accidents. 'They walk so daintily that one foot hardly steps a finger's breadth in front of the other.'

The subject of the ideal woman was also a favourite theme of Chinese novelists. As fiction was the chosen literary form for much that was regarded as too frivolous or 'unworthy' for scholars and serious writers, novels frequently extended the entertaining story into a detailed treatise. Li Yü, the great seventeenth-century novelist, who travelled round the Empire with his theatre troupe and was a notorious sex-conqueror, was obviously drawing on his wide knowledge of women when his characters gave their views on female beauty.

In *The Flesh Prayer-mat,* a middle-aged but active woman speaks eloquently on the subject:

'In my opinion', said Lady Chen. 'women can roughly be divided into two categories — those who please the eye and those who are meant for use. One does not necessarily mean the other, though there are a few women who qualify in both ways. Beauty will always possess the following qualities: a slender body, a certain delicacy, a fineness of line. The most famous painters give their women this appearance, never those of a coarse, powerful or large-boned creature. Yet these painters were simply admiring their beauty, hardly ever their usefulness as women. The women they did not paint, but who pleased them in other ways, were well covered and of good physique, seldom slender and delicate, always strong and lusty. And why did they prefer them like this? The reason is simply "use".

'The strong woman will be able to support his weight when he is on top of her, her body will more nearly be of the same proportions as his own, therefore his member will enter her like a foot into a well-fitting shoe, and she will be as soft to lie on as the bedding underneath her. And why should this be so important? Well, it's obvious. The thin woman is like a rock, a wooden log under his body. To lie on her will create aches and pains in a hundred places, and when she moves, her bony limbs will strike to left and right. How can a man find comfort and relaxation on this? On the other hand, with a woman for use, she is an extension of the soft bedding into which he sinks with total unconcern, confident that there will be no complaints, into which he can thrust knowing that he can go on for ever, as deep as he wants and as fiercely as he likes. With men of experience, then, the well-covered body is preferable to the slender beauty.

'But let us be even more detailed. The average man weighs a hundred *catties* [75 kilos], which is no mean load. To lie on a frail woman is like sleeping on an unsafe bed; it can suddenly collapse beneath you. If one of the pleasures of intercourse is to abandon oneself to furious activity, how can a man really throw himself into the sex-battle when he knows his opponent is too weak to make a fight of it? A robust plain girl is always better than a frail beauty.

'Fortunately for men there are many of us women who combine the qualities of both use and beauty, and a man who has found, say, eighty per cent of each can consider that he has a fine thoroughbred for the riding.'

This idealisation of the sturdier woman was not surprising in a society where most females were physically slighter and flatter than the seductively curvaceous beauties favoured by the men and artists of other countries. Any concessions to seductiveness were further diminished by the dress favoured by Chinese women — or perhaps inflicted on them. Her breasts were

'All men are free to have concubines, and class or fortune means nothing in their selection as the only standard of preference is physical beauty.' Matteo Ricci (1552-1610), missionary and explorer. Painting from a 17th-century pillow book. By kind permission of the British Museum.

bound by a crushing bodice, her gowns hung shapelessly from neck to foot, and the wide sleeves and general looseness made her seem lost in a mass of material. The only parts that indicated herself were the face, head and hands, and on these were concentrated her efforts to appear glamorous. The result was a face powdered and rouged like a mask, and a magnificent and lacquered hairstyle adorned with flowers and jewellery, combs and ribbons.

From about the time of the Mongol Dynasty (1280-1368), however, until China became a republic in 1912, an exciting new factor entered into considerations of feminine beauty. To the obsession with 'the one square inch' was added the sudden discovery of the sexual attractiveness of bound feet. Whether it is regarded as a fetish or a fashion, the historical fact remains that in a remarkably short time it had claimed women of all classes, except for a few maidservants and peasants, and since no revolts against the painful practice are recorded, there must have been very real (psychological) reasons for its adoption.

The bandages were usually applied in early childhood, the technique being to fold the toes and the front part of the foot underneath, very painful at first, more bearable as the deformity finally set into the pattern of a hoof. This hoof-like shape was given the romantic name of 'golden lily' or 'golden lotus', the ideal dimension being when the base measured only three inches. Apart from the physical discomfort, the result of foot-binding was to handicap movement and to make even walking an awkward exercise. There were no protests, however, from the Chinese male. If the Yin of the eternal sex battle wanted to handicap herself even further, why should he object? And to the colourful Taoist sex terminology was added another name for intercourse — A Walk Between the Golden Lilies.

A popular folk story suggests that the practice originated in the earlier Southern T'ang dynasty. The ruler was very much in love with a dancer called Yao-niang, and to give her an appropriate stage for her exquisite talents had constructed a golden lotus flower six feet high. To enable her to dance on the petals, Yao-niang had her feet bound with silk and, like a modern ballerina, performed on her toes. More widely accepted, however, was a conviction that foot-binding caused the thighs to swell, thereby making them more voluptuous to the male.

Another theory put forward to explain its popularity with the male was that her virtual immobility in the bedchamber reduced her to helplessness, and if it can be believed that love had previously been preceded by an exhausting chase round the room, there could be some truth in this. In the case of wives, certainly, her bound feet tied her more than ever to the home, and concubines and mistresses seeking a quick escape from a tyrannical master could hardly have done so unaided.

In Lord Macartney's Journal recording his stay in Peking at the end of the eighteenth century, he is told by a Mandarin attached to the Embassy: 'Footbinding might possibly have arisen from oriental jealousy, which has always been ingenious in its contrivances for securing ladies to their owners, and that certainly a good way of keeping them at home is to make it both troublesome and painful for them to gad about. I must observe, however, that the deforming of a part of the human body is to us Chinese less strange than such foreign practices as actually cutting pieces off as in circumcision ...'

The tightly bound feet were covered by decorative leggings tied round the ankles or sometimes rising to mid-calf, and the modesty surrounding the 'golden lilies' was such that a woman indulging in sexual intercourse would allow herself to be stripped of everything except her leggings. In erotic prints and paintings, usually in pillow books, the women are shown in every imaginable position, sometimes two or three with a single male, and the only garment invariably in evidence is the foot-covering. The almost sacred nature of the bound foot, however, gave it a special importance in courtship, and for a man to lightly brush the leggings with his fingers was the most direct invitation to sex. This was often managed with some pretence at subtlety, by the man 'accidentally' dropping objects on the floors when seated close to the woman of his choice, then whispering to be allowed 'to walk between the golden lilies'.

As the feet remained hidden even when the woman unconcernedly exposed her vagina, it was not surprising that they became the object of the deepest sexual longings and the commonest cause of male involuntary ejaculation. To be allowed to remove the bandages was a favour seldom permitted in the early stages of a sexual relationship, and an exciting love posture was for the man to have the embroidered leggings dangling in front of his face

as he thrust into the Jade Pavilion. To effect this added pleasure, lengths of rope were needed to suspend the feet from the ceiling or, if the couple were lying on a traditional bed, to tie them to the high frame. A compromise between keeping on the bandages and exposing the feet was to use the bandages for the tying-up, an arrangement that possibly allowed a glimpse of the crumpled toes.

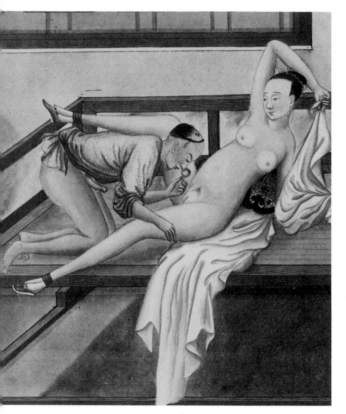

Male fascination with 'the one square inch.' 19th-century. Courtesy of the Bibliothéque Nationale, Paris.

While the element of fetishism is undeniable, the foot and the shoe being traditional sex images of the Chinese, the satisfaction in the physical helplessness of his partner related to the growing doubts the male was having in his manliness. The period of foot-binding coincided with the élitist character of Chinese society, the intellectual and cultural superiority of an educated minority compared with the peasantry, and the equally absolute supremacy of the Middle Kingdom over the more primitive states of the neighbouring barbarians. It also coincided with a parallel consciousness that the educated male might have paid a high price for his over-refinement and his academic honours.

To what extent was he losing his animal virility in his worship of culture and learning?

The crippling of his womenfolk to a point almost of immobility helped to restore his male ego, and as he witnessed their helplessness in face of physical assault, he enjoyed a 'make-believe' identification with the lustier barbarians and Tatars. At the same time, however, the refined Chinese male, further needing to assert his manliness, sought out vigorous peasant girls. This class of females was called 'chopping blocks' or 'the big-footed', and when they were purposely introduced into a household as maids, it was on the understanding that they retained their primitive ways.

In any study of the physical variations of the Chinese, the vast area of the country must be considered. Between north and south the racial differences are as marked as those between the Scandinavians and the Mediterranean peoples of Europe. Mongols, Tatars and Tibetans, tough, physically impressive and earthy by nature, are part of the same society as the smaller more sophisticated southerners who are ethnically closer to the Thais and the Vietnamese. Their faces and bodies, too, reflect these variations, the accepted standards of beauty of one region differing greatly from that of another. Skin colour, physical proportions, the shape of face and features, the degree of body hair, and even certain characteristics of the sex organs, are identified with distinct districts of the country. In an area of Kiangsu the local women are renowned for their fine and delicate noses. In Kweichow the women of one of the tribes are mostly without pubic hair, while in a district of Szechwan the females are reputed to have 'double-door' vaginas. This term refers to unusually thick *labia majoris,* giving the male a greater sense of penetration.

The wide differences between the physical characteristics of the peoples of this vast territory are also considered to be reflected in their behaviour and their degrees of passion. As in Europe, the individuals of one area are regarded as particularly virile, of another as rather dour, of a third as temperamental. A story is told, for example, of the Emperor who chose all his concubines from a certain area of Fukien. Although a virile man himself, he could hardly satisfy girls with such passionate natures, and gradually they began to lose their gaiety and vitality. He therefore consulted his doctors and was told that the best medicine for the girls' sickness was a company of the Palace Guards. The Emperor's sense of magnanimity prevailed and he agreed to this, and some days later he decided to visit his harem in person to see whether the girls were feeling better. He was at once delighted by the transformation, but as he turned from the radiant women he was surprised to see sprawling on the couches a number of prostrate and haggard men. On demanding an explanation for their presence, one of the girls exclaimed: 'Oh Dragon Ruler, these are the empty jars of the medicine you prescribed.'

In his *Ways of Sex* published in 1927, Yeh Tê-hui attempted to summarise popular beliefs on the subject, and in a section on 'The Choice of a Woman', in a form that might have come from the dialogue of the legendary Yellow Emperor himself, he offered the following comments:

First, let us take the buttocks. If they are high and protruding they provide a comfortable cushion for the sex battle. The woman will be demanding and hard to satisfy. On the other hand, if they are as flat as a featureless plain, she was not created for love but can labour tirelessly in the kitchen or about the house. If the buttocks are narrow she will seldom have orgasms, and if they droop over the back of the thighs she will be lazy and passive.

Of the vulva, this should be said. The preferred colour is a honey pink, the flesh soft and with a natural and constant warmth. Too red denotes too much of the raw animal, too pale, too little of the animal. The outer lips should be firm yet easily parted at a touch, and when open radiant like a flower in the morning sun. The Jade Gate should be exactly between the *mons veneris* and the anus otherwise it may not be in line for the Celestial Stem. If the Jade Gate flies open at the approach, she is sexually healthy. If it is a flat little aperture, the colour of pale ash, the welcome will be a cold one.

Of great importance is the Jade Step (clitoris) to the Pavilion. This should be round like a pearl, not protruding yet readily touched by finger or tongue. It should rise a little as it is unveiled, then retire when the activity moves elsewhere. The inside of the Jade Pavilion should be deep but not too wide, its walls formed in a series of folds that retain a constant flow of lubrication. This flow should be slow but endless; there should be no sudden deluge followed by a drought.

The pubic hair indicates the following:

Black like the feathers of a glossy bird — a strong and obstinate female.
Brown with golden tints — an easy and generous female.
Hair fine, silky and short — a quiet and retiring female.
A really thick growth sweeping down and under — a female with the abandonment of a waterfall.

Patchy and arid, like vegetation on hill tops — a female lacking warmth and sentiment.

The intellectual interest with which the Chinese male regarded the female organs was applied with equal diligence to his own parts. The consciousness of the mixed blessings of over-refinement, and the price paid in his loss of physical stature and primitive lust, caused him to devote his considerable intelligence to restoring what he regarded as his manly heritage. For the Chinese, with his concern for victory in the Yin-Yang confrontation, this simply meant the size and performance of his Male Peak. He was aware, too, not only of the formidable sex feats of his ancestors but of the fact that men like War God Kuang Yü rode into battle swinging axes weighing 80 *catties* (120lbs), that warriors of old engaged in single-handed contests with tigers, and that they were agile enough to catch arrows in flight. And now, as a scholar or a poet or a mandarin, he had lost those splendid manly qualities.

The need to retrieve his lost physical glory therefore encouraged him to substitute sex for other forms of heroism and masculine feats, and this was displayed in two ways. One was with the 'personification of the penis' (a kind of *alter ego*), the other with equipping that *alter ego* with a formidable arsenal of sexual aids. What over-refinement had taken away, he would provide for himself. The bedchamber heroes of sex-battles therefore took to the field wearing a penis-helmet known as the Cap of Eternal Desire, a breastplate termed a Sulphur Lust Ring, a carved jade or ivory ring at the base of the penis (for exciting the clitoris), and sometimes pennants of gay ribbons fluttering from the testicles. These adjuncts, together with passion-rousing ointments and couch-pleasure powders, are dealt with in a later chapter, but one may refer here to the 'battle-songs' of such encounters. The following, by a seventeenth-century writer, though it glorifies the weapon of the sex-war, contains a few lines of irony.

Jade-stalk stands high,
Capped by the mushroom helmet
Of blushing crimson,
Its base rising from a saddle
Of profuse black hair.

Under its glowing skin
Ligaments and fine veins
Throb with eagerness
For girls of thirteen or thirty,
For boys of fourteen or fifteen.

Position of Cicadas Clinging to a Tree. *The Most Noble Tung Hsüan in his* Art of the Bedchamber *states: 'This position is not for heavy women with weak men.' From the* Yanwo 5 *in the Mitchell Library, Sydney.*

The position of Silkworm Spinning *from the Most Noble Tung Hsüan's Thirty Heaven and Earth Postures. 19th-century. From the* Yanwo 5 *in the Mitchell Library, Sydney.*

But this menacing sea-cucumber
Has a series of short lives,
Each time collapsing
To resemble the shrimps
In the water around it.

This preoccupation with the penis, as well as creating a minor industry in sex instruments and battle array, also had its more worrying side. The Chinese male, at least those elevated to the class of administrators, scholars, merchants and the educated, was constantly troubled by a sense of inadequacy. This led to a flourishing demand for aphrodisiacs, an obsession with size and performance as if sex was a competition of Olympic rigours, and frequent fears of impotence. There are many accounts of such fears affecting the male population of different areas of the country, and these seem to rival the terrors of religious damnation. In Kwangtung province in the fourteenth century the villagers were convinced that a form of dehydration in hot weather was causing their penises to shrivel. They therefore devised a small water-bag, which hung round the waist, and the Jade-stem during the day was placed in it to soak. A more modern phenomenon is recorded of men in a large city being stricken by the horror of a regressive penis. Various methods were adopted for preventing it from shrinking into the stomach. These included strapping to the leg, suspending weights from the end of it, glueing wooden rings to the base and piercing the foreskin with wire rods. Men were also seen on the streets with the member firmly gripped between chopsticks or drawn up

with a string that was looped round the waist.

As physical exercise was considered unseemly for cultured men (one of the customs was to keep the back slightly bowed to indicate a learned and courteous disposition), the bedchamber was usually the only place where the educated man utilised his muscles. Then as now, muscle-building exercises were in vogue, and apart from aphrodisiacs for improving the performance, attempts to increase the size of the penis were conducted at two levels, one being by medicaments, the other by surgical grafting. The prescriptions could be taken orally, applied to the member or, in some instances, rubbed round the Jade Gate, and the favoured ingredients were: powdered deer-horn, sea-cucumber and human placenta (both dried and powdered), hawk excrement, sea grass, dog's liver and bull's genitalia. A diligent application of such potions, it was claimed, increased the organ by half its usual length.

The second area of experimentation, that of transplants and grafts, is not so incredible as it sounds. The eunuch was a common figure in society, not only at the Imperial Court but at less exalted levels, and since one of the methods of effecting castration was to remove the penis as well as the testicles, an organ 'bank' was always available to those scientists and surgeons working in that field. And not only would they be concerned with enlarging unsatisfactory members; their services would have been called on by those eunuchs whose fortunes and stations had changed and who sought later in life to recover what they had lost. Criminals and prisoners-of-war also suf-

A variation of Hovering Butterflies *from the Most Noble Tung Hsüan's Thirty Heaven and Earth Postures. 19th-century. From the* Yanwo 5 *in the Mitchell Library, Sydney.*

fered castration and were frequent victims of the 'transplant craze'.

As the novel gave the truest and least inhibited picture of traditional China, because of the greater freedom accorded to what was regarded as a vulgar literary form, it is not surprising that the subject of improving on nature was a common feature of sex-narratives. In the seventeenth-century work, *Jou-pu-t'uan,* Li Yü succeeds in capturing the mood of the men of the time as well as describing such a penis-graft in detail.

The hero of the story, the Night-time Scholar, having left his wife to travel widely in search of wisdom, spends a night at a lonely roadhouse. Here he meets a warm-hearted bandit called Kun Lun's Equal (after the great Kun Lun, famed for his success in abducting women), and they quickly become close friends. In fact the bandit adopts the Scholar as his younger brother ('hsiung' and 'ti'), and in conversation mentions all the women he knows who are not being satisfied by their husbands...

The Night-time Scholar reflected on the pleasing information of the failure of these husbands to conquer their wives. Kun Lun's Equal's colourful account of these tormented women, and his willingness to take his newly-adopted younger brother with him on his raids, promised adventures that would not only be exciting but which came within his pledge to his wife to seek every opportunity to improve his learning. Wishing, however, to prove himself worthy of the bandit's friendship, and to show that he was also a man of the world, the Scholar said with great authority:

'Let us seek the reasons for the failure of these husbands. It could be that their wives are frigid or that their implements are inadequate for the job. On the other hand, from my own experience, I know it's not just a trusty weapon that matters. A man's potency is like "capital" in the bank. There must be plenty to draw on.' The Scholar smiled with the utmost self-confidence. 'However, I can assure you of one thing — when you lead me to these women, I'll certainly be able to give them what they're missing.'

'From my personal knowledge of the two husbands,' observed Kun Lun's Equal, 'their husbands have implements and "capital" that are by no means inadequate. They are unimpressive only when compared with the largest and the most virile. But while we are on the subject, dear adopted younger brother, what about your own implement and stock of "capital"? Tell me something of its size, how long you can last.... After all, since I am being entrusted to get these women excited about you, you must give me some details by which to recommend you.'

The Scholar replied with serene confidence.

'My honourable elder brother need not imagine I am in any way lacking. My implement and capital reserves are more than adequate for the job. If described in the terms of a banquet, I will provide sufficient food and drink to make any woman incapable of rising from the table, and too tipsy to put her words together. After all, I hope I'm not the kind of host to offer my guests mean meals, a host from whose table they leave hungrier and thirstier than when they sat down.'

Kun Lun's Equal persisted with his searching questions.

'I am not for a moment questioning either your dimensions or your "capital", but I would be much happier to learn a few facts. For instance, my indisputably virile younger brother, when you are attacking the Pleasure Pavilion, how many blows can you strike in one unbroken assault?'

'I hardly take my writing equipment to bed with me!' protested the Scholar. 'I may not be able to quote figures but I can assure you that my guests are always well-filled. With me it's a banquet every time.'

'Then if you cannot give me an exact number of thrusts, at least tell me how long you last before withdrawing from the field of battle?'

In truth, the Night-time Scholar could seldom prolong it for more than an hour, but in order to impress the Bandit, he decided to double the period. After all, there were the ladies to impress as well.

'My performance lasts a quarter of the night,' he assured Kun Lun's Equal. 'that is without once withdrawing from the field.'

'And you call that exceptional?' the Bandit exclaimed. 'Your performance is no better than average — adequate for marriage and other domestic arrangements but hardly enough for orgies among strange women, for storming the headquarters, for taming them completely. No, before I can recommend you as an amorous companion, you must be better than average.'

The Night-time Scholar was becoming a little impatient, but he managed to speak with pleasant conviction.

'You needn't be concerned about me, I can assure you. Besides, I have recently bought some really potent aphrodisiacs. One I swallow and the other I apply externally to the implement. The real problem for me is to find the right women for my talents. I'm like a powerful cannon with no enemy to fire at, or with a target that's hardly worth the ammunition. So don't worry — between the pills and the couch ointment, I'll be able to last forever.'

'It is true that such ointment can prolong your performance,' conceded Kun Lun's Equal, 'but can it double the size of your implement? Let's face it, if you are lacking in dimensions, no amount of 'stiffening-pills' or 'endurance-ointment' will make up the difference. A person of inadequate size trying to compensate with aphrodisiacs is like an examination candidate with not enough knowledge. He can stimulate himself with ginseng or alcohol, work himself into a state of busyness and determination, but what will be set down on the paper? On the other hand, if the candidate is well-equipped and has all the material he needs, then the stimulants will give him just that little bit of extra encouragement. To come to the point, then, how big and how thick are you?'

'Bigger and thicker than most, I can assure you,' the Scholar said at once.

'You must either give me the dimensions or let me see it for myself,' insisted Kun Lun's Equal.

And observing that the younger man was reluctant to do either, he took hold of the Scholar's trousers with the intention of pulling them down.

'Here — what are you doing!' protested the Scholar.

After three unsuccessful attempts to discover the exact size of the implement, Kun Lun's Equal drew away impatiently.

'If you intend to be unhelpful you cannot expect your unworthy brother to advance your cause with these women. How would I feel if, after recommending you to them, you turned out to have only an insignificant little twig? And if the women cried rape as soon as you touched them, and it turned out that you had hardly enough to tickle them, how would they feel?'

The argument seemed indisputable but the Scholar tried to delay the embarrassing situation a moment longer.

'It's not that your unworthy brother's implement will not bear inspection,' he explained. 'It is simply that for a scholar it is somewhat inelegant to pull it out as if it is no more than my writing brush or my handkerchief.'

Having said this, however, he unfastened his trousers, placed his hand under his vest and took hold of the instrument. Then he flattened his hand like a platform and raised it for Kun Lun's Equal's better inspection.

'This is your unworthy younger brother's Male Peak. Take as good a look at it as you wish.'

The Bandit stared down with an inscrutable expression, then moved to view it from a number of angles. The Scholar waited some moments for the man's opinion, but when Kun Lun's Equal seemed unable to utter a word, he decided that the splendid dimensions of his implement had reduced the man to speechlessness.

'And you should see it when it is roused,' the Night-time Scholar added proudly. 'It's at rest now — in fact really shrivelled up.'

Kun Lun's Equal spoke at last.

'The best thing you can do with that is to keep it in your trousers — out of sight,' he said briefly.

The Scholar did not immediately understand.

'And what do you mean by that?'

'There is an outside limit to everything, and it's pretty obvious that what you've got can never really amount to much.'

'But my wife and concubines have never complained...'

'My dear adopted younger brother,' said the older man before the Scholar's dismay could really express itself. 'Your implement is hardly more than a third the size of a real man's. Do you honestly think that's enough for raids on other men's private property? Your earlier stories, all those amorous adventures, made me think you had a cudgel in your trousers. Instead, what do I find? Something that might be all right for brushing the undergrowth but is hardly up to the job of storming the headquarters. No, you have clearly been leading this unworthy elder brother up the garden path.'

The Scholar's shock at last turned to the need to defend himself.

'On most occasions it is received with approval and on some it has even roused women to applause. Even now, my wife trembles with delight and fear at the sight of it.'

'If you have ever received a compliment on that thing, it could only have come from a virgin you were deflowering or from a young boy taking a man for the first time.'

Kun Lun's Equal spoke with such scorn and authority that the Scholar was at last prepared to believe that he might not be so well-endowed as he had imagined.

'You honestly mean to say I'm hardly even average? It's unbelievable!'

'I'm giving you the opinion of someone who has seen at least a thousand of them and I can truthfully say that not one of them was so small as yours.'

The Scholar reflected wretchedly on this information, then remembered that his intention was to accompany the Bandit on one of his raids.

'Let's get back to the subject of those two frustrated wives. How do the weapons of their husbands compare with that of your apparently undersized younger brother?'

'I haven't much of an opinion of their implements, either, but at least they're twice the size of yours.'

This seemed incredible, unbelievable, and the Scholar raised his voice.

'You're only saying this because you've changed your mind about wanting me to join you. Perhaps you haven't really got these conquests after all? Besides, how can you know so much about the dimensions of the husbands when you only glimpsed them for a second when you were raiding their homes?'

'In the case of the silk merchant I made further enquiries and learnt from a friend, who had seen him on hot summer days, that he had an implement of impressive size, as big as a large eel. If you haven't something at least as big as his, how can you possibly be welcomed by his wife?'

The Scholar became more depressed than ever.

'What about my good looks, my charm and intelligence — don't they count with a woman? Assuming my equipment is slightly stunted — is that all women are after? I beg you in the name of friendship to give me a chance with the two wives. I'm sure I can make up in other ways for any discrepancy of length.'

'Well, it's all very well to have good looks and intelligence — they'll certainly get you through the doors and into the bedroom. But what do you do once you're inside? Once she's taken you into the Examination Hall, you either pass or fail. No, put out of your mind such big ideas as carrying off other men's wives, raping their daughters... Keep your limited talents for your own wife and forget these dreams of yours.'

The following day the Night-time Scholar had managed to locate a certain Master of Medicine, an elderly man of distinguished appearance and wide reputation, and confided the nature of his private shame. If what the Bandit had told him was true, this was the only way of correcting what was clearly a physical malformation.

'Master,' said the Scholar, 'I have seen your advertisements in which you claim to increase the size of a small member. Perhaps you will kindly explain how this miracle is performed and whether you can guarantee one of giant proportions?'

'That all depends on the original material,' replied the Master of Medicine. 'First on its dimensions, secondly on what size you want it to be. Then there's a third consideration — will you be able to adapt yourself to the drastic change?'

This explanation greatly excited the Scholar.

'Please tell me more. I really hope you can do something for me.'

'I trust you will be able to follow the language of a medical explanation. To begin with, do you need simply a couple of inches on the end? If so, I can give you an ointment that will bring about this marginal change without difficulty,' explained the Master.

'First it makes the implement insensitive to heat and cold and temporarily stops the need to urinate. In this state it is then 'washed', 'smoked' and 'pulled'. Please excuse these professional terms. The 'washing' is for enlarging, the 'smoking' for toughening and the 'pulling' for lengthening. This treatment continues for three days and nights. As you see, then, it is very straightforward, and for this reason is the most popular method of all.'

'And what is the most ambitious of your methods?' asked the Night-time Scholar,

'If it has to be enlarged out of all recognition, such as in the case of a really diminutive Male Peak, then a major operation is necessary. This is the "Jade-Stem Graft" and requires a total restructuring of vessels, sinews, skin and flesh. But such surgery is only recommended to those who feel that the chance to have a super-size implement out-weighs all other considerations of life. I would first have to be satisfied, by judging his character, that he has the purpose and courage to face the prolonged treatment. If he fails this test, then the best advice I can give is for him to forget the matter altogether. On the other hand, if the patient regards sex gratification as the most important thing in life and is of the right disposition, then I will gladly perform the graft.'

The Scholar had listened with incredulity. Now he said: 'But is a graft really possible?'

'Again I must explain in medical terms,'said the Master. 'First I find a large and healthy dog, then a bitch who is on heat. I place them in adjoining kennels and feed them well. After a few days I bring them together. Now a dog's implement is a remarkable thing. It is capable of great enlargement and this erection will last a very long time. Even after the dog has enjoyed the *Clouds and the Rain,* because of its remarkable implement, it will remain stuck in the bitch for half a day. My operation consists of this — I wait until the mounted dog is about to ejaculate, when his implement is most swollen, then take out my surgeon's knife and slice it away with a single cut. As it is lodged in the bitch, I then carefully carve it out of her.

'The operation depends on great speed. In a matter of moments, I first cut lengthwise down the enlarged penis, quartering it into long segments. Then the patient's member, after being anaesthetised, receives four incisions. Into each of these long cuts I slot a slice of the dog's member — the flesh must still be warm — rub the assembled strips with a special healing ointment, then bind the lot in tight bandages. With luck, there will be a perfect grafting of man and dog.

'The one danger is the possibility of cutting into the urethra. Once the waterway is damaged, the patient may never again achieve a full erection. However, if all goes well, the healing should take no more than two months, and when the bandages come off, you will hardly notice any scars. After a further month of recuperation, the new implement can be pressed into service.'

Instruction of a young concubine. Lord Yang and his mistress try to reassure the timid virgin. The scrolls and brushes in the vase imply a learned household. 19th-century. Courtesy private collection, Paris.

The erotic fan could present a pattern of irreproachable good taste when opened in one direction and a tableau of lovers when the ribs were reversed. 19th-century. By kind permission of the British Museum.

'But what will the dimensions be?' inquired the Scholar, a little dazed by the medical description.

'Outwardly it will only appear two or three times the normal size, but once brought into action it will swell much more than the usual ratio, and its total volume and power is probably twenty times that of the average organ.'

Ever since the Scholar had suffered Kun Lun's Equal's scorn, he had felt broken and shamed. Now, with a cry of delight, he dropped on to his knees and made a full kowtow to the Master. In his heart he could hear the songs of a thousand birds.

'Oh, great Master of Medicine and Surgery,' begged the Scholar on his knees. 'This operation means more to me than life itself. What must I do in return?'

The Master helped him to his feet.

'If you wish it so much, then we can arrange for it to be done.'

The Scholar responded with a speech of great sincerity.

'Woman is the whole point of man's existence on earth, yet I have learnt that I am lacking in the part that is meant to make the most of that existence. Now you promise to correct this ill-endowment of nature ...' He fell on his knees again. 'What can I do except face north and kowtow with gratitude.'

He called his servant to bring forward his treasure-box and drew out a bag of silver.

'Here, Master, is a modest token of my appreciation. When the operation is over and the grafting successful, you will receive a further proof of this unworthy one's gratitude.'

'A number of points still remain to be clarified,' the Master now explained.

'Then let us clarify them. I will pay any price to be the proud possessor of a super implement, and I will endure any pain. And if the knife should slip, ending my days on earth, I will bear you no ill-will.'

'I have no doubts about my surgical ability. My failures are very few and never fatal. However, I wonder whether you are prepared to make the Three Sacrifices.'

'And what are these sacrifices?' the Scholar asked instantly.

'First, for three months there must be total abstinence from sexual intercourse. To ignore this will cause the seams to come apart. The slices of dog will simply fall off, that which is your own will become septic along the whole length of the incisions. The second sacrifice is that the possessor of such a formidable implement must forego certain categories of girls. First are young females with little experience. Secondly, virgins. To transfix such virgins with the grafted giant is nothing short of murder.'

'And the third, Master?'

'This is the inevitable sacrifice of some of man's normal potency. By adding a dog's organ to the patient's equipment, one also dilutes man's potency with the animal's lesser preoccupation with sex.

Also, records show that your children will have shorter lives, which means that future generations will also pay for your decision. So think carefully — can you abstain for three months, can you control your desire with virgins, are you prepared to forego having children?'

The Scholar made this weighty decision without a moment's hesitation.

'Such sacrifices I will bear with fortitude, Master. Have no doubt about that.'

'Then I will leave you to obtain the animal of your choice, and bring it to me when you are ready.'

The Night-time Scholar searched the district for three days before finding a dog enormous enough to suit him. He also purchased a bitch in a fine state of health, fed them with the choicest provisions and kept them in separate parts of the house. When the appointed day arrived, his servants led the animals to the residence of the Master of Medicine which was situated in a secluded area of town and therefore ideal for such unorthodox surgical practices. Other servants brought with them enough food and wine for a banquet.

The Master of Medicine, on the arrival of the Scholar, immediately started his preparations. The unsatisfactory implement was rubbed with an ointment that instantly numbed it. After a few moments it was difficult for the Scholar to believe it was joined to his circulation, and after pinching and pulling it, he was confident that he would feel nothing when the Master sliced into it.

The dog was introduced to the bitch and they took an immediate interest in each other. It was a closed courtyard, and with some time to wait, tables were brought out and the banquet laid. Soon, however, the Scholar and the Master, between morsels of delicious food, were watching the preparatory stage of the imminent penis-graft. After a chase round the courtyard, and some strenuous love-play, the dog fastened himself securely to the bitch, and with unsuspecting indifference towards those seated at the table, the animals proceeded to enjoy their own variation of the *Clouds and the Rain*.

At last the Master gave a signal to the servant to tighten the leashes and pull the animals, who had turned tail to tail, in opposite directions. The dog's fine implement, now behind him and locked inside the bitch, was therefore taut and stretched, and in an excellent position for the Master's knife. Experience had made him expert in the hazardous matter of timing, and judging his stroke perfectly, the Master severed the implement at the root. With an equally skilful slash, he had cut into the bitch's rump and successfully released the member.

As the servants dragged away the howling animals, the Master cut the prize into four long strips, then told the Scholar to assist him by holding out his own member. With some trepidation, the Scholar obeyed the order, but so swift and skilful was the surgeon's art, that the lengthwise incisions made no sensation at all. The slices of the canine organ were still hot as they were slotted into the cuts, and the Master paused to admire his handiwork. He then rubbed on the healing ointment and made a very neat job of bandaging the segments together. Finally, the servants were called to clear away the evidence of the operation, and since the Scholar appeared to suffer no ill-effects, he invited the Master to return to the table and to continue their interrupted banquet. And over the food and wine, the Master gave the Scholar further advice on how best to use his new acquisition.

It is interesting to reflect that the preoccupation of the Night-time Scholar with dimensions was similar to that of the Yellow Emperor. A period of four thousand years separated them yet they were joined by a common and enduring obsession. And the continuity did not end in the Ming dynasty. The timeless questions asked by the Yellow Emperor, his self-doubts and curiosity, are those revealed to the sexologists and psychiatrists of the twentieth-century.

The simple language, too, seems to defy the millennia, as the excerpt from Section 6 of of Su-nü-ching shows. The title is: *On the Large and the Small, the Long and the Short:-*

Yellow Emperor: Why is it that with 'Man's Most Precious Thing', it should vary so much in size and vitality?

The Wise Maiden: The difference between Precious Things is part of the great variety of creation. If heads and bodies differ, why not the parts of those heads and bodies? Some men are tall, some small, some strong, some weak. So it is with their Battle Implements. Some are formidable and aggressive, others puny and timid, some look angry, some look gentle. The most important thing, however, is that they are put to use.

Yellow Emperor: Does the difference in size and expression affect the pleasure derived by the man during intercourse?

The Wise Maiden: Such differences are purely external. The real pleasure is the inner one of satisfaction and the achievement of harmony in the Ultimate. Man and woman contribute to this by their *love* and *respect* for each other, they proceed further by their *desire* for each other, and they consummate it by their *passion* for each other.

Yellow Emperor: What variations are there between hard and soft?

The Wise Maiden: A long member which remains in a semi-hard condition is less satisfactory than a short member which is iron-hard. A short iron-hard member that is rough and inconsiderate in operation is less satisfactory than one used more expertly and carefully. As with all things under Heaven, one should achieve the Golden Mean.

Yellow Emperor: Is it true that with the right medicine, the small can be made big, the soft can be made hard? And what are the effects of such special nourishment?

The Wise Maiden: When the couple are in harmony, and the passions equally aroused, the small and the short will become larger, the soft and the weak will become stronger. Harmony of the spirit and the passions can sustain one through one hundred sexual acts with one hundred women without risk or fear to the health. The nourishment to male powers comes from the Yin Essence which is absorbed by their Yang Essence. As men and women indulge themselves, exchanging all the fluids of the body and breathing into each other's mouths, it is like the meeting of water and fire in such equal quantities that neither defeats the other. Man and woman should move and blend in intercourse like the waves and the currents of the seas, one way then another, but always part of the great tide of Harmony. Thus they will continue all night, their precious Essences preserved and constantly nourishing, curing the ailments and contributing to longevity. If this harmony is not achieved, then not even medicines distilled from the Five Minerals, the use of passion-rousing drugs or Jade-Fire herbs, can be of help. And once the Vital Essences have been consumed or have dried up through over-use or neglect, they can never be revived.

The curiosity — or his inexhaustible thirst for knowledge — of the Yellow Emperor then turns to what he calls the Conditions of Ripeness of the Precious Implement. Nearly five thousand years ago the male obsession was the same as it is today, and the Wise Maiden's answers defined the Conditions of Ripeness in the ascending order of (1) Slight movements of the male member, but not reaching its full extension. (2) Extended but not really hard — thus denoting that the Yang spirit had not yet been fully aroused. (3) Hard but not yet hot and throbbing — a sign that the Yang spirit was lacking only the last ferment of the soul. (4) When it was hot as well as hard, yet the dam holding back the Vital Essence was standing firm, then the Four Conditions of Ripeness had been experienced.

Through the Jade Gate we enter this life,
Once born we are forever seeking to return.
How many men wake in the night
Their Iron Rod stiff with desire;
And with this eternal truth, that other
    message —
That the joy of life and everlasting youth
Are found in the same place as his creation.
Lewd Tales From China (1927) Yoneda Yutaro

CHAPTER FIVE

The Assault on the Jade Pavilion

As has been previously stated, the methodical approach to sex of many Chinese lovers was to have it catalogued and illustrated in books and on scrolls. These collections demonstrated the various positions of the sex act and were called pillow books or albums. Frequently they were constructed concertina-fashion or as a long scroll, and when opened allowed a fine choice to be surveyed at a single glance. Their Taoist origins were revealed in titles such as *Play of the Clouds and the Rain* or *Precious Moments in the Fair Field*.

The great number and variety of pillow books naturally resulted in the repetition of many of the sex positions, even if there was no limit to the exotic and descriptive names given to them. The practical Chinese, however, as distinct from Indian and Arab handbooks on the subject, made sure that the positions were both credible and feasible for bodies of normal human limitations. The books were literally laid on the pillow, to be consulted frequently and with great attention to detail, and their usefulness thereby depended on their practicability.

In this, many Chinese were no doubt helped by their slight and lithe physique, and such

A bridge between two garden seats, the softly entwined limbs contrasting with the hard supports. In winter, however, the porcelain was heated by lamps placed inside the seats. 17th-century. By kind permission of the British Museum.

manuals were frequently as much a part of the bedroom as cooking utensils in a kitchen. The illustrations often included the presence of a third person, usually a maid or another concubine, and though some of the juxtapositions of the three might seem amusing to western minds, the trio seemed a very sensible arrangement to the Chinese. The male was naturally the central figure in these tableaux, with the second female having a subservient role, inserting the master's member or, with a similar wish to conserve and concentrate his efforts, taking over the need to excite the other woman with loveplay. Some prints show the second woman standing naked at the bedside and reciting from a book of poems.

The illustrations evolved into a favourite art form, though they were never exhibited outside

The painters of erotic albums, when they were not anonymous, adopted pseudonyms. This picture of a methodical lover, with a hard garden seat to support his back, was painted by a Mr. Lewd Hero. 19th-century. Courtesy Yasha Beresiner, Intercol, London.

the bedchamber. The size was usually 20-25cms in depth, and from the seventeenth century they were printed in four or five colours. Before that date simple woodblock techniques gave a cruder appearance to the figures, particularly to the genitalia, though earlier hand-painted or multi-woodblock printed scrolls provided examples of the highest craftsmanship. Such craftsmen also worked with ivory, jade and steatite, carving into flat plaques which were then mounted on silk-covered card and bound into an album (usually of concertina design). The rather lifeless flat figures were given a little more realism by colouring the faces and sex organs.

In his study of a dozen erotic albums of the Ming period, with a selection of about three hundred colour prints, R.H. Van Gulik draws up a comprehensive table of the sex positions of the lovers. About a quarter depict the male lying on top of the female or kneeling between her thighs, her legs resting on his shoulders, gripping him round the waist or simply apart in total abandonment. The next favoured variation shows the woman in the upper position, either facing his head or his feet as she straddles her lover. A surprising number of pictures, almost one-in-seven, show a traditional Chinese position, that of a seated woman with her legs hanging over the arms of a large chair, permitting introitus by a standing or kneeling lover. Also popular according to the illustrations were those of the male *making love behind the mountain,* either with the female kneeling in front of him, bending over a table or sitting on his lap, and the lovers facing each other in the side-by-side position. A high proportion, eight per cent, depict cunnilingus or fellatio, though this could be because these positions permit a fuller exhibition of the sex organs, while artists also favoured 'love in the garden' with the woman seated on a swing, her legs apart, descending towards a lover, his penis erect, waiting to 'pierce' The Flower Heart.

Van Gulik makes a valid and authoritative comment: "I think that sexologists will agree that the table ... represents a good record of healthy sexual habits."

Pillow books also contained poems and instructions (sometimes written in verse), the choice of words being in good taste and avoiding any hint of vulgarity. This refinement was equally apparent in the pictures, an aspect of the art being the total composition and the sensitive arrangement of the figures. The sex organs were usually stylised, the female pubic hair forming a fan-shape above a pronounced vulva, the penis, unlike certain Japanese prints, keeping within the limits of human dimensions. The faces of the lovers displayed a uniform serenity, eyes and mouth smiling slightly, as though the artist also hoped to project their higher Confucian principles.

The manner in which the novel was used to embrace subjects and aspects of life considered too vulgar for learned writings has been mentioned earlier and the following is an extract from Li Yü's *Jou-pu-t'uan* which beautifully portrays the importance of the pillow book. In this scene, the Night-time Scholar (mentioned in the previous chapter) has just married a very puritanical young woman and finds that she is only prepared to make love in the most customary position. He therefore produces a pillow book to reassure his bride that there is nothing improper in a little variety in the marriage bed, but consulting such uninhibited illustrations is an approach that he has to handle with the greatest delicacy...

'If what you say about love not being a reason for shame or shyness is true,' said Delicate Scent, 'why is it that my honoured parents never indulged in the act during day-time?'

'How do you know they didn't?' asked the Night-time Scholar.

'If they had done it in the day I would've noticed it. I spent the whole of my sixteen years with them and in all that time I never saw or heard a thing about sex.'

The Scholar laughed.

'Well, that just goes to show what a child you really are, not noticing things like that. Even the maids would've seen your parents, or at least noticed your parents retiring at odd hours and closing the doors behind them.'

Delicate Scent reflected on this for some moments.

'It's true, I agree, that my parents retired from time to time during the day, and closed their doors — but who can be sure what they were doing? All the same, I can't believe they saw each other naked.'

'You're wrong, my dear,' said the Scholar. 'One of the reasons for practising the arts of the bedchamber during the day is to have a good view of things. Nothing rouses the passions like a good sight of each other. However, I agree that "sexual matinees" should be avoided by two types of people.'

'And what types are they?' Delicate Scent asked curiously.

'Those couples where the husband is an ugly monster and the wife is a delicate beauty, and those where the husband is handsome and his woman just the opposite.'

'But if they've accepted each other,' persisted Delicate Scent, 'why should their appearance stop them from making love in the daytime?'

'Why? Well, because it all starts as desire, with a spark that fires the blood. For the act to be pleasurable they must be drawn to each other. With these two categories, the pitch black night is better.' The Scholar found himself becoming eloquent, though possibly this was from the stirrings of lust. 'Imagine a beautiful wife, her skin smooth and soft, and as fragile as porcelain. Then the husband removes her clothes one by one, at last revealing this beauty. She sits on his lap, his Male Peak gets bigger and bigger, and she at the sight and feel of him gets similarly excited.... Then imagine an ugly man doing this, all his deformities shown up in the daylight — why, instead of the ten per cent ugliness in the night light he is now two hundred per cent ugly.'

'But this cannot apply to us,' Delicate Scent observed confidently. 'My own beauty is matched by your own, whether it's night or day we are equally pleasing to the eye. If there are people who should be indulging in love-making during the day and not hidden in darkness, then surely it's us'.

The Scholar inclined his head as if congratulating her on a very profound remark, then said:

'This is absolutely true — so why should we be the exception? I can assure you that you will find it ten times more pleasurable than at night.'

Delicate Scent had blushed faintly and her body appeared to be trembling. It was evident to the Scholar that only a little more persuasion was necessary, but being of a refined nature, he had no desire to show crude impatience. Besides, she might well react like a starving person given a good bowl of food — it would be gobbled up without any appreciation for the cooking or flavour. With this in mind, to keep her waiting a little longer, he seated himself in his comfortable Mandarin chair, drew her to his side then on to his lap. Then he picked up the Bedchamber Book, which was within reach, and nonchalantly flicked over the pages so that she would receive a quick impression of colourful illustrations. The Night-time Scholar had chosen this volume with care. Not only was it a collection of pictures, but opposite each one was an explanatory text. This text was divided into two, the top half giving a detailed explanation of the sex-position, the lower half commenting in a learned way on the artistic merits of the illustration. The Night-time Scholar began to turn the pages more slowly, concentrating his attention on particularly revealing pictures. Then he started to read aloud from the text. It was clear that Delicate Scent was trying to follow the meaning, and though he was sure that she understood the words, he doubted if she had gathered the deeper sense of the passages.

The first picture was described as *Butterflies Seeking the Source of the Scent:* 'The Lady is sitting on a boulder by the Tai-hu Lake', he read. 'Her legs are held apart and her partner is fluttering his Jade Stem round the heart of the Flower. Both Man and Woman are still at the frontier of the Land of Pleasure and Passion, which is why their facial expressions are relatively calm, though it should be noted that their eyes are wide open and their eyebrows raised.'

The second picture was described as *Bees Making Honey:* 'The Woman lies on her back, her legs raised and parted as if hanging from ropes. Her two hands are holding on to the male Thrusting Root, guiding it downwards into the Flower Heart instead of allowing it to get lost in the bushes.'

The third position was *The Hungry Horse Devouring at the Feeding Trough:* 'The Lady lies on her back, her arms round her partner's neck. He raises her feet and places them on his shoulders and presses the Golden Lilies against his cheeks. At the same time the Jade Stem is driven in to the hilt, not a hairbreadth remaining outside. Yet he still manages to burrow deeper. Both their faces carry the expression of total preoccupation and their tongues are interlaced.'

The fifth picture read: *Two Dragons Exhausted by Battle:* 'The Lady lies sideways on the pillow, her body limp and her legs and arms thrown around her. The Man has collapsed over her, his face in the hollow of her neck, his body as lifeless as hers. The Flowery Battle is over and the Scented Souls are clearly at rest. Yet there are signs that the bodies are not totally exhausted. The Lady's Golden Lilies are still held by him, and they occasionally flicker in the hope of arousing him.'

At this point it was clear to the Scholar that his wife was beginning to understand what was being read to her. Her face was very pink and she was looking distinctly angry.

'What rubbish are you reading — what pictures are they?' she demanded, jumping from his knees.

'It is the *Collection of the Spring Palace*. Let me tell you about the sixth picture.'

'The more you look at them, the more excited you get. You can study the dirty things yourself. I'm going to bed.'

As she started to walk from the Inner Hall, he shouted after her: 'The later ones are even better. We can go to bed as soon as we've studied them all.'

'Why don't you leave some of the pleasure for tomorrow,' Delicate Scent said sarcastically. 'You'll be in the same state then, won't you!'

The Night-time Scholar rose from the Mandarin chair and caught his wife in the door opening. Her lips were pouting with annoyance and her body was rigid with disapproval. It was a particularly attractive pose and he kissed her passionately on the mouth.

Then — what a surprise! They had been married for one month and whenever they had kissed and he had sought to insert his tongue, it had been met by the guardian barrier of her perfect teeth. But this time it was different — he had hardly touched her lips with his own moist tongue when hers flicked out to meet him. Soon they were interlaced and playing the busiest of love games. When their mouths parted, the Scholar's voice was shrill with excitement.

'My dearest heart — no, my dearest liver! Let's forget about retiring to the bedchamber — come over here by the Mandarin chair! We can pretend it's the boulder by Tai-hu Lake.'

'You mean make love here!' exclaimed Delicate Scent, though her indignation seemed a little forced. 'That would hardly be proper for respectable human beings!'

'Your're quite right,' agreed the Scholar. 'It's not for human beings. But if we were gods — you and I — and who can say we're not? Aren't we more handsome than most couples ...?'

As he spoke those flattering words his hands were feeling along the sash holding up her trousers until he found the silken knot. Delicate Scent expressed her disapproval with a gasp and a frown but made no attempt to push him away. When the garment fell round her feet, he noticed a darker patch of dampness in the centre of the material, and from its extent he concluded that her secretions had started not with the kiss but with the readings from *Spring Palace*.

Still unprotesting, she allowed him to lift her feet from the silken pool, then he quickly threw off his own trousers. A look of hesitation crossed her face, and instead of proceeding to remove their upper clothes, he lifted her into the Mandarin chair and placed her legs over the wooden arms. Before she could recover from his initiative, his implement was pressed between the Jade Gates, and only then, when it was apparent that she was not protesting, did he remove her jacket and his own upper garments.

This technique was known as 'occupying the headquarters first', a lesson well-learnt from the Handbook. If he had dallied by first removing the upper garments, there might well have been a change of heart. Now, with the headquarters occupied, there was no way for her to escape, the surrender was unconditional and all that remained was the 'mopping-up' operation. And why not begin with the embroidered socks covering her bound feet?

Delicate Scent was now naked except for the coverings round her ankles and feet — yet why should he waste time down there when he was already being welcomed at the Jade Gate? And further, women knew that their feet when bound excited the man, yet stripped they revealed misshapen toes and unsightly stumps. Delicate Scent also possessed the ideal 'Three-inch Lotus' dimensions, so attractive when bound, so forlorn when naked. No, to remove them, decided the Night-time Scholar, was like seeing the head of a flower on a stalk without leaves; somehow it was too naked.

He therefore returned to a direct assault, using his 'male club' with an upward swing, pausing after two initial duels to observe the effects. He decided to raise his wife's legs from the arms of the Mandarin chair and place them on his shoulders, a variation that facilitated his movements, particularly in the

A variation of Two Swallows with a Single Heart. *The narrow chests of men indicate their learning and good class. 17th-century blockprint.*

Hovering Butterflies, *one of the* Thirty Heaven and Earth Postures. *17th-century blockprint.*

side-to-side swing, so necessary to capture the secret chamber of the Flower Heart. It pleased him, too, to observe that they were exactly as the Position One illustration.

For her part Delicate Scent had not only surrendered; she was now assisting the enemy. Her hands gripped the chair and her body moved forward to meet his thrusts, and when he indulged in side-to-side variations, she knew instinctively how to position the Jade Gate. Suddenly, and for the first time since their marriage, Delicate Scent felt a fierce sensation that was both unbearable yet wonderful at the same time, and though she had no idea what it would be like, she knew she was reaching the Ultimate. In her desire to enjoy this ecstatic state without further delay, she therefore begged the Scholar to thrust deeply and straight rather than to indulge in side movements, an instruction which he immediately obeyed. He made one hundred charges at the Flower Heart before Delicate Scent bit into his shoulder and clutched him wildly; the cloud had at last burst.

'It was too beautiful, too beautiful,' she sighed.

Her expression was one of wonder and contentment, but the serenity, to the Scholar's surprise, was rather more brief than he had expected. In fact, Delicate Scent at the moment of sublime peace had suddenly realised that the invader of the Flower Chamber was not only still in possession; he was clearly only allowing her a short rest before continuing the assault. She therefore placed two hands behind his buttocks, preparing herself for further battle, locked her legs round his neck and blocked his line of retreat.

The Night-time Scholar, far from considering retreat, immediately flung himself into the fight. His Jade Stem was bigger than ever, as if the pause had allowed it to soak up her Vital Essence, and as he took her slender waist in both hands, he realised that the entwining of arms, legs and bodies was exactly as Picture Number Two in the *Collection of the Spring Palace*. But Delicate Scent, who had seemed to relish this next stage of the battle, suddenly went limp, as if she had fainted. Her eyes were closed and her high and ornate hair-style had collapsed to one side.

'Dearest heart and liver,' cried the Scholar, 'clearly we should move to the bed where we can continue in comfort.'

The suggestion caused Delicate Scent to rouse herself.

'No, no,' she murmured.

The protest, however, was really because moving to the bed would allow the rascal inside her to escape. She felt she should not be denied the rightful triumph of gaining his hot secretion and so enjoying the enriching effect on the earth of her Fair Field.

'Dearest heart and liver, is it because you can't move?'

She nodded her head.

'Well,' said the Night-time Scholar, now intent on pursuing his day-time studies, 'I shall have to carry

This position was called Leaping White Tiger, *from that animal's form of attack, or* Making Fire Behind the Mountain. *The dutiful servant supports the lovers. 17th-century blockprint.*

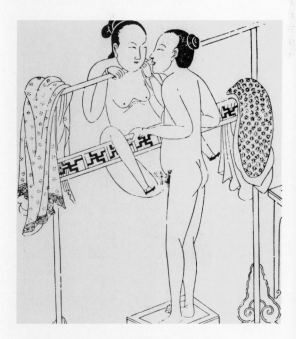

A variation of Spider Trapped in its own Web. *Whether suspended by ropes or hanging from a frame, the woman is helpless, a state that many Chinese males found exciting. 17th-century blockprint.*

you to the bed.'

The Scholar was a skilled lifter of women, particularly when they were still transfixed by his spear, and to be precise he only half-lifted her, pivoting her on the end of it and keeping her legs wrapped round him. In this manner he proceeded to the bedchamber, making small movements above and below, which served to keep him as stiff as ever and which were not unlike reversing a chariot or carriage. As he reached the bedside, however, and bent forward with her underneath him, Delicate Scent suddenly cried: 'Dearest! Dearest — I am about ... I am about to ...'

She was now gripping him as if he were saving her from falling into an abyss, breathing so hard that it might have been terror — except that the Scholar was aware of a sudden flood of Female Essence. He plunged his Male Peak into the moisture, as deeply and as fiercely as he could, then knew that he, too, was rushing over the waterfall. He felt himself submerged in a hot and frothing whirlpool, then began to float to the surface, and once he seemed able to breathe the air, he contented himself with the sensation of floating.

In the position known as Bouncing Infant, *one of the* Nine Glorious Postures, *Lord Yang reflects on the wonders of the Mountains of Wu. 19th-century album. Private collection, Paris.*

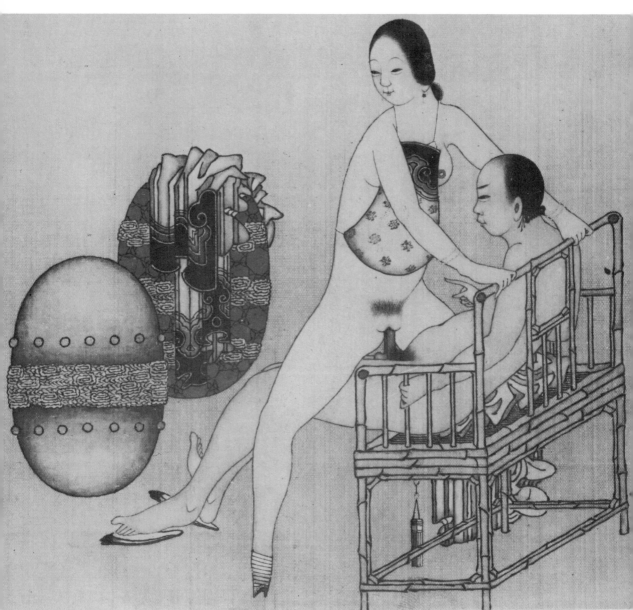

Delicate Scent was the first to recover.

'Did you know that a moment ago I was actually dead,' she said.

'You were more dead than dead,' replied the Scholar. 'What you experienced was Heavenly Oblivion.'

'But why do you give it such a strange name?'

'Because we both have our own kinds of essence. When those essences are released, which coincides with the enjoyment of the Ultimate, our whole body, be it the skin, flesh, limbs, blood or bone, is so relaxed that we are no longer aware of these parts as our own. That is why it is called Oblivion, and is exactly as Picture Number Five in the *Spring Palace Collection.*'

Delicate Scent had now fully recovered.

'How wonderful is the state of Oblivion. And how wonderful to waken again. It is like a resurrection.'

'And that's exactly how it should be,' said the Scholar, very satisfied with his skill as a teacher and Delicate Scent's progress with the lessons. 'This Oblivion should come every time man and woman make love. And with some really talented men the woman will release her essence twenty times before he surrenders his own Life Force.' The Scholar laughed happily. 'Was I right in describing the album as a most useful book?'

'It is a very precious book,' Delicate Scent said with conviction. 'Definitely a very precious book.'

The Chinese reverence for their ancestors caused them to regard the older sex handbooks with special respect. The positions in the pillow books, and even those featured in what must have seemed outrageously 'avant-garde' novels, sought to give the impression that they were drawing on the wisdom of the ages, and Most Noble Tung Hsüan's sex guide was a favourite source of such knowledge. As a classic of the T'ang Period (618-906), its popularity was assured for many centuries.

In an earlier chapter Most Noble Tung's *Art of the Bedchamber* was quoted at length except for the sex positions, and the following is a catalogue of his *Thirty Heaven and Earth Postures*. He regards them as a basic minimum from which other variations should proceed, and which lovers should follow in sequence before indulging their own impulses.

SECTION 9

The Four Fundamental Positions, from which all follows, need hardly be described in detail, and I simply give their names:
1. *Deepest Embrace*
2. *Open Fish-gills*
3. *Horn of the Unicorn*
4. *Rolled Bedclothes*

The 'love-and-battle' variations on these can now be described:

5. *Silkworm Spinning*
Lady Yin lies on her back facing upwards. Her arms are placed round Lord Yang's neck, her legs round his waist, crossed behind him. Lord Yang places his arms round her waist, his knees under her thighs. He pulls her forward and on to the Celestial Implement.

6. *Forcing the Dragon*
Lady Yin remains on her back with her knees raised and bent. Lord Yang kneels between her thighs and raises the Golden Lilies until they are above her head. She then holds her own feet while he forces the Dragon Jade Gate.

7. *Fishes Eyeing Each Other*
Lord Yang places Lady Yin on her side, then lies down facing her. He takes her upper leg and pulls it across his thigh, at the same time inserting his tongue into her mouth. Lord Yang then draws her leg above his waist and Lady Yin returns his kiss. When their tongues are interlaced, he inserts his Male Peak.

8. *Two Swallows With a Single Heart*
Again Lady Yin is on her back. Lord Yang pushes her legs sideways, as far as they will stretch, to resemble open wings. Then he leans on to the Vermilion Valley and introduces his implement.

9. *Copulating Kingfishers*
Lady Yin holds her own feet apart, facing upwards and shaking the Golden Lilies. Lord Yang sits on his haunches between the fluttering feet, clasps her waist and draws her up his thighs, his Jade Root in line with the centre of the 'lute strings'.

10. *Mandarin Ducks*
Lady Yin lies on her right side, Lord Yang directly behind her, his body curved to hers. The left legs are raised in unison, the right legs stretched straight down. The sex parts pressed together tremble with small movements until they are united.

11. *Hovering Butterflies*
Lord Yang now takes a position on his back and faces upwards. Lady Yin seats herself on his stomach, placing her feet firmly in the bedding. She reaches behind for his Jade Root, then slides on to it with a backward movement.

12. *Tandem Ducks in Flight*
Lord Yang remains on his back but this time Lady Yin sits on his stomach and faces his feet. In this position she can use both hands to guide the Male Peak into the Golden Gully.

13. *Crossed Pine Branches*
Lord Yang and Lady Yin sit on the bed, she placed on his feet, their legs extended, his under hers. Her feet are pressed against his stomach and as the desire increases, they draw each other forward, her legs separating round his waist until he finds the Jade Gate.

14. Bamboo Bridge to the Pavilion
Lord Yang and Lady Yin now rise to their feet and stand facing each other. They embrace tightly, their tongues bridging the separation of faces and, soon after, the Jade Root forming a lower level bridge. Once deeply inserted in this position, the Male Peak will reach the Upper Yang Terrace.

15. Pair of Swooping Eagles
Lord Yang and Lady Yin embrace in a lying position, then roll first to the right, then to the left. As they roll they constantly rub against each other until the erect Male Peak is ready for the final swoop. This should be when he has rolled into an upper position.

16. Phoenix Seizing the Chicken
[This passage of the ancient manuscript is illegible but it is believed to be a position for large and heavy women with small and thin men.]

17. Seagull Wings on the Edge of a Cliff
Lady Yin is placed on the edge of the bed, her upper body lying flat but her legs raised against Lord Yang's chest, who is standing upright. As he inserts himself into the Flower Paradise, he takes her feet and opens and closes them as a seagull in flight.

18. Bucking Horse
Lady Yin stays in the same position but her Golden Lilies remain on Lord Yang's shoulders, tight to his ears. As their bodies thrust together, Lord Yang jerks the legs upwards.

19. Kicking Mule
Lady Yin is placed in the centre of the bed, lying on her back. Lord Yang places his left hand under her head, his right hand under her right leg, raising both together as the Jade Thrusting Root is inserted . The right leg is then raised and lowered to the rhythm of the thrusting.

20. Horse Pawing the Air
Lady Yin remains on her back but her left foot is placed on Lord Yang's shoulder as he covers her with his body. If the thrusting is slow and controlled 'this position can give indescribable pleasure' (Most Noble Tung).

21. Leaping White Tigress
Lady Yin now kneels in the centre of the bed, her legs apart, and Lord Yang kneels immediately behind her. He clasps her waist, pressing her on to his lap, her hand reaching underneath her to direct the way to the Jade Gate.

22. Cicadas Clinging to a Tree
Lady Yin lies with her face down and Lord Yang occupies a kneeling position between her Golden Lilies. He grips her waist and draws her towards him, her legs separating further as she is pulled up his thighs. This position is not for heavy women with weak men.

23. Goat Butting a Tree
Lord Yang seats himself in his favourite chair, drawing Lady Yin facing away from him, on to his lap.

Flowers and birds and plants on wall and screen designs helped to create a sense of belonging to the great universal Yin-Yang. *17th-century blockprint.*

As she looks down at his erect Jade Stem, he pushes her towards it and inserts it fiercely. Then he holds her in position for a series of butting movements.

24. Pheasants Sporting
Lady Yin is joined by Mistress Precious Peony. As Lord Yang sits cross-legged in the centre of the bed, both women touch and tease him. When Lady Yin finally places herself on his Jade Stem, Mistress Precious Peony continues her touching and teasing. ('Very entertaining,' adds Most Noble Tung.)

25. Phoenix Sporting
Lady Yin, dismissing Mistress Peony, lies on her back and raises her Golden Lilies above her shoulders. Lord Yang holds on to both sides of the bed and with motions of raising and lowering his body, repeatedly enters and leaves the Precious Crucible.

26. Double-Winged Bird
Lord Yang kneels between Lady Yin's thighs, and placing his two hands under her buttocks, helps her to raise her body from the bed. In this arching position, he enters the Soft and Warm Country.

27. Monkey Swinging from a Branch
Lord Yang places one arm round a bed post then invites Lady Yin to seat herself on the Jade Stem, at the same time placing her legs behind him. He then presses on the bed with one hand, and pulls himself up by the arm round the post, continuing these movements until exhausted.

28. *Cat and Mouse in the Same Hole*

Lady Yin kneels and places her forehead on the bed. Lord Yang takes up a position behind and plays cat and mouse in the two orifices offered for his pleasure.

29. *Mule in the Springtime*

Lady Yin walks to the high couch and bends over it. Lord Yang stands behind her, holding on to the couch, and keeping her imprisoned until she has yielded to his Warrior Club.

30. *Autumn Days*

Lord Yang lies on the bed, his hands at the back of his own head, and Lady Yin sits on his stomach but with her face to his feet. As they have enjoyed twenty-nine positions without pause he contemplates her back, and since he cannot see her face, he imagines her to be the Great Yin Spirit herself. Her hands have also encouraged this illusion, and as the Jade Stem stiffens, she raises herself on to it.

Although there is an intellectual exactness about sex positions as described in the pillow book, and constant references by lovers to its pages, it must not be imagined that they were not enjoyed without a sense of fun and pagan delight. The atmosphere of the Chinese bedchamber, whether in palaces or in modest homes, was a busy, noisy affair, the air filled with chatter and singing, with squabbles and movement. And the interior of the bedchamber, apart from its bright décor, formed an essentially Chinese background to the act of love. In the following passage from the sixteenth-century novel, *Chin P'ing Mei,* the restless wife takes the initiative in persuading her husband to indulge in the game of *Hovering Butterflies* ...

After washing her whole body, Golden Lotus loosened her hair and entered the bedchamber. The silver lamp had been turned very low and the outlines of everything were soft and cosy. The shape of Hsi-men Ching under the coverlet quivered as he snored, and she sat on the edge of the bed and pulled on her bedshoes.

She lay down and placed her head on the long pillow but her mind was too active for sleep, and before long she reached out and placed her hand on his male implement. It was as soft as a ball of cotton-wool and showed no immediate reaction to her persuasive touch. The wine she had drunk earlier, and which had not so far affected her, seemed now to go to her head, and with a feeling of reckless passion she plunged under the coverlet. After a moment she managed to turn the sleeping Hsi-men so that she could take the *turtle-head* in her mouth, concentrating on tickling the rim with her tongue. When her husband woke up, he said:

'Have you just come to bed? Where have you been?'

Mountains and rocks, with their mystical and phallic associations, were also favoured as interior decorations. 17th-century blockprint.

'We've been drinking in the courtyard. Third wife Meng brought out two trays of food and wine and we had quite a feast.'

'What are you doing down there, you wicked woman?'

'We played the finger-game, and when I lost to Graceful Tower, I had to drink three cups of wine.'

'You'll find my love-belt at the bottom of the bed. Can you reach it?'

Not only did she reach for it, she helped to fit it. The results of her efforts under the coverlet were now visible for all to see, and she tied the belt round his waist then fastened the stiff sheath under and round his Jade Stem. A little more fondling made it grow another two inches, and since he seemed in a lazy mood while she felt very active, she suggested that he place a pillow under himself and she would do all the work. In the end Hsi-men had all four red pillows under his buttocks, and without wasting time on the preliminary embrace, Golden Lotus bent her knees, squatted across him and took the sheathed implement in her hand.

'Did you remember to take your medicine tonight?' she asked.

'I took it,' said Hsi-men Ching. 'I hope the wine won't make you sick.'

'We are going to enjoy the position called *Hovering Butterflies.*' And without showing any mercy on the Jade Gate, she immediately transfixed herself on his spear. 'There,' she exclaimed proudly. 'It was so big tonight yet it's all inside. Feel for yourself.'

Hsi-men placed his fingers between her legs and tested the truth of the statement. All that could be felt were his testicles, and this at once inspired him to slap her thighs, which was taken as a signal to start moving. As her rump rose and fell, and her squatting knees made similar movements, the lower part of her body was exactly like the hovering butterfly.

'Which do you find better — the sheath or the silver cap?' asked Golden Lotus. 'The trouble with the silver cap is that it makes me sore.' She then paused to stroke his cheeks. 'Dear heart-and-liver — in this position you seem to pierce my whole body.'

This confession was followed by a renewed and vigorous assault on him, and when she had completed three hundred ups-and-downs, she screamed at him to bite her neck. In this position they simultaneously enjoyed the *bursting of the clouds.*

As their bodies seemed to flow with the flood of their vital essences, she felt that a herd of one hundred deer were lightly leaping through her thighs, and when they had passed on, her body was left as limp as crêpe silk.

'I'm going to sleep,' said Hsi-men Ching.

'That position is really my favourite. Can you pass the towel. We're both soaking.'

They went to sleep in each other's arms, and before hardly any time at all, the East was getting lighter and the dawn was already reaching out to them.

Such handbooks as the Most Noble Tung's formed the basis of later interpretations of the Bedchamber Art, and in his celebrated *Sex Methods* (Peking 1927), Yeh Tê-hui (of Chang Sha) brings it up to date with a number of colourful variations. The Chinese had frequently indulged in sex without too much self-consciousness about the presence of others, and through the ages the garden and the bamboo grove had been favourite settings for their games. Yeh Tê-hui's departure was therefore to catalogue the open-air positions and though some of them extend the imagination, they have certainly appeared in the older pillow books. The following is a representative selection:

1. *Flying Through the Clouds*

The man and woman, both naked, seat themselves on garden swings hanging from the same branch, the man below and behind the woman, she crouching on her seat. The swings are drawn back by ropes held by servants so that the man and woman remain close together. Once union is effected, the swinging sensation adds to the pleasure. Yeh Tê-hui then adds: Only much practice can effect such union when the swings are moving in opposite direction.

2. *Lovers on the Tightrope*

A tightrope is stretched just above the ground. The lovers stand together until union has been achieved then, helped by servants, they step on to the rope. If intercourse is all-consuming, their preoccupation will help them to reach the other end of the rope.

3. *Monkeys in a Fruit Tree*

The woman climbs a leafy fruit tree. When she has found a solid footing, she throws fruit at her lover below. He immediately gives chase and overcomes her among the leafy branches. Very enjoyable in sunny weather.

4. *Spider Trapped in its own Web*

The woman is suspended by ropes and pulleys from the ceiling, the height of her outstretched body according to the wishes of the man. If he wishes to enjoy 'Swinging Union', the ropes should be of stout Kiangsu fibre.

5. *Floating Porpoises*

An ideal position in the swimming pool. The man floats on his back with the woman above him, the dog-paddle necessary to keep afloat causing their naked organs to rub together. When union is effected, their concerted movements prevent them from sinking. The water, stesses Yeh Tê-hui, must be warm.

6. *Hangman's Rope*

Divide the woman's long hair into two, then plait and fasten round the man's neck, bringing their faces together. A servant then binds their hands together, left to right, leaving them to effect union as best they can. Their difficulties increase the excitement.

7. *Awakening the Sleeping Beauty*

The woman pretends to be dead. Her body is limp, her eyes closed. The man undresses her and there is still no movement. He then teases her by fondling her breasts and the Pearl on the Jade Step, while she fights to remain limp. Suddenly she springs to life and the Iron Implement strikes at the Gate.

8. *Blind Man's Buff*

Both partners are blindfold, then search for each other round the bedchamber. When the woman is caught, the bandages remain in place during intercourse.

9. *Steady-Head Lovers*

The man and woman balance a bowl of tea on their heads and attempt union and intercourse without spilling a drop.

In another chapter of *Sex Methods,* the author states: Variations in love-making distinguish men from animals, the educated man from the ignorant. To conduct one's sexual battles with as little sophistication as two horsemen charging at each other is as tasteless as the flavour of wax and as boring as a diet of dry rice. The following positions are particularly recommended:

Waters of the Fountain

The woman sits astride the man's lap. They face each other then lightly flick their tongues together and, below, the Jade Stem across the Lute Strings. There is no insertion, just light touches above and below.

As the Vital Essences being to gush, however, he plunges between the Gates.

Over the Rainbow
The man kneels on the bed and places a pillow on his upturned feet, then sits back on it. The woman sits astride his knees and throws herself back, her head reaching the bed and her body arching. He strikes upwards, from the end of the Rainbow.

The legendary Yellow Emperor (Huang Ti), however, in his searching conversations with the three knowledgeable maidens, was not one to overlook this aspect of Yin-Yang relationships, and *The Nine Glorious Postures* were hardly to be improved on in the later pillow books. The Wise Maiden, in her description, also stresses the therapeutic qualities of the positions and the need for a rhythm of shallow and deep thrusts by the male. These postures, which form part of the *Hsüan-nü-Ching,* are as follows:

1. *Dragon in Flight*
Lady Precious Yin lies on her back with her legs raised and her feet together. Great Lord Yang parts the feet and lowers himself over the body. She then slides down, causing the Jade Gate to widen, and he moves into the Golden Pavilion. He then creates the 'eight deep and six shallow' rhythm until both are overwhelmed and the clouds burst. This posture, with the feet facing the sky, resembles a flying dragon and eliminates sourness in the stomach.

2. *The Gobbling Fishes*
Lady Precious Yin and Mistress White Jade lie on top of each other, their Jade Gates press together. They then move in a rubbing and jerking fashion against each other like fishes gobbing flies or waterplants from the surface. As they become more excited, the 'mouths' widen, and choosing his position carefully, Great Lord Yang thrusts between them with his Jade Root. They then move in unison until all three share the Ultimate simultaneously. The triple flow of Vital Essence will strengthen bones and sinews as well as the breathing. It will also assist the Great Lord Yang to avoid the Five Overstrainings and the Seven Sex-injuries.

3. *Tiger in the Forest*
Lady Precious Yin takes up a kneeling position, her head lowered on to her hands, then practises the 'five shallow and six deep' method for one hundred thrusts. At the end of this period the Jade Flower will be flowing with secretions, which will wash away the cares of life. This posture also benefits the heart and liver.

4. *Swinging Monkey*
A chair is placed under a low tree in the garden. The Great Lord Yang then seats himself and holds a branch overhead. Lady Precious Yin sits on his lap, sliding the Jade Gate up and down the Male Peak without allowing it into the Inner Chamber. When the excitement becomes unbearable, she then inserts it herself and indulges in the 'nine deep and five shallow' method while he remains holding the branch. This will benefit the spirit and the longevity.

5. *Cicadas Mating*
Lady Precious Yin lies facing down, stretching the left leg straight and drawing up the right leg. The Great Lord Yang takes up a position behind, buries himself in the Cinnabar Heart, and practises the 'seven deep and eight shallow' method. When they enjoy the Ultimate, all blockages will have been cleared.

6. *Floating Turtle*
Lady Precious Yin relaxes on her back, apparently resting, as a turtle floating on water. The Great Lord Yang raises her legs, keeps her feet to his ears, and passes through the Vermilion Gate. His movements should resemble those of the turtle's head, short and in quick succession. This will release the unwanted gases from the five organs.

7. *Phoenix in Flight*
Lady Precious Yin holds her feet and pulls them as far back as possible. The Great Lord Yang then circles her thighs and body in a tight embrace. He then presses at the Jade Gate, and once passing into the Pleasure Chamber, moves to left and right but to the rhythm of 'nine shallow and eight deep'. This method to the outside observer is like watching a Phoenix flapping its wings, and will enhance the marrow.

8. *Bouncing Infant*
The Great Lord Yang lies back on a couch and Lady Precious Yin sits astride his Jade Stem. She then bounces up and down in a carefree manner while he reflects on the wonders of the Mountain of Wu. Their spirits will eventually float among the Nine Clouds.

9. *Standing Bamboos*
Lady Precious Yin and her Lord stand in front of a couch. She place one foot on the edge of it and he slowly penetrates the Golden Valley. He moves to a rhythm of 'nine shallow and one deep' until the Flower Heart is completely open and the Perfumed Dew covers it. The 'standing bamboos' then bend to the wind and complete the act by lying on the couch. This position banishes hunger and promotes longevity.

The terminology and the precision with which sex postions are explained owe much to their association with the idea of intercourse being a battle for ascendancy. Out of the Yin-Yang contest would come the wonderful peace of the final Harmony — though usually in a manner that favoured the male ego and his pleasure. Both the Taoist and the Buddhist influences in his life, drawing much of their message and their wisdom from nature and a deep sense of the universe, accepted the belief of conflict within harmony. Whether the sexes were equal, or one was superior to the other, the Chinese acknowledged certain realities very early in their history, namely that there was an eternal War of the Sexes. Of all civilisations it was the last to be drawn into the whimsical conception of romantic love, and even today, behind the apparent Chinese conformity to modern practices and customs, the differences between the sexes and their adherence to the opposing traditional polarities remain a continuing truth.

Sex as battle has therefore been a feature of novels and epic stories almost as frequently as the wars of the Chou states and the fights against Tatars and Manchus, and the following passage is quoted to give the flavour of such encounters. It has also been selected because it features the Night-time Scholar's first sexual battle after the successful penis transplant described in the previous chapter. The author of *The Night-time Scholar* eloquently conveys the martial spirit with which his hero pushes his formidable new cannon on to the field of battle. The author addresses the reader directly:

Are there really any differences, apart from the numbers involved, of battles between armies and those fought in bed? In each instance the first requirement is for the commander to survey the terrain and to assess his opponent. In sexual encounters the man's first curiosity is about the hills and valleys of the woman, and hers about the size and fire-power of his armaments. Which of them is to advance and which is retreat? As in war, to know oneself is as important as knowing the enemy.

For the battles that lay ahead the Scholar now possessed a piece of equipment not only of remarkable dimensions but as yet of untried power. How would he manage it? Could he control it? Would it turn savage with the spirit of its former canine owner? As the Scholar contemplated the body of Scent of Love lying on the bed, and saw both terror and delight in her eyes, he decided, in fairness to her, that he must resort to the technique of placing a pillow under her buttocks.

The use of a pillow for difficult sex battles is worth a more detailed study. If the woman's head remains on a pillow it is a mistake to introduce one under her rump because the result is to cause her to sink in the middle like a sagging bridge. For a man to lie over such a bridge will shape him in the reverse manner, therefore making it difficult for him to achieve contact at either end. To kiss the woman will give him a neck like a camel, to enter the Jade Gate will force him to go forward on his knees.

The solution is to remove the head pillow, thereby allowing the bodies to curve to each other like a double rainbow. The woman's hair will spread beautifully on the sheet, her smiling eyes will look up and her mouth will be well-positioned for the kiss. In the centre of the rainbow the Jade Gate is thrust upwards and is in the ideal position to receive the mightiest of visitors. As the Scholar removed the head pillow, therefore, Scent of Love was consoled by the idea that he was a man of great experience.

He proceeded to display this proficiency by raising her feet and resting them on his shoulders, then, in a kneeling position, used both hands to ensure that the way was already opening for him and thoroughly moistened. His eyes momentarily came off the inviting Golden Valley and he was delighted to observe that the colour of his restructured Jade Stem was a uniform honey-pink with no evidence of the segments from the grafting. In fact, the closest inspection by a woman would have failed to reveal that this fine implement was not other than had been bestowed on him by nature.

With great difficulty, but with no more than a gasp from Scent of Love, the Scholar inserted the mushroom head. He paused a moment, but only a moment, knowing that the advantage had to be pressed. But if he plunged forward too fiercely with this massive instrument, she would scream and cry out, alerting if not the help of neighbours, certainly their curiosity. He therefore decided to advance in a series of gradual rhythms.

This he did with some expertness, each small advance causing his Jade Stem to be gripped by the tightest of collars. But when these seemed to slacken, he was able to push forward a little more. After a period of minutes he realised that he had reached the inner chamber of the Pleasure Palace, and Scent of Love, surprised by her own remarkable resilience, began to move and mount a counter-attack as though her confidence was returning. It was the signal the Scholar needed. His cannon began a barrage on her defences of unprecedented violence, reaching a depth that seemed even beyond that of the inner chamber. And he swung from side to side, penetrating every crevice, pursuing the enemy into every corner and hiding place. Her intention to return his first attack reverted to a hurried defensive action. She writhed and whimpered and gasped under the fierceness of his barrage. She moaned and cried: 'My dearest heart and liver-what are you doing to me! Your're killing me!' Then her cries turned to: 'Something is coming! Something is coming!'

The Scholar pretended to be incredulous at the information.

'So soon? But I'm only warming up. Besides, I have only a most miserable "piece of flesh".'

'It's enormous! The biggest I've ever known!'

This, from Scent of Love, was the greatest of compliments.

'But what about the neighbours? That's what is holding me back.'

'Never mind the neighbours,' Scent of Love replied urgently. 'On one side of the house there's empty ground, and on the other is the kitchen, where nobody sleeps.'

Variation of Deepest Embrace, *one of the* Four Fundamental Positions *of the Most Noble Tung Hsüan's sex guide. 19th-century album. Courtesy of the W.H. & Elizabeth M. Deane Collection, University of Sydney Library.*

Encouraged by this information, The Scholar decided to have no mercy on his lovely enemy. The couch suddenly began to shake as if the house was collapsing from an earthquake. The struggle was instantly one of life and death, the most furious of bodily collisions, roars of fury from himself, squeals of delighted pain and pleasure from the woman. She writhed and convulsed, she bucked and collapsed, but the Scholar plunged forward without pause. A sex battle had to be fought to a finish, and like an audience with the Emperor, no interruptions were permitted. And this was how it was until Scent of Love, having soaked the couch with floods of moisture, cried:

'Dearest heart — can you now come with me!' But she showed her awareness of the Scholar's vanity and the need to let him feel he had won the battle. 'You are the most wonderful lover in the world. If I were ten women I couldn't stand up to your attack. If you want me to be of any use tomorrow night, then please finish me off now!'

Conquest was part of the pleasure, and since he himself had been brought to the point of surrender, he was ready to accept her suggestion. He mounted a final and extra-deep attack and soon they both clutched each other in a rigid and final *bursting of the clouds.*

As well as the handbooks that gave advice and recorded the wisdom of the ages on the subject of sex, not to mention the thinly-disguised use of fiction, there was a more intimate genre of instruction known as *chia hsün*. This term meant *Family Guidance* and was written by the head of the family as he approached the end of his life in the hope that his sons, as they prepared for marriage, would learn from his experience. What the writings lacked in literary style, however, was balanced by the rich realities of life. The instructions were personal and practical and, quite unconsciously, gave some rare pictures of the domestic background.

This was particularly true when the father of the family was unconventional. One Ming dynasty *chia hsün,* for example, reveals an unusually liberal attitude to women, at least for the society of the time. The writer begins by observing that his wives and concubines have boring lives in which the only relief is sexual intercourse. Their days are devoted to the menial tasks of the home, and apart from the diversions of music and parlour games, and attending to their appearance, the only meaningful joys are those conferred on them by their master. He therefore has a duty to give them *complete fulfilment* every time they indulge in *The Clouds and the Rain.*

This philosophical gentleman illustrates his advice by describing two contrasting neighbours. 'To the East of my street a handsome and vigorous young man quarrels all day with his wives. They have no respect for him and he cannot keep order. Yet to the West lives a frail old man, greybearded, whose women are obedient and attentive. Why is this? The secret is in the old man's knowledge of the Art of the Bedchamber, something that the young man has yet to learn.'

As well as general advice on how to keep his wives contented, the old man writes about specific routine problems such as introducing a new concubine into the home without making his other women jealous, and the correct way to beat them when they misbehave. 'There was the case of an official who acquired a new concubine and immediately locked himself away with her for three days. His wives and concubines were outraged by this inconsiderateness, which later made it more difficult for the new woman to be accepted by them. Instead of behaving as he did, the official should first have enjoyed copulation with his other women in the presence of the new concubine, who should have been made to stand respectfully by the Ivory Couch. Only after four or five nights, during which time she has learnt her place among the women, should the new girl be taken by her master. And then only with his wives and concubines witnessing the introduction. In this manner, Harmony between the women will be maintained.'

The writer then turns to punishment. If the offence is repeated, '... she should be caned. But this has to be done sensibly. The woman should lie face down on a bench, having first loosened and dropped her trousers, and be given five or six strokes. The cane should never strike as low as the thighs or as high as the coccyx. It is wrong to go to the extreme of binding a concubine naked to a pillar and flogging her until the flesh is split and the blood flows. That is the way to turn the women's quarters into a torture chamber.'

CHAPTER SIX

Prolonging the Pleasure

THE FERTILE yet practical mind of the Chinese male, at least those with the advantages of education and wealth, regarded sex as a suitable subject for study as well as pleasure, as a science as well as an art. The ideal of the equality of the sexes was unimaginable. Woman had been created for certain specific functions, to bear children, particularly sons, to please her master in the bedchamber, to obey his commands. Romantic love was alien to both his way of life and to his emotional needs, and the social opportunities to indulge in it were even less available. The conditions were therefore favourable for Lord Yang to regard Lady Yin as part of his household possessions, to be used or enjoyed as the mood took him.

This emphasis on use and practicability was inevitably directed towards experimentation and to widening the whole area of sexual pleasure. The Yellow Emperor, whether a mythical figure or not, had created an early and time-honoured precedent, both in legend and in records purported to have been inscribed by him, for pursuing Harmony by all possible means and methods. The handbooks and the writings that followed, from the Chou

period to the Ming, stressed the same message, and since Harmony, in such a male-orientated society, was wholly related to the sex act itself, it was on this that most attention was concentrated. How could one extend the experience and how could one prolong its duration?

The Yin-Yang theory had always given it a quasi-religious significance by regarding the sex organs as one of the elemental forces of the great cosmos. The Earth, Woman and the vulva were all Yin, the Sun, Man and the penis were Yang, and out of the Chaos that preceded Creation, the union of these opposites was meant to lead to Harmony. It was possible, by the same logic, to believe that the Sun and the Earth consummated their relationship every time Man and Woman indulged in the act. The prolongation and the exaltation of it could therefore be seen as a deeply meaningful ritual.

There were three obvious courses for adding to the significance of the ritual, and they were pursued with industry and imagination. One was by a methodical approach to sex positions, the second was by instruments, aids and aphrodisiacs, the third by glorifying the primary sex organs.

A long history of custom and superstition had added a complex framework of beliefs to every aspect of life, and sex was as affected by these as were burials, births and ancestor worship. There were lucky and unlucky days for intercourse, good weather and bad, favourable and unfavourable directions in which to lie. The physical characteristics of women also carried their signs and portents, and of particular importance were the principles laid down in the Confucian Book of Rites (*Li-chi*). These were concerned with 'right behaviour', the Rules and Regulations covering every aspect of social and personal life, from the relationship between various members of the family and the observing of festivals to such stipulations as the wife's 'right' to see that a concubine left her husband's bed once the act was over.

The use of aphrodisiacs against such a background of beliefs and superstition, of ritual and custom, explains much of the success attributed to them. It is commonly accepted that faith is the most important ingredient of any form of sexual stimulation, and the Chinese male was always eager to supply this essential part. Those stimulants taken orally were for men only, it being conceded that the woman could play her part on the battlefield at any time while Yang's ability to participate depended greatly on the condition of his Male

Peak. Ointments and powders, however, were distributed with less partiality, in the case of the male to encourage his erection and to slightly insensitise his member, with the female, by exciting the Jade Gate. This hastened the woman's receptiveness and so reduced Yang's need to indulge in love-play when he was impatient to attack the Pleasure Pavilion.

The basis of both external and oral aphrodisiacs was usually herbal, the commonest ingredients being ginseng, sulphur, cinnamon, cedar seeds, seaweed, pine-needles and powdered charcoal. To these were added one or more of the following: liver extract of various animals, distilled urine — human or animal — secretions from the human sex organs, from tame bears, goats and bulls, hymenal blood, and the excreta of certain animals and birds notorious for their powerful or predatory characters. A third popular constituent was related to shape, its likeness to fertility symbols, and in this category were the horns of various animals, plants, fungi and cacti of penis-like mould, and certain marine objects. These were powdered and sieved before being swallowed.

The term 'aphrodisiac' had a much wider application, however, than a concocted stimulant, and covered the whole category of beneficient aids, techniques and elixirs. In a Ming period work, by Teng Hsi-hsien, much is made of the restorative power of the woman's fluids when imbibed by the man, and in the *Great Medicine of the Three Heights (Levels),* we are told:

The first and highest level is called Red Lotus Peak and its medicine 'jade liquid' or 'honey fountain'.

A rhinoceros-horn cup, 9 cms. high. The edge has been broken away, possibly to be ground into a powder that was a favourite aphrodisiac. By courtesy of the Wellcome Trustees.

This flows from under the woman's tongue, is green in colour and should be sucked by the man into his own saliva. This fluid rises directly from the 'vermilion pond' and will nourish his Five Organs, his Vital Essence and his blood flow.

The middle-level is called Land of the Twin Peaks and its medicine Exotic Peach, Liquid Snow or Coral Cream. It exudes from exactly between the two breasts, is white in colour and sweet to the palate. The man should lick it as it appears. It will benefit his stomach and his gall-bladder and improve his tempers. By drawing it from the woman, her menstrual flow will be helped, and if she is a mother lacking milk, this will help in the same way.

The lowest level of the Three Heights is the Purple Mushroom Peak, also called White Tiger Cave and Moon Halo. The beneficial fluid lies in the Flowery Pavilion when the Gate is closed, and only flows once the woman is excited by intercourse. To draw this vital essence into himself, the man must press in fiercely but withdraw slowly, so dragging it into the skin of the Male Peak.

Those who nourish themselves on these medicines will know the full pleasure of serenity. Their fiercest desires will be enjoyed calmly, those whose hair has turned grey will find it restored to black, and those who have grown old will again know the joys of youth.

Faith in aphrodisiacs had always to be accompanied by the *sine·qua non* for a successful confrontation, the *right mood,* and handbooks old and new were unanimous in stressing the importance of this. Modern sexologists have not advanced on the ancient wisdoms of the Chinese. When the Wise Maiden said that many of man's weaknesses and worries were the result of unsatisfactory sexual relations, or even a determination to ignore sex, she was stating the teachings of Freud, Kinsey and others many millennia later. 'To retire to the bedchamber in the wrong mood' is the commonest form of impotence, a condition shared by the Yellow Emperor and the over-stressed business executives of the twentieth-century. The need to banish the *'wrong mood'* was therefore an essential part of the ancient dialogues of the *Su-nu-ching:*

Yellow Emperor: Now there is this problem of the Jade Thrusting Root failing to rise and stiffen. When this happens my face reddens and I am soaked in sweat. I breathe hard, my desire is strong, I press furiously at the Gate — yet there is no sign of life. How can I avoid this mortifying situation?
The Wise Maiden: This is a problem that afflicts many men. Unless one is physically exhausted it is because one has retired to the bedchamber in the wrong mood. With a harmonious spirit the Jade

93

Stem will always stiffen, with a mood that is dark or bitter, it is like a thorn piercing one's own flesh. The way to induce the Right Mood is to follow the Five Natural Humours of the Male and to be guided by the Five Responses of the Female.

Yellow Emperor: And what are the Five Natural Humours?

The Wise Maiden: He should be relaxed and calm, which is proof of his UNASSUMING nature. As he wishes to give his male implement to another, his mood must be one of GENEROSITY. His body contains cavities which can be expanded, and by correct breathing this will induce the correct CAPACITY. Fourthly, his body is constructed in rings and circles, from the foreskin to the ears, and his mood must therefore be of total SERENITY. The fifth of the Natural Humours is that which will excuse the failure of the Jade Stem to stiffen — the only excuse — and that is LOYALTY. If the Male wishes for solitude, then nothing must prevent him from thus being loyal to such a noble mood.

Yellow Emperor: And what are the Five Responses of the woman that should guide a man?

The Wise Maiden: First, she flushes and is pink in the face. This is the sign that he can approach her. *Second,* her nipples rise and harden, and perspiration appears on her nose. This is the sign that he will be welcome at the Jade Gate. *Third,* her mouth opens and she breathes faster, her nostrils spread and her hands tremble. This is the sign to thrust forward. *Fourth,* the Golden Gully is profusely lubricated, and this is a sign that one must be carried by the current. *Fifth,* the flow is now spreading over her thighs and she seems to have lost all strength. This is the sign to relax and pause before returning to the attack.

Yellow Emperor: I have heard it said that with the Five Responses, one should also know the Ten Revealing Movements of Women. What are these movements?

The Wise Maiden: These are the revealing movements:

First, if she clasps the man in her arms, she wishes their bodies to press together and their genitalia to be one against the other.

Second, if she raises her knees from the bed she wishes the outer parts of the vulva to be touched and rubbed.

Third, when her back arches she is ready for the first thrusts of the Jade Stalk.

Fourth, when her buttocks convulse more urgently, that is a desire for more speed.

Fifth, when her legs kick in the air or rise high, that is a desire for deeper penetration.

Sixth, when she convulses to right and left, she wants the member to jerk in the contrary direction.

Seventh, when her thighs press together that is the moment of stillness before the Great Typhoon.

Eighth, if her body thrusts up so violently that the man is pushed back, that is the supreme moment of the Ultimate.

This domestic scene illustrates the Confucian ideal of pursuing lofty thoughts while dutiful concubines attend to the master's physical needs. His detachment does not, however, preclude casual pedicatio. 17th-century blockprint.

Ninth, when her body goes limp it is a sign that all her organs and limbs have shared the Ultimate.

Tenth, if her secretions continue to flow, this is the sign that the Vital Essence is wholly released.

If these movements are observed, the man can be assured that the woman is satisfied. But one should also be familiar with the Nine Urges of Woman.

Yellow Emperor: And what are the Nine Urges?

The Wise Maiden: First, when the woman pants and swallows in quick succession, it is an urge coming from the lungs.

Second, when she sucks at the man's tongue, it is an urge from the bones.

Third, when she screams and shouts, it is an urge from the heart.

Fourth, when she seizes the Jade Stem and grips it tightly, it is an urge from the spleen.

Fifth, when the Jade Gate is draining with fluid, it is an urge from the kidneys.

Sixth, when she raises her legs, it is an urge from the sinews.

Seventh, if she plays lightly with the man's nipples, it is an urge from the flesh.

Eighth, if she plays lightly with the man's implement, it is an urge from the blood.

Ninth, if she plays lightly with her own nipples or organ, it is an urge from the Dark Ancestor.

For the mandarin society, and for many other Chinese, life was a leisurely devotion to pleasure and culture. After a peaceful social order, the priorities of the good life were food and sex, and not necessarily in that order. The idea, therefore, of food as an aphrodisiac seemed a natural connection. Without food, man died. Similarly, in the case of a drooping Yang spirit, the right preparation taken by mouth would quickly revive the weakening member. Recipes for aphrodisiacs were therefore simply part of the culinary arts. The correct ingredients, first, and then close attention to the preparation and various signs and auguries would create the Secret Elixir. These preparations usually meant pulverizing and sieving, mixing with wine and taking with a spoon or kneading with wax to make pills. One aphrodisiac had a further propensity. It promised to lengthen the penis by three inches but for this liver extract had to be obtained from a white dog killed during the First Moon of any year, the resultant ointment rubbed over the penis three times, and the residue drunk with fresh well water.

Two popular recipes were *I-tu Potion* and the *Bald Chicken Tonic.* The first is mentioned in an old medical treatise, the *Yin-yen-fang,* in which a noblewoman charged with murder revealed it to the Emperor. In her defence, her story was that her troubles began when her eighty year-old husband learnt of a secret remedy to cure his impotence but had died before it had restored his virility. A seventy-five year-old slave, I-tu, whose hair was white and whose body stooped pitifully, then decided to try the elixir. In twenty days the powdered concoction of cinnamon heart, liquorice, yam, lacquer and various herbs had given him black hair, a straight body and a young face. He was so virile that he decided to marry two of the noblewoman's maids, and so happy were they that their mistress was overcome by desire for the rejuvenated slave.

'Although I had reached half a hundred years and had retired from the *flowery battle,* his wonderful Yang force restored my own youth and every day, in the company of his wives, we devoted ourselves to the *Clouds and the Rain.* But one day, in a fit of shame at my enjoyment with a slave, I killed him. I therefore petition Your Majesty to spare my life in exchange for the secret medicine.'

Bald Chicken Tonic was regarded as a regimen as well as an aphrodisiac and the story is told of the seventy year-old Prefect of Shu who remained so virile from taking it that one of his wives suffered from a sore vagina and could not sit down. In despair she threw the elixir into the courtyard where it was consumed by a cock. The cock at once jumped on a hen and continued to copulate without pause for a number of days, pecking at the hen's head until it was bald, so giving the potion its name.

The ingredients of Bald Chicken Tonic were mostly herbs mixed with wax and taken as pills, and such 'wonder drugs' were naturally a common feature of Chinese novels, particularly since most of the literate population were male. In the *Chin P'ing Mei,* the indefatigable hero, Hsi-men Ch'ing, always eager to improve his performance, meets a Tibetan monk:

As Hsi-men Ch'ing passed through the temple he paused in that part named the Hall of Contemplation. Against one wall a number of couches had been placed, and on one of these reclined a monk of most distinguished appearance. He had the fierce head of a leopard, the lines of his face emaciated, the deep-set eyes staring blindly into space. His robe was flesh-pink in colour and his hat had a ridge to it like a cock's crest. His beard was long, hanging from underneath his chin. This man is a Lo-Han God, decided Hsi-men. The One-Eyed Dragon himself.

A magnetic force drew him to the man's side, and as he stared down he was surprised to see two long drips of snot like a pair of green-jade chopsticks hanging from his nostrils. But this carelessness about his appearance served to confirm Hsi-men Ch'ing's certainty that here was a monk of extraordinary powers.

In an excited voice, he cried: 'Oh, holy man, where are you from? How is it that you have wandered into this particular temple?'

The questions were asked three times before he received an answer. Then the monk sat up, wiped his nose with his wide sleeve, and said: 'Why do you pose such meaningless questions? Of what importance is it from where I come? Am I not the same person wherever I am?' He looked at Hsi-men Ch'ing with his piercing eyes, and seemed encouraged to be a little more forthcoming. 'Does my name change with travel? Does it alter if I choose to stay in

a place? But since you ask from where I come, let me inform you that I am from Tibet, from the remotest part of the pine forests covering the lower slopes of the highest mountains. My monastery is called The Windy Courtyard of the Cold Peaks.'

'But what brings you to my humble district, my Elevated Holy Man?'

'I have entered the world of ordinary men to bestow on them the special medicines and remedies of the Cold Peaks. Why, my honoured young official, is there something you seek?'

'I am always ready to avail myself of medicines of special nourishment,' admitted Hsi-men. 'Do you have anything for replacing the daily spilling of my Vital Essence?'

'I have,' said the monk. 'That is a very common request.'

'If you would care to accompany me for dinner at my humble abode, perhaps we could talk about it.'

'I shall be honoured to eat at your table.'

'Then let us go,' said Hsi-men, concealing his eagerness.

The monk from Tibet picked up his iron staff, and threw over his shoulder a long leather pouch which contained bundles, jars and gourds of medicines. As they left the Hall of Contemplation, Hsi-men Ch'ing invited the holy man to mount his horse, but the monk refused, saying that he saw no reason to exchange his own legs for those of an animal. Hsi-men then ordered his servant to accompany the monk, and turned the horse towards the main highway.

To his surprise, he arrived to find that the monk and the servant were already outside his home.

'My honoured holy man, you must really be a god to have travelled so quickly!' exclaimed Hsi-men. 'But let us go upstairs to the Upper Hall.'

As soon as they entered the library, servants removed their outer garments, and Hsi-men called for his scholar's cap. The fierce eyes of the long-bearded monk looked round the hall as if he had never seen such a place, and Hsi-men maintained a humble silence. The walls were covered with scroll pictures, the bamboo rods being decorated with jade and cornelian, and the curtains across the entrance were of such fine threads that the material was called 'Shrimp-whisker Silk'. The rugs on the floor had designs of lions and phoenixes, and the chairs were exquisitely carved from southern blackwood. A marble table top was set below the Ancestral Tablets.

'Do you drink wine, Esteemed Master?' Hsi-men inquired at last.

'Wine I drink and meat I eat,' the monk said, as if disclosing to his host that his self-denial did not extend to food.

Hsi-men Ch'ing then turned to his servant and told him that they would not be needing vegetarian dishes and that the usual food could be served. As it was the *Festival of the Great Li's Birthday,* the kit-

A Taoist interlude. Near the waterfall, the travellers pause in their journey. Inevitably, there is the humour of watching eyes. 18th-century painting. Courtesy private collection, Paris.

chen had been busy all day preparing dishes for the occasion, and within a short time three servants were setting them before their master and the visitor from the Cold Peaks of Tibet.

'Let us eat,' said Hsi-men Ch'ing courteously.

The formidable monk then ate for over an hour without uttering a word. He stared with the four 'Wine-accompanying' dishes, braised fish-head, savoury duck cooked in wine-sediment paste, skinless chicken on turtles' eggs, and a dish of sea-bream from Kiangsu. These were followed by the four 'Rice-accompanying' dishes, lambs' tripe filled with walnut and goat-horn powder, wet-fried Anhwei snake, dry-fried buffalo meat and onions, long simmered eels in the Sea of Cosmic Flavours.

Chinese humour. Old man being teased by two shorn Buddhist or Taoist nuns. Monks and nuns had a reputation for depravity and hypocrisy. 19th-century painting. Courtesy Bibliotheque Nationale, Paris.

The monk then went on to enjoy the three 'Savoury soups,' Dragon Playing with Two Balls, Tears of the Princess Shan-yin, and Supreme Yang-essence of the Kitchen God.

The servant, between almost every mouthful, refilled the monk's lotus-leaf shaped cup, breaking open the red-earth seals of wine-jar after wine-jar. In all, before the monk sank back in his chair, thirty seals had been broken.

Chinese humour. Is the watching woman one of the master's older wives? Is her raised hand hopefully tidying her hair or expressing disapproval? Private collection, Paris.

'This disgrace to his Holy Vows has imbibed to the point of drunkenness and eaten to the point of surfeit,' the monk mumbled unsteadily.

'Clear everything away,' Hsi-men said to the servants. And once they were alone, he roused his visitor and asked: 'Tell me, holy man, about this medicine that will constantly renew the Vital Essence.'

The request served to revive the monk, who sat up and reached for his leather pouches.

'These pills were concocted by the Ancient Emperors and handed down by the Fair Goddess,'

he explained in a deep voice. 'We holy men are pledged to give them only to those whom we consider worthy of such powers. Since my honourable host has been so generous and his kitchen so excellent, he is certainly worthy of such powers.' He tilted one of the medicine gourds and poured a heap of large pills on to the table. 'You take only one at a time, otherwise I cannot be responsible for the dragon effects of their potency.'

The monk counted one hundred pills, each the size of a cherry, then produced a small container of red ointment.

'Should you feel weak and dizzy, rub this on the

inside of your thighs. After one hundred rubbings the weakness will have disappeared.'

Hsi-men Ch'ing was delighted by this information and by the heap of pills that promised even greater victories in the battles of the bedchamber.

'May I ask how this medicine will affect me, oh holy man?' he inquired humbly.

The guest's rather drunken speech instantly cleared, and in a voice that was a musical chant, and in words that might have been a poem, the monk sang:

This remedy in the shape of a hen's egg,
The yellow of a duckling's down,
Was concocted by the Triple-process
Of our Ancient Emperors,
And by the Fair Goddess
Brought down through the Ages.
Its taste may be that of dung or soil
But its value is that of precious jewels.
Which man would not prefer it to gold,
Choose it rather than jade,
Exchange it for his silk purple robe
Or his coat of finest sable?
To swallow this aphrodisiac
Will turn winter's night into spring morning,
And like a whirlwind in the bedchamber
You will sweep all before you.
Two women or twelve, five or fifty,
Not one will remain without contentment.
And stronger not weaker will be your response,
The gall-bladder nourished, the testicles untiring,
The Jade-Stem ever-rigid, and the appetite keener.
In one hundred days grey hair will turn black
In one thousand old men will be young,
Each lover worthy of the Fair Goddess herself.
If all I claim seems beyond belief
Try out this pill on the oldest tomcat.
Within three days he will be mating unceasingly,
Within four he will be after dogs and rabbits,
His colour will change from white to black; and finally
He will fall dead from forgetting to shit.
So remember the fate of this cat,
Do not from ardour neglect the bowels
And do not in winter forget the icy wind
Or in summer disregard the exhausting heat.
To revive yourself after the fiercest battles
Simply gulp mouthfuls of cool mountain water.
And with this pill the Flowery Field
Will seem illuminated on the darkest night,
Older women will tremble at your approach
And even the harlot will wonder at your power.
So use them well, these first hundred,
And with their help enjoy your fullest manliness.

The recital had carried away Hsi-men Ch'ing but as soon as the deep voice stopped the practical side of his nature encouraged him to say:

'My honoured holy man, to obtain a medicine is not always enough. When you return to the Windy Courtyard of the Cold Peaks, how will this humble

and faithful convert to your greatness renew the prescription? For a copy of that prescription, I would pay whatever you ask.'

He immediately instructed his servant to open the treasure box and present to the monk twenty taels of 'White gold' (silver).

'What use do I have for money!' exclaimed the monk, gesturing to the servant to ignore his master's order. 'I have given up worldly wealth and ambition — so I would hardly be grateful for the burden of your white gold.'

'But surely you will at least take a fine piece of cloth measuring fully forty feet?' said Hsi-men.

The monk thanked him but again refused.

'I float like a cloud over all the areas of the region — why should I encumber myself with a piece of cloth?'

The monk then wrote out the prescription, repeated his warning about over-indulgence, and before Hsi-men could adequately thank him, the impressive figure had thrown his long leather bag over his shoulder and was striding through the Outer Hall.

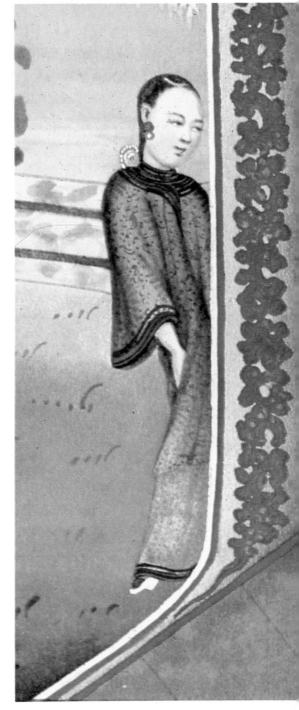

Drinking wine by a mountain path
I wave as she passes on pony-back —
Pretty Maid of Wu, hardly fifteen.
I offer her the wine jar
And she jumps down to drink with me —
Pretty Maid of Wu, hardly fifteen.
Her manner bewitching, her eyes blue-lined,
She gets drunk on my lap
Then yields to my passion.
Oh that morning by a mountain path
The warmth of the wine and her caresses —
Pretty Maid of Wu, hardly fifteen.

Li Po (701-761)

The hero of the Chin P'ing Mei was not one to waste time in putting to use his latest sex acquisition, and from the following account the monk had not exaggerated its effect on both the performance and on the Jade Stem. It also describes anal coitus, a surprisingly rare phenomenon in Chinese erotic literature:

Hsi-men Ch'ing needed a long draught of Shiu Hsing wine to wash down the monk's yellow pill, and not wanting to waste a moment of the effects on him, he immediately removed his clothing and began attaching the contents of his leather case of sex instruments. The pretty harlot of the Golden Willows and Silver Waters establishment, Pearl Moon, sat on the edge of the bed and watched with interest.

'What was that enormous pill you took — are you up to some wicked scheme?' she asked.

'I have taken one of the dragon potions of our great Ancestral Emperors,' he replied. 'And now permit me to prepare for our battle.'

His member was still at rest but he succeeded in attaching the open-weave silk sheath. Then

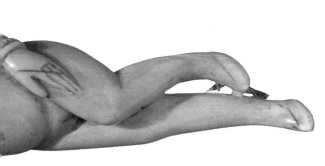

A 'medical ivory' about 10cm. long. The Confucian code prevented doctors from examining women patients, apart from feeling the pulse of an arm stretched through the bed curtains. The doctor's ivory was therefore used for the husband or female relative to indicate the area of the illness. 18th-century. Courtesy of the W.H. & Elizabeth M. Deane collection, University of Sydney Library.

The maid stands ready to be summoned, either to serve refreshments or to join in such positions as The Gobbling Fishes. *19th-century pillow book. By kind permission of the British Museum.*

he slipped a sulphur ring round the base of the 'turtle head', took a pinch of the red-powder ointment given him by the monk and pressed it into the 'tiny slit' itself. To his amazement, and clearly to that of Pearl Moon, the limp flesh instantly reared up like an angry dragon. It had turned from a honey-pink to the purple-red of pig's liver and was quivering as if overwhelmed by a fierce rage.

'Why aren't you undressed?' demanded Hsi-men.

Intimidated by both his voice and the angry dragon, the young woman threw off her clothes and at once lay on the bed. As Hsi-men Ch'ing was eager to test the monk's potion he did not waste time with love preliminaries but placed the two pillows under her buttocks and took up a kneeling position between her legs. The 'turtle head', however, was so enlarged that he was forced to request her help; while he held open the Golden Valley, she took the angry dragon and gardually managed to accommodate it.

'You are killing me,' she gasped. 'I feel quite drunk after that wine.'

Hsi-men Ch'ing was also flushed from the wine, and once her secretions had begun to flow, managed to practise 'short-and-long' movements and those known as 'seven shallow and two deep'. But the fever of intoxication was more wonderful than anything he had known before and this, he decided, must also be from the monk's pill.

'I feel indescribably happy and I am going to attack you from behind,' he cried.

He withdrew his implement and roughly pushed her over. Then he made her press her forehead on the pillow and took hold of the mounds of her buttocks. This time penetration was even more difficult than before and was accompanied by a rubbing and tearing sound.

'That's enough!' screamed Pearl Moon. 'I haven't had so much wine that I can take that!'

Hsi-men Ch'ing speared her more deeply than ever while she moaned and struggled to escape, but the monk's pill also filled him with a great benevolence, and he said, 'Do you think we should go back to the normal way?'

'If you will only do that,' pleaded Pearl Moon, 'I will hold the lamp over us so that you can watch. You certainly have a *wong-pa* (turtle) worth watching.'

Hsi-men Ch'ing felt pleased with both the suggestion and the compliment, allowed her to turn and passed her the lamp. This she held with one hand, and once he had raised her Golden Lilies above her shoulders, she used the other hand to help him return to the Flower Heart. He was again aware of the audible sound of their love-making, and he made her hold the lamp so that he could ascertain that all was normal with the Jade Pavilion; when he was reassured about this, he adopted the position known as Phoenix Sporting and made two hundred thrusts without pause. And his delight at the effect of the monk's pill made him cry:

'Tomorrow my servant will deliver you twenty yards of the finest silk and a bed coverlet embroidered by my wife's own hands.'

In the nineteenth-century the Chinese addiction to opium became widespread. As an aphrodisiac it affected the mind rather than the body, inducing sensual fantasies while inhibiting a more sustained physical role. As smokers were invariably men, however, and usually reclined on a mat in the company of another male, a certain number of homosexual relationships were encouraged. It has further been suggested that the addiction of so many males was related to the servile state in which he kept his womenfolk, their inferiority and Confucian sense of obedience restraining them from taking a greater initiative in controlling the self-destructive habits of their husbands. The social custom of keeping a wife out of sight of the public, of hardly ever allowing her to accompany him when visiting friends, also attributed to his arrival at the opium-shops.

The addiction affected all classes of society, reducing merchants to penniless paupers, causing poor men to sell off their children and even their wives, and those from the lower classes to die of neglect. Any illusions about the sex-stimulant properties of opium should be weighed against the following nineteenth-century description of the addict:

The first signs of ruin come with sneezing. Mucus runs from his nose and eyes. Gripping pains seize him in his bowels. His whole appearance indicates restlessness and misery. After smoking, he usually falls asleep, but it is not a sleep that refreshes. On being aroused, he is himself again, provided he can immediately have his opium. If not, he begins to suffer and the pains multiply. Diarrhoea of a most painful and dreadful kind, peculiar to smoking, sets in, and he is without strength or disposition to stir himself. Eventually, the agonies become unbearable, only relieved by ever-increasing recourse to the drug. Few recover once their pains have reached this excruciating stage.

J. Doolittle (1867)

Women were not disregarded in the search for aphrodisiacs and a Taoist manual called *Guide to the Jade Room* lists many concoctions for exciting Yin. The ingredients were invariably herbal, plants of penis shape and such additives as musk incense and sulphur. Their names, not unlike modern aphrodisiac products manufactured by pharmaceutical companies, were meant to add to the stimulation, some being: Happiness Powder, Gate Opens Wide and Smiling Golden Gully. The method of application was to rub the powder or ointment inside the Jade Gate. The result was claimed to be immediate but this was probably due to a mixture of the irritant effects of the stimulant and the woman's desire for success.

The woman, however, had to overcome traditional ideas about the actual physical characteristics of the Flower Heart. Wisdom — or ignorance — had sent down the ages preconceived notions that lay outside the effectiveness of aphrodisiacs. Had not the Yellow Emperor, for example, asked: Why is it that the Jade Gate is sometimes nearer the front than the back, and sometimes exactly in the middle? And which is the best position for intercourse?

These 19th-century lovers relax with their opium pipes, the maid versatile in her skills. By courtesy of the Wellcome Trustees.

To which the Wise Maiden had replied: 'The suitability and the responses of the vulva do not depend only on its position. Whether it is high, low, or in the middle, each will contribute equally to the pleasure of the Flowery Field. However, there are distinctions, and these I will explain. A woman with a high vagina, that is to the front, is better for intercourse in the winter season. The man can be on top of her immediately on going to bed, drawing over his back the embroidered coverlet. He can enjoy intercourse without dismounting, convenient for himself, and since she will be benefiting from his warmth, she will not complain. In the summer it is an advantage to copulate with women with low vaginas. She can be laid on a cool marble slab in the shade of bamboos, reclining on her side, and the man can take up a position behind her. Her vagina is in the ideal position for this variation, the position called *Making Fire Behind the Mountain*. A woman for the Four Seasons is one whose vagina is in the middle, a careful study of positions enabling her to be adapted to Spring, Summer, Autumn and Winter.'

The Clouds and Rain have passed
From the heights of the Jade Mountain —
The loving is over and slowly she dresses,
Her weak fingers fasten her robes,
Arrange her hair. And her dazed eyes
Still reflect the passionate hours.

Tung Hai (Scholar — Seventh Century)

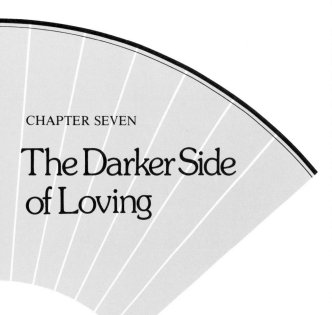

CHAPTER SEVEN

The Darker Side of Loving

The pattern of a civilisation determines certain sexual practices, and in Chinese history the social inferiority of women, the cerebral inventiveness of the men, and the pagan guilt-free element of Taoist beliefs, were three of the most obvious influences. The idea of normal sex behaviour varies from period to period, from society to society, and any study that regards one approach as correct and others as perversions, is simply applying the criteria of its time and place.

The Chinese custom of footbinding, for example, was widely considered by westerners as a cruel fetish, though the Chinese male was delighted by the woman's helplessness and the accompanying sense of dominance, while the female displayed a masochistic acceptance of the discomfort and humiliation. Yet the Chinese, for their part, could not understand Christian disapproval of fornication, of masturbation and their relating the most wonderful of pleasures to sin. Nor would they have followed the Muslim horror of hymenal blood or their employment of special 'stud males' to deflower virgins, an initiation which medieval Arabs apparently found distasteful.

The Chinese attitude to circumcision was one of terror, to clitoridectomy bewilderment, and to kissing and casual love-play that did not advance to the natural and ecstatic climax an insult to both Yin and Yang.

In societies both ancient and modern, sin and guilt determine the nature of what is acceptable and what is to be condemned, and the existence of such taboos frequently excites men and women to seek those pleasures explicitly because they are forbidden. Among the Chinese there were no rigid religious or ethical reasons for condemning homosexuality, masturbation, 'flute-playing' (fellatio), transvestism, lesbianism, polygamy, masochism or voyeurism. As most of these choices of gratification, if they were practised with the consent of all concerned, were regarded as a matter of individual preference, there seemed little reason to turn them into social crimes. In the case of sadism, the perversion that could lead to the most destructive and painful effects, there are few recorded instances to suggest that the Chinese resorted to it for sexual ecstasy. At least not within the four walls of the bedchamber. Beating and whipping were common punishments for many offences, even for minor infringements of the Book of Rules, and public torture was a common spectacle, but any gratification for the flogger or the onlookers would not have been displayed as overtly sexual.

It would be more correct to define Chinese sexual perversions as socially acceptable deviations, and to approach the subject with the toleration and the good humour, not to mention the element of cerebral delight, which

The ladies of the household consider the itinerant trader's merchandise. 19th-century, gouache on paper. Courtesy of the Library of the University of Indiana, Indiana.

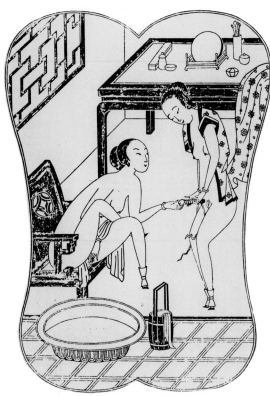

Love between women was a popular theme in erotic albums and a wise master tolerated it as a way of keeping them contented. Following a bath, evidence of cleanliness, the illustration shows women preparing to use an imaginative sex-aid. 17th-century blockprint.

usually prevailed. As has been stated, the idea of casual kissing seemed a profitless sexual encounter, and when westerners began to settle in Shanghai and other cities, and husbands and wives were observed to greet each other with a kiss or an embrace, those Chinese witnessing the affectionate gesture waited expectantly for the European to produce his Jade Stem and to leap into battle. Even more confusing for the ever-watchful Chinese was to see two Frenchmen greeting each other with kisses on the cheeks; this, too seemed a pointless sexual preliminary.

Such an unromantic approach on the part of the Chinese, and the role of the concubine as a sex-slave rather than as a partner, meant that he was not over-concerned with placing her gratification before his own or too worried about a show of western-style gallantry. The perfunctory mouth-kissing would therefore soon be followed by a request to his female to 'play the flute', and this was regarded as no less an art than the musician's. A skilled concubine would have a full and varied repertoire of songs, playing gently or vigorously, tremolo or basso, as she felt her master's mood required. A scatological side to the practice was common to most intimate relationships, though the concubine probably did not go so far as the ever-

willing Golden Lotus in the novel *Chin P'ing Mei* by Wang Shih-cheng (sixteenth-century):

The two-week separation from her husband, Hsi-men Ch'ing, had inflamed her desire so much that in the morning she refused to let him leave the bed. His member had been in the Jade Pavilion or in her mouth all night, and when he said that he must leave her side to relieve himself, she could not bear the idea of separation.

'Your body is so warm and it's so cold outside,' she protested. 'I wouldn't want you to catch a chill. Why don't you aim it in my mouth?'

Hsi-men Ch'ing was both moved and pleased by her consideration.

'I am sure no other woman would spoil me like this,' he said.

Golden Lotus opened her mouth a little wider and he aimed down her throat. She hastily gulped every mouthful, not a drop spilling on her face.

When he had finished, he asked: 'How did it taste?'

'A bit salty,' said Golden Lotus. 'Have you any scented tea leaves to take away the flavour?'

'The tea is in a pouch in the sleeve-pocket of my jacket. Help yourself.'

Golden Lotus reached for the white jacket on the bed-post, found the pouch and poured some of the leaves into her mouth.

The harem was inevitably associated with love between women. In some instances, where hundreds of women lived together, methods of mutual satisfaction were methodically organised, frequently with the blessing of an understanding master who accepted his human limitations, particularly if he were ageing. Apart from mutual masturbation and love embraces, a great variety of instruments were used by the women. The most-favoured artificial penises were of polished ivory or lacquered wood, with a pattern creating a corrugated effect. In a Ming period painting one of the girls, in a revealing love scene, is wearing the dildo strapped to her thigh, a location inconsistent with the male anatomy but which required less effort from the wearer. A further development of this instrument illustrates the inventiveness of the Chinese. A double-ended dildo, twelve inches long and with two loops of silken cord in the middle, allowed the sapphic lovers to gain simultaneous pleasure. By adopting a position which brought their Jade Gates facing each other, tugging alternately on the cord loops caused the same movement to gratify them both.

Early Chinese classics recall that the Imperial physician to the Empress Wu Tse-t'ien, a certain Ming Ch'ung-yan, presented her with a 'lively limb' for when she wished to have pleasure in solitude. This was a penis-shaped instrument made of rubber and which was attached with cords to the back of the ankle. Once the recumbent Empress had inserted the 'limb', it required only the minimal movement of her foot to make it 'lively'. As the use of rubber became more advanced, a scrotum was added to the instrument. The pouch was filled with warm milk and squeezed to simulate the male climax — or the defeat of Yang in the Flowery Battle.

An attachment, or perhaps it could be called an insertion, in frequent use was the Burmese Bell. This hollow silver sphere, the size of a berry, was placed in the vagina before intercourse, and because of the curious effects of warmth and movement on the pellet inside the 'bell', a constant tinkling was heard. Another variety contained a drop of mercury and a tiny 'striker'. Two such bells were frequently placed under the outer lips of the vulva, lodged with cotton packing, and once the lovers started moving, played a merry tune. This toy was also favoured by lesbians, and its insertion together with other instruments, when used for prolonged periods, sometimes caused deformities to the labia minora and distention of the clitoris. Chinese medical books of the Middle Ages describe a complaint peculiar to male-neglected concubines in large harems. It was termed 'coxcomb clitoris', one of the indications of Harem Nymphomania (*W'ei-T'ung-Sh'ih*).

If one had to define a single area of sexual nonconformity in which the Chinese excelled, it would certainly have been in the use of sexual aids and instruments. As their sophisticated society developed, and as a lusty naivety gave way to the intellectual's inventiveness, there evolved what might be described as the pedantic lover. In his satchel, with presents of perfume and silk for his female, he carried his pillow books; in his pocket, with his personal necessities, he carried a pouch of love instruments. These included couch-pleasure powder and other stimulants, equally exciting unguents to lubricate the hinges of the Jade Gates, sulphur rings, silver collars, clasps, caps and 'Jade-step Polishers' (clitoral massagers), and a rather primitive assortment of birth control devices. For those who suffered from a loss of erection once intercourse had begun, the use of ribbons tied tightly round the base of the penis to prevent 'the return of the semen' was recommended.

A description of such a scene, the serio-comic interplay of the animal and the intellectual in man, is given in the following passage from the *Chin P'ing Mei:*

Miss Heart's Delight invited him into the bed-chamber where a whole feast had been laid out. On the table was a variey of chicken and duck dishes, meat and delicate savouries. He loosened his clothes as he sat down, in anticipation of the feast, and she filled his wine-cup. They ate and drank for some time, not conversing much, but towards the end of the meal the intoxication of the wine created a more relaxed mood. They moved their chairs together and embraced sitting up, then she placed her feet on his lap, and he touched them. With this signal of his readiness, they stood up and undressed each other, then he carried her to the bed.

She had prepared the bed with care. There was a double layer of down underneath so that they could roll in comfort, and the coverlet had been sprinkled with strong-scented powder. A painting of the Green Dragon and the White Tiger sporting together had been hung above their heads and bells tied to the bedposts. These wanton preparations were quickly appreciated, Miss Heart's Delight was pleased to observe, because before he had lain down beside her, she could see that he was fully roused.

'I shall be with you in a moment,' he promised, then pulled out an embroidered silk pouch.

He opened it carefully and laid the following items along the edge of the coverlet:

A silver love-clip
A Cap of Everlasting-Desire
A sulphur Lust-ring
Medically treated passion-ribbons
Jade Penis-ring
Lust-rousing ointment
Tatar Love-bell

'There, what do you think of my whoring instruments,' he asked.

She was too speechless to reply and lay back on the pillow, a picture of fear and anticipation. Her mouth had dropped open and her breathing had quickened, her hands felt weak but her knees were already rising into the air. When he had fixed the silver clip to the Jade Stem, he covered it with ointment, then moved between her knees. He tried out the position with a brief pressing at the Jade Gate, then withdrew and added the sulphur ring and a yellow and blue ribbon. Thus reinforced, he made a purposeful entry into the Pleasure Pavilion, at once causing her to scream with pain and joy, as if a blade was driving deeper and deeper inside her.

In a society where justice was often swift and summary, where the Book of Rules and other authorities had clearly defined the nature and consequences of offences, the infliction of corporal punishment was a common feature of life. The bamboo rod grew in profusion, as if Nature intended it to be used to enforce discipline, and the fatalistic character of the people accepted this and other forms of violence. Such fatalism was encouraged by the absolute authority of the Emperor and his governors, and by an innate sense of the established order of life and respect for their ancient traditions.

European merchants and seamen of the 19th-century, fearing disease, occasionally adopted this position. As the girls would have been Fallen Flowers, the variation would have been passed on to other clients. From Yanwo 5, in the Mitchell Library.

Indisputably there was an element of sadism in every swing of a father's arm, the teacher's rod, the executioner's sword or the soldier's foot, but the custom of the liberal use of corporal punishment was no more to be questioned than family relationships or social practices. It was just one element of a much greater whole. An old Chinese maxim states that when a son knows he has offended his father, he can do no more than carry to him a stick for his own punishment. Equally, it is said that Po Yü, two thousand years ago, wept bitterly when flogged by his old mother. As he was almost a man, and had not wept for years, his mother asked the reason for this. Po Yü then confessed that it was not pain that had reduced him to tears but the fact that the bamboo fell so feebly that he knew that she was becoming infirm with age.

These and other stories not only sentimentalised about retribution and the time-honoured acceptance of the deserved and the unavoidable, they were part of a conception that the punishment should fit the crime. For this reason sentences were often inflicted in public, and the human sympathy for the victim did not necessarily shake confidence in the system. This included many complex and brutal forms of torture. The Code of Laws (*Ta Ts'ing-luh-li*) was drawn up during the Sung dynasty (960-1127), and the number of strokes fixed as penalties remained in force until the twentieth-century. Most offences calling for beating were infringements of behavioural customs or breaches of filial piety rather than

misdemeanours of a more criminal kind. Sixty strokes of the 'long stick' was the penalty for evading mourning for a grandparent by keeping the fact a secret, for 'ignoring' grief and making music, or for prematurely putting aside mourning dress. Eighty strokes was the punishment for a wife or concubine disobeying a husband (should he take them to law), and a similar punishment with the 'short and thick stick' was inflicted for failing to observe certain public festivals. The Code of Laws, it has been claimed, purposely regulated every offence within the clan, tribe or family, as a way of achieving social harmony and balance, and the aristocracy was expected, by its correct behaviour, to set an example to the lower classes. In such circumstances — made more complex by the continuity of exacting traditions — the nature and degree of sadism passing as forms of discipline or punishment are difficult to define. If sexual sadism was less prevalent among men, however, it was often in evidence between women, particularly when the polygamous pattern of the household created tensions and jealousies of an unbearable kind. A common situation, which must have been repeated very often, is recounted in the *Patterns of Light and Shade*, an early Ch'ing novel. The scene describes the

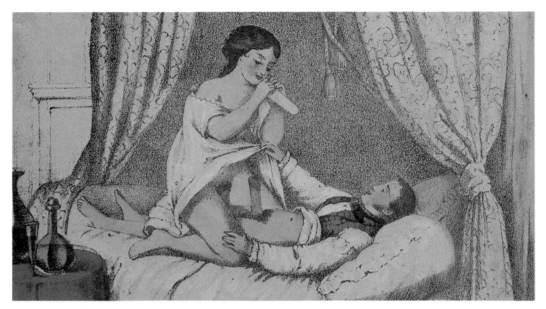

This 'Western' picture has been added to the erotic album Yanwo 5. Its interest is because the Chinese artist sees the European woman (testing her master's condom) in the traditional role of a dutiful concubine. The 19th-century merchant also typifies oriental ideas of bullying Europeans. Courtesy of the Mitchell Library, Sydney.

delight with which a dominant wife tortures one of her husband's concubines. Two servants are ordered to truss Sweet Spring to a wooden post, then the savage beating begins. It lasts most of the day, during which both the wife and the concubine eat two meals. The wife's passionate application of bamboo and leather strap finally reduces the victim to helplessness, at which point her hair is cropped and the wife enjoys the paroxysm of an orgasm.

An accepted variation of this occurred in court circles when the new favourites of rulers were often given the displaced consorts and concubines to torture as they thought fit. The malicious assault was usually directed at the sex organs, the unfortunate victims being beaten to a pulp, having irritants such as sand poured into the vagina or, even more brutal, having it pierced with red-hot rods and similar devices. Slicing of the breasts and buttocks was also a common occurrence, as was the coupling of the girls with goats, rams and even donkeys, an exhibition staged before a jeering crowd, the most vocal of which were their fellow females.

Although the worst outrages were committed in the courts of all-powerful kings and princes, or of tyrannical governors, the households of more modest families were not spared scenes of violence. This did not, of course, go to the extremes of bloody torture and killing, but the following account from *Chia-chang-yieh-shih* (Unusual Family Stories), a Ming dynasty novel, gives a picture of a sudden eruption of violence in the home. Ti-jen's wife, Fragrant Blossom, is jealous of

his favourite concubine, but unable to direct her fury at that well-protected female, chooses to attack her maidservant, Pure Crystal. The servant has the misfortune to spill some oil on her mistress's new shoes:

'You clumsy donkey,' screamed Fragrant Blossom. 'Look what you've done to my best shoes!'

Pure Crystal leaned across to look and received a blow from one of the shoes on her cheek, which started to bleed. As she stepped back, partly from shock and partly from the pain, her mistress jumped forward.

'So you're running away from me! You find me objectionable, threatening,' she cried. 'Spring Flower! Spring Flower!' The older of the two servants came from the Outer Court. 'This brainless slave has insulted me — fetch the leather whip!'

Spring Flower obeyed with the full knowledge that her mistress's fury could quite as unpredictably turn against her, and when she returned with the whip, she was at once ordered to strip the now whimpering Pure Crystal.

'Hold her hands — and if she gets away, you'll get the rest of the beating!' raged Fragrant Blossom.

Pure Crystal seemed too terrified to resist Spring Flower's haste to undress her, but as soon as she was dragged over the high couch, and her mistress wrapped the writhing leather round her bare back, she began to squeal like a half-slaughtered pig. After the fourth or fifth lash of the whip, Fragrant Blossom paused and said,

'This hurts me more than it hurts you!'

This sounded so ominous that the girl began to scream more loudly than ever.

'Isn't that enough?' Spring Flower ventured to ask.

The whip again fell across Pure Crystal's back, and from the noise the room might have been an abattoir. Her cries had already woken up Grandfather Wei in the next room, and as he sat up Fairy Coral in the other bed shouted: 'Go and stop that daughter of yours before she wakes up the baby.'

Grandfather Wei immediately ordered his wife to leave the warm brick bed and have the noise stopped, and when the old woman arrived in the next room, Fragrant Blossom had already brought down the whip thirty or forty times.

'Your elder sister is afraid you'll wake up the baby.' said Mother Wei. 'I don't mind you whipping that donkey, but at least you might consider the infant.'

The request instantly added to Fragrant Blossom's fury. She gave her old mother a push that sent her into the mandarin chair, then stood over her.

'Are you telling me how I should treat my own slaves! I won't have anyone coming in to my room and interfering with what I want to do!'

'I only came for a bowl of cold rice,' the old woman said timidly. 'But I don't think I want any now.'

As Mother Wei withdrew, Fragrant Blossom seized the screaming girl on the couch, turned her over, and scratched her face. Her nails were so sharp that they left long gashes down both cheeks, but the girl suddenly managed to slip behind the couch where only the soles of her bare feet showed. This was enough for Fragrant Blossom, however, who snatched the bamboo blow-pipe from the fireplace and began to beat the exposed feet. When she had exhausted herself, rather than her victim, she dropped on to her bed, told the servant to get back to her quarters, and lay waiting for the return of Ti-jen. She realised that perspiration was soaking her, but even more moist than her body was that part of her anticipating the return of her errant husband.

For Western religions the Ten Commandments emanated from an almighty and sacred deity but for the Chinese, who also had many moralistic texts based on the number 'ten', their commandments came from less divine sources. They were usually Confucian or Buddhist in origin and seemed to have received an extra impetus during the Yüan or Mongol dynasty (1279-1367). It was in this period, when the Empire was under the domination of the Mongol conquerors, that a new sexual morality evolved among the Chinese. Taoism and a more relaxed approach to sexuality gave way to a secretive and conservative form of behaviour, this more withdrawn society being a common reaction to invaders.

The Chinese equivalent to the Ten Commandments (or Ten Precepts, as they were often called), though not the work of any one particular moralist, frequently incorporated a system of merit marks or penalties. The purpose of this was to protect the Eternal Values of what they regarded as their unique heritage. The marks awarded by such texts, called *Kung-kuo-ku* (Tables of Merits and Demerits), covered almost every virtue or offence, though since it was for each individual to decide on his or her behaviour, the exercise was a little similar to the religious practice of the confessional. How did one assess one's own sins? An objective judgement required a rare degree of self-honesty and willpower, and there is no evidence of any lasting improvement in the individual's behaviour.

Of the various categories, or Precepts, the one relating to sexual behaviour is the most pertinent to both this study and a chapter devoted to 'the darker side of loving'. Examples are as follows:

Selection of Demerit Marks from Ching-shih-kung-kuo-ko

Violating a chaste woman	-1000
Turning a housemaid into a prostitute	-1000
Producing pornography or painting lewd pictures	-1000
Inviting a nun or a widow to become a concubine	-500
Abortion to hide an illicit affair	-600
Abortion in the case of a wife	-300
Taking a prostitute or young boy (each orgasm)	-50

Much is written about the distinction between 'violent rape', that is assaulting a woman against her will, and 'crazed rape', which indicates that the man is overwhelmed by blind passion. Such offences against virgins and widows are considered twice as sinful as against married women, but with prostitutes the demerit marks are relatively low. On the other hand, to fall in love genuinely with a prostitute was very sinful because it established beyond dispute the profligacy of the man.

There was also a long list of offences drawn from strict Confucian sources, which predated the Yüan or Mongol dynasty, and a selection of those relating to the conduct of the head of the family are:

Having more wives and concubines than one can satisfy	-50
Suggestive behaviour to rouse women outside the bedchamber	-20
Showing favouritism among one's women	-20
Going whoring and gambling with friends	-50
Boasting to one's women about other love affairs	-10
Putting erotic pictures on public display	-10
For purposely displaying oneself when urinating	-1
For keeping aphrodisiac incense in one's pocket	-1
For base dreams, masturbation etc. (each time)	-1

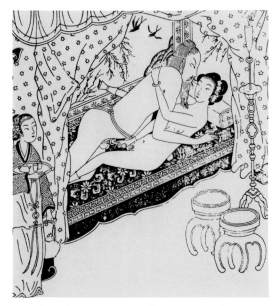

The 'dragon' ring ready to begin the yin-yang battle. The faces express a sense of confrontation. Ming dynasty blockprint.

One print in twenty, from a survey of erotic albums, had a theme of cunnilingus. The master's bare foot, suggesting pedicatio, complements the erect Male Peak. 17th-century blockprint.

Sweet girl not sixteen years
Soft breasts white and smooth
But between her legs a vicious trap
That strikes at manly ardour.

Hers is the cunning called passion
For which man dies with pleasure
His blood and essence drain away
For that girl of sweet sixteen.

Wang Shih-cheng

The most cruel aspect of the darker side of loving concerns a practice — a custom — that was both heroic and tragic. It was prevalent until the beginning of the present century and one can do no better than quote the relevant passage on sutteeism from Justus Doolittle's work on Chinese social life, published in 1867. He wrote:

Two singular customs which relate particularly to widows who do not marry again will now be described.

Some widows, on the death of their husbands, resolve not to survive them, and proceed to take their own lives. Chinese sutteeism differs from Indian sutteeism in that it is never performed by burning. The manner of doing it is various. Some take opium, and lie down and die by the side of the corpse of their husband. Others commit suicide by starving themselves to death, or by drowning themselves, or by taking poison. Another method sometimes practised in this place is by hanging themselves in public,

near or in their own houses, having given notice to that effect, so that those who desire may be present and behold the act.

The real reasons which induce some widows to practise sutteeism are various. Some, doubtless, are moved in a great degree to do it by a devoted attachment to the dead: others by the extreme poverty of their families, and the difficulty of earning an honest and respectable living; others by the fact or the prospect of unkind treatment on the part of their husband's relatives. Occasionally, when poor, the brothers of her deceased husband advise or insist that the young widow shall marry again. In one of the cases which occurred here about a year ago, the inciting cause why the young widow decided to kill herself by public hanging was that a brother-in-law insisted that she should marry a second husband. On her refusing to do it, he insinuated that the only way for her to gain a livelihood, in the indigent circumstances of the family, was by her becoming a prostitute. This unkindness maddened her, and she resolved to commit suicide. She appointed a certain time for its accomplishment. On the morning of the day appointed she visited a certain temple, erected to hold the tablets and perpetuate the memory of 'virtuous and filial' widows, and located near the south gate of the city. She was borne to and fro through the streets, seated in a sedan carried by four men, dressed in gaudy clothing, and holding in her hand a bouquet of fresh flowers. After burning incense and candles before the tablets in this temple, accompanied with the usual kneeling and bowings, she returned home, and in the afternoon took her life, in the presence of an immense crowd of spectators.

Actors played many roles and not always in public. 18th-century painting. Courtesy of the Library of the University of Indiana. Indiana.

On such occasions it is the practice to have a platform erected in the house of the widow, or in the street before it. At the appointed time she ascends the platform, and sprinkles some water around on the four sides of it. She then scatters several kinds of grain in different directions. These are done as omens of plenty and of prosperity in her family. After being seated in a chair on the platform, she is generally approached by her own brothers, and by her husband's brothers, who worship her. This is oftentimes accompanied by the offering to her of tea or of wine. When everything is ready, she steps upon a stool, and, taking hold of the rope, which is securely fastened to a high portion of the platform or the roof of the house, adjusts it about her own neck. She then kicks the stool away from under her, and thus becomes her own murderer.

Certain officers of government used to sanction the self-destruction of widows, not only by being present on the occasion, but also by their taking a part in the worship. Once, it is related, a woman, after the honours had been paid to her, instead of mounting the stool and adjusting the rope about her neck and hanging herself according to the understanding, suddenly recollected that she had forgotten to feed the hogs and hastened away, promising to be back shortly, which promise she omitted to keep. Since that hoax no mandarin has been present at a

suttee at this place. A public suicide by a widow always attracts a large crowd of spectators. Public sentiment encourages the practice enough to make it considered honourable and meritorious, though not to make it a very frequent occurrence. The brothers and near relatives of a widow who thus immolates herself soon after the decease of her husband regard it as an honour to the family, and not unfrequently feel gratified in having themselves referred to as her brothers or relatives.

Sometimes a girl who has been betrothed to a man who dies before the marriage-day resolves to take her own life by public hanging, in view of his death, rather than be engaged again in marriage, or live unmarried. If she cannot be persuaded to take a different course, she is allowed to appoint a day for her suicide, visits the temple referred to above, if not too far distant, mounts the platform provided at the house of her affianced husband, and launches herself into eternity, in much the same manner as do those widows who resolve not to survive the loss of their husbands. The coffin of the girl, in such cases, is interred by the side of the coffin of her betrothed, and at the same time.

There is little evidence that either sadism or masochism was greatly favoured by Chinese men though there are instances, both in history and in literature, of some very colourful excesses. Records from the Han dynasty mention a Prince Chien who punished his erring concubines by having them sit naked in trees for a number of days or, similarly naked, sentenced them to beat the 'time drum' in the court until they dropped from exhaustion or starvation. The prince also found amusing the drowning of young people in the palace lake.

The Emperor Hsiao-ching and Prince Tuan of the same period were notorious sadists with a predilection for incest with their sisters, while the prince, during a period of impotence, turned to catamites whom he frequently strangled for such invented offences as secretly visiting his harem. There was also the case of Prefect Lü of Hsüan-chou who took every opportunity to have prostitutes whipped in public — until he fell in love with one. This conversion was the subject of a famous poem by Mei Yao-ch'ên, the message being that a lovely prostitute, if driven away by cruelty, will always find other patrons.

One example of sadism is described in the novel *Chin P'ing Mei,* and the quietly cerebral excess seems more in keeping with traditional attitudes. But first the hero must be put in the right mood:

The effects of so many days of continuous love-making had weakened Hsi-men Ch'ing's legs so much that he realised that he could either take a rest or take the longevity and aphrodisiac potion. He chose the latter course, then remembered that human milk had to be added to the herbs. Lady Any-Way-You-Like-It was in her room, flowers in her hair and looking very desirable. He instantly asked her if she might squeeze him a little milk, since he needed it to blend with the potion. This she readily agreed to, and as the liquid dripped into the powder, she called out to the maid to bring tea and some tasty dishes.

When the girl had gone, and the tea had washed down the potion, Hsi-men Ch'ing closed the door and lay on the couch. Then he unfastened his white silken trousers and pulled out his Jade Root, which was held rigid by a silver collar. He indicated that he would like Lady Any-Way-You-Like-It to encourage it with her mouth, a suggestion to which she agreed, and while she was busy he proceeded to eat from the various dishes.

'You certainly work well with your mouth,' he said. 'I'll buy you the best embroidered jacket I can find. You can wear it on the Twelfth of the First Moon.' He watched her busy mouth for some moments, then added: 'Would you let me burn passion incense on your body?'

Snuff bottles frequently had erotic motifs, possessing them adding to a man's yang *power. Chinese ink on white porcelain. Collection Gèrard Lèvy, Paris.*

'That's entirely up to you,' said the lady. 'I'm in the mood for anything.'

He sat up and told her to lock the door, and from his sleeve-pocket produced three pyramid-shaped knobs of passion incense. Then he removed her skirt and her shift, unbound her breasts and laid her naked on the couch. One knob of incense was stuck to her just above the navel, one between her breasts, the third among the glossy hairs of the 'Silken Fan'. He then lit each one with the tip of a burning incense-stick.

The sight of the three tiny spirals of smoke, and the effect of the potion he had taken earlier, were enough to stiffen his Male Peak, and his delight that he was not so exhausted that he would have to forgo the pleasure for a day or two, made him plunge at once into the Inner Chamber. After a few minutes of furious activity he reached for a hand-mirror and placed it below the field of battle so that he could better view the assault. By this time the knobs of incense had half burned away and the lady was beginning to feel the heat.

'Please stop — it's burning!' she cried, biting into her lip with the pain.

'Whose whore are you!' Hsi-men Ch'ing demanded.

'Usually I'm Hsiung Wong's, but for today you can call me yours,' she gasped.

'You are Hsiung Wong's whore!' he shouted, busy again in the Jade Pavilion. 'It's only your body that you're giving me!'

'But I want to be all yours . . . . Please, it's burning!'

'Do you find me better at it than Hsiung Wong?'

'You've got the greatest implement in the world!'

As he was indulging in these vulgar exchanges, Hsi-men Ch'ing continued to plunge into the Golden Valley and to study the view in the mirror underneath. The parted pink lips of her vulva looked like the open mouth of a tropical bird and the black hair at either side was damp and glossy as if its feathers had been soaked. Inspired by this extra perspective, Hsi-men Ch'ing lifted her legs higher

Households supporting many women shared a common practice with the ladies of the Green Bowers. Male dominance and egotism made them seek gentler comforts from each other. 19th-century album, gouache on paper. Private collection, Paris.

than ever while she continued to scream with the ecstasy of pleasure and from the burning pain of the incense. Her pleasure and pain were at their zenith when his own *cloud* burst, and as he fell forward he remembered to brush away the last of the burning ash.

'You will certainly have the best embroidered jacket I can find,' he promised her. 'And you must wear it on the Twelfth of the First Moon.'

The ferocity of the sexual battle itself was not without sadistic significance, particularly its association with battle and the need to triumph. In such Ming-period pillow books as *Battle Manoeuvres for the Flowery Field*, women were openly termed the 'enemy' and much of the Yellow Emperor's talks with his three goddesses was concerned with the need to enforce her submission. The idea of Yang prevailing over Yin was not confined to the bedchamber, however, and in a universe that was divided into male and female elements, the idea of sexual domination was extended to the inanimate. Fu Chien, a military commander, boasted that he had the power to stop the flow of a stream (Yin). He lined up a brigade of men on the banks, each with a whip in hand, and ordered them to lash it (her) into submission. By nightfall the men had exhausted themselves but the water merrily continued to flow. A second anecdote concerns Shih Huang (271-200 B.C.) who wished to build a stone pier into the sea so that he could observe from the end of it the rising and the setting of the sun. The pier was almost completed when it suddenly col-

lapsed. It was reconstructed but the same thing happened. Shih Huang then had the stones whipped 'until they shed blood', after which 'Yin was obedient' and the pier was completed.

The writing apparatus of a Chinese scholar consists of a square or cake of ink, a small black slab of polished slate with a slight cavity at one end to hold water, a finely pointed hair brush and a supply of paper. These four articles are called 'the Four Precious Implements'. Such is the reverence paid by the Chinese to letters and literary pursuits that they will not tread upon written or printed paper.

Ten Thousand Things Relating to China,
W. B. Langdon

As in many communities, the incidence of homosexuality was related to social factors as well as to the nature of the individual. Impressions gained by foreigners that Chinese men were more predisposed than Westerners were often due to immigrant communities of imported labourers and others being compelled to live without their womenfolk. The Ch'ing scholar Chao I (1727-1814), however, states that during the Northern and Southern Sung dynasties, homosexuality became more fashionable and that there were so many male prostitutes that new laws were brought in which added a hundred blows from a bamboo to the usual heavy fine. This was not enough to drive them from the streets and for their protection they organised themselves into a guild. They made themselves even more conspicuous by adopting transvestism, and since many Chinese men had little facial hair, the heavy make-up used by them often made it difficult to decide their sex.

The palaces of the emperors had always had a complement of young boys, powdered and rouged, wearing gold-pheasant hats and be-jewelled girdles, and they were therefore part of the 'sexual' entourage of eunuchs, concubines and palace maidens. This early introduction into the excesses of the Dragon Ruler's sexual programme meant that by adolescence the youth's vocation had already been decided for him. To the more conventional love stories were added those concerning rulers and boys, and one such liaison, that between Emperor Ai-ti of the Han dynasty and Tung Hsien, became immortalised. One day, exhausted after love, the youth was sleeping with his head across the loose sleeve of the Emperor when a courtier summoned the ruler to urgent state business. Not wishing to disturb his young lover, the Emperor reached for his

The neglected concubine. Fresh from her bath and stimulated by the pillow book on the table, she enjoys her solitary pleasure. Gouache on paper. 19th-century. Private collection, Paris.

sword and sliced off a part of the sleeve and then soundlessly departed. From this came the expression 'the cut sleeve' (*tuan hsiu*), which became a synonym for homosexuality.

Centuries later, as a genre particularly favoured by writers, one collection of fifty stories of homosexuals had the title *Records of the Cut Sleeve*. A larger edition was called *Collected Writings on Fragrant Elegance* and was published in Shanghai in 1910. It contained the story of Lung-yang-chün, Minister and lover to the Prince of Wei (4th century B.C.), and the term *lung-yang* was adopted by literary circles for homosexuality.

There was an engaging tolerance towards most human weaknesses and deviations but this did not extend to monks and nuns, particularly Buddhists, who had the reputation of being venal hypocrites. Their religious duties apparently included sexual instruction to the young, match-making, messengers in illicit love-affairs and similar opportunistic dealings. In an early Han dynasty handbook, T'ao Tsung-i warns against nine classes of professional women who, 'for the sake of peace and quiet, should be kept out of the house:'

"I write of the three 'aunts' and the six 'old hags'. The three 'aunts' are the Buddhist nun, the Taoist nun and the fortune-teller. The six 'old hags' are the sorceress, the match-maker, the procuress, the pious-ly dishonest, the so-called healer and the midwife. When such women descend on the household, they should be regarded as the 'three punishments' and the 'six curses' because the result will always be licentiousness and roguery. If the man wants to keep his home clean, let him drive away such snakes and scorpions.''

For those rulers who came under the influence of Buddhist monks, one of the duties of the religious men was to teach the young princes the love arts and how to be invincible in the Flowery Battles. The Buddhists were rather more successful than the rival Taoist monks in being employed by the courts as sex-instructors, and the Mongol ruler, Emperor Shun-Ti (1323-1368), went so far as to employ them to improve his own performance. The period of instruction lasted many months in which the convert to *Joyful Zen Buddhism,* obeying his Tibetan monks, had assembled the most beautiful of his concubines and palace maidens and, to the accompaniment of chanted sutras and the sound of drums and gongs, proceeded to follow the teachings of the holy men.

Monks also played their part in the problem of barren marriages because there was a widespread belief that women who received 'the Buddha's seed' would soon fall pregnant, and provided the act was done with discretion, so that the husband would receive the credit, the practice was tolerated. With such duties forming part of the religious life, it was not surprising that many 'aliens' dressed up as monks, and in the thirteenth-century it was calculated that half a million men were claiming the privilege. The result was such caustic poems as 'The Wickedness of Monks and Nuns' (*Seng-ni-nieh-hai*) by T'ang Yin (sixteenth century):

Rumour has it that Monks lead saintly lives
A race of men straight and strong like pillar or beam.
They shave their beards and cut their hair
The top of them as shiny as their bare bottoms.
Yet neither is quite so shiny as the implement
They are forever producing from their robes.
The Monks' eyes are like rats coveting wax,
And their hands grab everything that's offered.
In pretending to be saintly and above the flesh
They reveal the deceit of Buddha's Holy Tooth,
And surrender to lust at every opportunity,
Their holy cloaks flapping between the ladies' legs.

When caught at such moments they are quick to proclaim
    That they have nothing to fear from Heaven or Hell —
    But let them await the Final Reckoning!

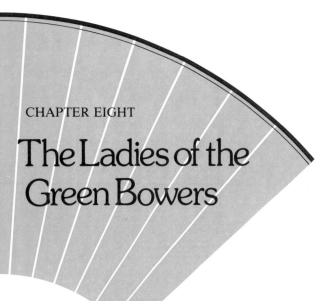

CHAPTER EIGHT

The Ladies of the Green Bowers

Women disrobing. Under very loose trousers and robes women usually wore a tight mo-hsiung *(brassiere). This was either buttoned at the front or tied with cords at the back. It was a garment not always discarded during love-making, modesty often being related to the smallness of many women's breasts. 17th-century blockprint.*

Saying farewell after ten years of dreams in Yangchow
The girls of the Green Bowers shed tears
And charge me with forsaking them. . . .
Tu Mu (803-852)

With all its inequalities, cruelties and sufferings, traditional Chinese society survived until modern times because of the complex balance of its institutions and a belief by high and low, scholar and peasant, that they were part of a superior social order of people. These institutions and this balance were achieved by a long and careful application to detail, the legacy of many generations of sages and scholars, and of rulers and ministers who usually respected, and sometimes shared, their wisdom. Their early civilisation had taught them that a society of different tribes, some settled, some nomadic, of different cultures and beliefs, could only be bound and held together by a common allegiance to its institutions, and these became the framework within which the pattern of life functioned. Emperors ruled, fathers were obeyed by their families, one's Ancestors were worshipped as gods, students and scholars who did well in the Imperial Examinations were automatically superior citizens to those who could not use a writing brush.

In this rigidly evolved system the definition of the place of women was subject to a similar calculating design. In a society dominated by men this inevitably meant not only a status of inferiority but of doing exactly what was required of them. As one needed wives to perpetuate the race and to run homes, certain women had to be nominated for that function. They were not required to do more, however, and they were not expected to; breeding and good home-management was a full and worthwhile occupation and precluded them from those activities that might detract from their application and purpose. For a housewife to be a musician, to be able to dance, converse eloquently, to write poetry and to be coquettish in the sweetest sense of the word, would have been regarded as a violation of her destined role.

Man, on the other hand, could hardly be expected to deny himself the more passionate, inspiring and colourful pleasures of body and mind, nor would he submit to restraints that limited him to the rigid and even dreary role of faithful husband and father; he always demanded the freedom to be a lover. To this end his personal and family life was made flexible enough to accommodate the concubine, consorts, courtesans and 'serving girls'. The 'second-status' female enjoyed more intimacy with him than did his head wife, gave him more delight and served as his companion when he visited his friends or received them, but she was always legally and socially inferior to the First Lady.

Within the home the concubine obeyed a wife without question, but since the time-honoured system had created this necessary place for her, she was regarded as one of the family. She was, however, subject to the inevitable system of Chinese customs. Her purpose was to please her master, and she would therefore be promoted over other concubines if she served him well. Similarly, bearing a male child would improve her rank and bring many privileges. Her fundamental role, however, was to be desirable and pleasing, and for this she perfected her talents as zealously as the mandarins taking their higher examinations. The most gifted concubines played the lute and the mandolin, played chess when the master was in a pensive mood, sang and danced when he was gay, fenced or boxed (Chinese-style) when he was feeling energetic, and wrote poetry to record their shared pleasures.

These qualities, nevertheless, were secondary to her ability as a sex partner. Not only was she skilled in the techniques of love and in offering her master the pleasures his wife could not offer, the concubine had constant need to be indispensable to the male by keeping him active sexually, by reviving him when he was tired, soothing him when he was worried, and even seeking to share some of his problems — an unthinkable intrusion on the part of a wife. The concubine would also be skilled in the concoction of aphrodisiacs for keeping him drinking at the Jade Fountain, his *Yang*-strength, by definition, constantly needing the revivifying powers of the *Yin* waters.

Resident concubines, however, were a luxury for most men. With the very rich, this was not an unbearable burden, and the household frequently supported as many as the courts of the lesser princes, but as the population increased, and as more humble men coveted women other than their wives, a demand for cultivated and exciting females who need not necessarily be established in the home was created. Again Chinese society adapted itself to the changed situation, and a new class of professional woman emerged. Whether as a higher courtesan, however, or as a prostitute, the new

category of sex partner, and the importance of her profession, was accepted with both respect and toleration.

The growth of this professional class was most apparent in the T'ang dynasty (618-906), which was not only the Golden Age of Chinese art but also a time of great social change in which family discipline became less rigid and migration from district to district became more common. In this more fluid society girls were offered their first chance of independence, and those who were prepared to seize it found that they were not without the means of supporting themselves. And prostitution, if the girls were reasonably attractive, not only afforded them a good living, it granted them what no other class of women enjoyed, a degree of personal freedom.

The girls, as social favourites and the source of inspiration for some of the greatest poets, were affectionately called *Fallen Flowers* or *Flowers on the Wall,* because they could be picked by anyone. They were also known as *Women of the Wind and Dust* since they were creatures who could be blown anywhere. The brothels themselves, similarly, were given such romantic names as 'Hostels of the Sing-Song Girls' (*ch'ang chia*), 'Ladies of the Green Bowers' (*ch'ing-lou*), and 'Beauties of the Blue Chambers'. This last term came from the blue shutters of the brothel windows, a version of the more universal 'red light', and was frequently eulogised in song and poetry.

For the man who simply wanted sex on a commercial basis, the street-brothel was a convenient institution that had the advantage of economy, and if he required girls to help him entertain at home, or to provide him with pleasant company, flexible arrangements were easy to make. It was also possible for men to commission a girl for a trial relationship with a view to promoting her to concubine if she proved satisfactory. Prostitutes ranged from the high-class courtesan, with her own servants and her own 'foster-mother', living in palatial circumstances, to sing-song girls, dancing girls and 'barracks whores' (*Ying-chi*) for soldiers in camps. Lowest of all, however, were 'saltwater whores', who not only worked in the brothels of seaports but allowed their exalted Chinese bodies to be possessed by foreign sailors and other species of 'foreign devils' (*kwai-lo*).

As with the more elevated concubines, courtesans and prostitutes, if they were to rise above the lowest categories, had to apply themselves to their training, and for this they relied on a 'foster-mother' (*chia-mu* being an 'adopted-mother'). In turn the girls were given the title of 'adopted-daughter', and since no reason for shame attached itself to the profession, the relationship between 'mother' and 'daughter' was often as close as that within a family. The 'mothers' were also known by the slang term 'buzzard' (*pao*), and were usually retired Fallen Flowers who had invested their savings in their protégées.

As astute businesswomen, they were ever watchful for the opportunity of selling their 'daughters' to any suitor who might see in one of the girls a prospective concubine or wife. The girl's release would not only cost the man the expense the *pao* had invested in the debutante's training, it would have to cover her future earnings and possibly the original cost of the girl if she had been bought from her father. Within the brothel itself, assisted by 'strong-arm men' (*pao-piao*), Madame's word was law even to the customers. In the more civilised and sophisticated establishments a strict ritual was laid down, tea-drinking ceremonies, musical recitals, conventional introductions and sometimes protracted courtships preceded the eventual admission to the bed-chamber. 'Sex-only' brothels on a 'quick-cash' basis were regarded as an outlet suitable for only the roughest and least educated of men, and such customers were bundled in with the next prostitute to fall available. Even in better-class 'Green Bowers', the powers of the *pao* were such that she not only regulated matters to the last detail, she usually assigned her customers to the girls she thought most suitable, an aspect of the art of 'match-making' that was an important attribute of running a successful establishment.

One of the reasons why prostitutes were accepted in society and why there was no stigma to the profession was because of their role as the sweetheart of young Chinese males. The importance of virginity in all classes above peasants and labourers, and the rigid traditions that made a romantic courtship impossible for unmarried men because of the total seclusion of respectable girls, encouraged youth to direct his feelings to the Fallen Flowers as a substitute for courtship. His father, eager that his son should excel both as lover and husband, often introduced him to courtesans for a course of love-instruction, paying generously for the best education. With the right courtesan, and if she inspired the romantic side of his young feelings, the young man frequently enjoyed a courtship approaching the real thing — the full cycle of promise and denial, of hope and despair, his spirit at once poetical or suicidal. When he was finally allowed into her bed-chamber — perhaps after weeks of waiting — the innocent 'spring chicken' (*tung-t'ze-ch'i*) would face his sexual initiation with the same confusion of emotions as a young man with his first sweetheart.

Old Chinese Proverbs:
A youth entering the Blue Chambers for the first time is like the dogs of Szech'uan who see so little of the sun in that district that when it chooses to shine they bark back in terror.
The nervous lover is like the idiot cattle of Kiangsu. They tremble at the rising of the moon thinking it to be the sun.

The reputation of the more famous courtesans was such that emperors were known to prefer them to their own thousands of concubines, one aspect of the characters of such women, their independence, being particularly attractive to those Chinese males bored by submissive partners. Some of the courtesans, because of their freedom, distinguished themselves in the arts and excelled even the men as poets and song-writers. One such woman was Yü Hsüan-chi (844-871), who had the advantage of friendships with some of the most brilliant men of her time. As a sixteen-year-old girl only concerned with physical survival in a very competitive profession, she soon picked up the basic art of calligraphy, went on to study the Classics, learnt three musical instruments, discovered herself to have a voice of unmatched sweetness, and finally brought together these varied talents to become a much-admired poetess.

In this early phase of her life, she wrote:

Brief Company
Each man a prince
Each man a beggar
Each wearing a crown
Each asking for love.

They arrive like masters
But soon become children
They depart with a bow —
My smile never changes.

What brought them here
What took them away —
What are their memories?
My smile never changes.

As a woman who was 'larger-than-life' Hsüan-chi liked to match her physical prowess with that of her lovers, and there are many stories of her debauches, her extraordinary consumption of wine and alcohol, and the fatal attraction of lawless characters and criminals. In the company of such men she eventually deserted her high standards, found she was unable to support herself in her usual style, and became the concubine of one of them. The man's household, however, and particularly his wife, could not tolerate such a self-willed and passionate woman, and Yü Hsüan-chi withdrew to a nunnery.

Here she became interested in Taoism, and as such monasteries, behind their thick walls,

The 'flower boats' of Swatow often supplemented their income by transporting goods and passengers along the rivers. A certain distinguished scholar, innocent of the true nature of the boat, called for one of the crew during a rainstorm to repair his leaking cabin roof. The crew member turned out to be a lovely woman attired only in a red-satin bodice. After replacing the roof-mats, the woman remained with the scholar for the rest of the voyage and, after his departure, was able to charge higher prices for having had the great man as a client. 19th-century gouache. Private collection, Paris.

were centres for the high-spirited as well as the holy-spirited, she was soon caught up in orgies and drinking bouts as demanding as any she had ever known. The monks who ran these establishments expected such beautiful and talented courtesans to help support not only

Attempting to revive the debauched in a 19th-century brothel. Courtesy of the British Museum.

themselves but the monastery as well, and one of the men to visit Yü Hsüan-chi in her apartment was the poet Wên T'ing-yun. In his company she soon abandoned whatever restraints a nun's life might have imposed on her, and departed with Wên on a pleasure-seeking journey round the country. her love for Wên was the final passion of her life, and when it had taken its inevitable course, she returned to the monastery, an exhausted and broken-hearted creature, to write her sad yet immortal poem 'Selling wilted peonies'.

Another courtesan to inspire legends was Liang Hung-yu, who started her life in a small town and became a heroine in the eleventh-century wars against the Tatars. It was the custom at that time for the prostitutes to get their permits renewed by the Governor, and she was approaching the gate of his palace when a tiger seemed to materialise before her eyes. She momentarily fainted, then found herself being picked up by the soldier on guard duty. He was the only other living thing in sight. When she returned home, she reported the remarkable vision to her 'foster-mother'. The *pao* was a

practising astrologer and immediately consulted her charts and omens, then announced that the soldier had been the Celestial Tiger Star. Raising her from the dust was symbolical of his real purpose on earth, which was to offer her a new destiny.

The two women hurried back to the young man and invited him to dinner. At the table the 'eight characters' of the young couple were read, and when the *pao* informed the soldier of his real identity, he did not contradict her. The old woman then informed them that they were destined to marry and that she would release her 'foster-daughter' without the usual compensation. It was an inviting proposition for a poor soldier, and the girl had her attractions, and Han, his name, accepted the offer. Once married, however, his modest fortunes immediately changed and within a short period he was promoted to command the army.

When the wars with the Tatars demanded his presence at the front, Hung-yu insisted on accompanying him. She took part in every battle, fighting bravely at his side, and in a naval clash on the Yangtze river was responsible for saving the Empire. Han had put himself at the head of an armada of fighting junks, but these had come under such heavy assault from the invading Tatars that he was on the point of signalling the retreat. Hung-yu, overhearing his decision, ran up to the deck of the command ship and began to beat the war-drum to advance. This was taken up by the other ships, the fleet went on to the offensive, and the Tatars were chased down the river.

A thousand years before Hung-yu, the fashion for women to be attached to the fighting forces had been established when the Emperor Wu (190-87 B.C.) set up a commission to inquire into the mysterious disease that had struck down his best officers. The Taoist monks, to whom this was entrusted, reported that the *yang*-spirit of the officers, for long deprived of *yin*-essence, was greatly diminished, and that their health and fighting spirit would only return when their inner harmony was restored. Girls were quickly mobilised, not only to provide *yin* for the officers, but for his ten thousand troops as well.

In later periods the recruitment of *ying-chi* (barracks harlots) became more systematised and they were employed on a salaried basis. When there were not enough volunteers, the womenfolk of criminals, and the female relatives of those out of favour with the authorities, were pressed into service. These

Government brothels led to later refinements, and in the Ming period (1368-1644) houses were set up for the many grades of the civil service. Those for senior government personnel were particularly luxurious, the girls the most talented and beautiful in the country. An account of one such de-luxe establishment describes the variety of furniture and silk drapes as coming from every corner of the Empire, and that the temperature was controlled throughout the year by the installation of large copper heaters in winter and by enormous ice-boxes in summer, the ice being successfully stored and preserved in deep pits.

Marco Polo, too, in the thirteenth-century, succumbed to the charms of the Fallen Flowers and in his account of life in Peking (Khan-balik), after describing the beauty of the city, with its palaces and fine mansions, broad avenues and gardens, he writes: 'With regard to the prostitutes, they are made to reside in the suburbs, and there are no fewer than 20,000, all selling their bodies and charms for money. It is an established part of city life and they are organised into groups of one hundred and then one thousand, each under a leader. One of the reasons for such organisation is because visitors and ambassadors to the Emperor are provided with women for every night of their stay, the choice of the girls being left to the leaders. The visitors, who have a different girl every night, are not expected to pay, this being one of the ways in which prostitutes render their taxes to the Emperor.'

The pleasure houses of other cities also evoked Polo's admiration, particularly those of Kinsai (Hang-chau), and travellers returning home after enjoying the unforgettable charm and delights of the local girls, used to repeat the words: 'We have been to the City of Heaven. Oh, Kinsai, when shall we see you again?'

The Chinese prostitute retained her romantic image through the ages, and this goodwill and affection was not confined to her own countrymen. Cecil Clementi, in his Introduction to the translation of *Cantonese Love Songs* (Clarendon Press 1904) relates the story of one such girl with a poetry and a sympathy similar to many generations of Chinese writers before him. The tragedy of the prostitute who is still pure at heart and who pines to death at the parting of a favoured lover is a constantly recurring theme. He states:

Marriage in China, as in other countries where the patriarchal system is strong and where ancestor-worship is the chief cult of the people, has become little else than an institution for the birth of legitimate children. The principle of sexual selection does not decide marriages in China: and, since bride and bridegroom frequently have never met before the wedding-day, when the bargain made by their parents is ratified, love before marriage is almost impossible, and love after marriage is rare enough. Accordingly, in view of the fact that honourable love is hardly ever a theme of Chinese poetry, it is possible to regard much of the imagery ... as euphemisms, forced on the poet by the nature of his subject .... 'Arbours of flower and willow', 'haunts of vapour and flowers', 'rouge and powder', 'the world of flowers', and other such expressions, have only one possible meaning to a China man and thereby lose something of the delicacy which they retain for English ears.

... We are told in the Chronicle of Sundry States that in the seventh century B.C. a certain minister named Kwun Chung 'originated and developed the practice of prostitution as a masterpiece of political economy, making it a source of revenue to the country. Tshai Kwok, the modern Shantung, is described as being then a place of great gaiety and festivity, and likewise a great commercial emporium; strangers and merchants coming thither from all parts of China, and finding there a ready sale for their merchandise. Kwun Chung, dreading lest the silver of the country should be taken away by these traders in exchange for their merchandise, and be entirely lost to the state, thought it good policy to legitimise and encourage prostitution, and hoped these traders would be induced to squander their earnings in profligacy so that their money, or a great portion of it, might by this means be left in the country, and gradually filtered into the exchequer.' This economic aspect of the question has remained unchanged, though the centre of the evil has shifted from the state to the household. It is as the solution of a problem in domestic economy that the father sells his unknowing child, or the husband pawns his wife, though in the latter case the victim must be a consenting party to the bargain. Debt has been known to make a woman mortgage her person: while on occasion the Chinese Government has sold, as a source of revenue, girls who for their own fault have been discarded by their family. But it is always economic necessity, and scarcely ever free choice, that sets women to walk in 'Willow Lane and Flower Street'.

For this cause an intense sadness broods over the lives of these young girls. 'Wide, wide is the sea of bitterness: ill-fated be more than half therein.' Escape is wellnigh impossible. It can be attained only by one of two means. Either the girl must by her sin save money sufficient to ransom herself from the life to which she has been destined; or, if more fortunate, she may, before her maidenhood is lost, meet a 'true-hearted guest-gallant', whose love will 'bring her safe to shore', either as his wife or concubine. This is the one ray of hope which lights up the gloom.

In a series of varied pictures the *Cantonese Songs* describe for us the life of such a girl. We see her at the toilet-table braiding her hair, with the significance of a love-spell in every action: for, as she parts her hair so will her lover part all troubles and come to her: the centre of her head-dress symbolises the concentration of her heart: the roots of the hair and the ends of the tresses are signs that she will follow her love to the end; the flowers she wears are emblematic of her flower-debts, and will win her the favour of the Flower King; the 'moon roses' will gain her the protection of the Old Man in the Moon. Again, we see the girl, in the brief hour of her happiness, weaving words with her lover as they stand beside the ring-fence, while he writes on the whitewashed wall the lotus-flower song which they have sung together. Suddenly she overhears the chill words of men saying that the peacock and his mate will soon be torn apart. The spring dream is shattered and she bravely takes up the burden of her predestined sorrow. Her lover is a young and brilliant scholar, whose debt to his books summons him to pass examinations at Peking.

The girl who loves him so tenderly cannot let her love stand in the way of his advancement. She hopes to see him one day arrayed in academic robes and returning home in honour, but the hour of parting haunts her .... She whispers in his ear on the pillow her message of good-bye; 'My love, fair though Peking may be, yet forget not your sweetheart!' Swiftly the hours pass, hope as she may that the forest branches would arrest the setting sun. In a moment his carriage and horses will be at the door. She forces herself to mirth and laughter, so that her lover may go with a light heart; then he is gone northwards. With yearning eyes she follows the carriage on its way, and when he is out of sight, the girl retires to her chamber and at last finds relief in long and heavy weeping. Nature tries to comfort her, but the song of the oriole, the fragrance of the flowers, and the vernal season only add to her woe. In a lonely bedroom she faces the red lamp set on her table, and in futile effort raises in her hand a cup so that its shadow on the wall may delude her into seeming less forlorn. Then she seeks rest in sleep, and in sleep she dreams of reunion with her lover.

Hark! the sudden scream of the goose has divorced the wedlock of her dreams. It is the carrier-goose, but come without a letter from her lover. Is he, then, grown careless — or was it mere indolence in writing? If her lover has unsent letters written in his mind, let him send the empty cover so that, spreading out the blank paper, the fond girl may imagine it holds ten thousand words. He promised to write but, as she counts up the days upon her fingertips, she reckons that a full half-year has gone by without news. In time comes despair. She thinks of suicide but fears to die amiss, lest dying she should say — 'Would I might live once more!' The flower-debts [to her 'foster-mother'] are not yet paid in full, and her only hope is in the life to come. So, forced back into her vile life, night after night she is paired with a mate, but ever feels a very loneliness. Lovers quarrel over her but her heart remains true to her departed.

Would that all men seeing her might come to hate her or, if that cannot be, would that they ceased from hating her for jealousy of other men! Then come the reproaches of her 'pocket mother', who sees old acquaintances draw back and no new guests arrive. The ledgers show debts only, no payments. The Magistrate and his Police storm and threaten as they levy the 'Rouge-tax', to supply pin-money for ladies of the Imperial Palace, and amid this strife of tongues, old age begins to blight the beauty of this flower. An instant's dullness makes her threefold viler in men's eyes, white hairs hasten upon her, and she grows so frail that she can scarce bear the weight of her garments. At last she dies and her dainty feet tread the wide path of hell.

But hell has no inn; where then can she rest? Perhaps a lover will cast paper-money on her tomb, so that bearing money to the Lord of Hell, she may purchase a place in Heaven's sanctuary ....

As most high-class courtesans were women of some culture, they freely granted their favours to poets and artists and felt well-rewarded to receive a poem or a sketch in return. 'Poetic power' was a real belief, not only out of respect for the writers but because their verse was set to music and could become widely popular. Tales of heroism and love, starting as poems, often became the 'pop' songs of the people. This power of the poet was also something to fear, as the beautiful courtesan Li Tuan-tuan discovered. She gave great offence to the popular poet Tsui Hei by transferring her favours to a high official, and he struck back by immediately writing a poem which dwelt on her duplicity and her ugliness. So convincing was his condemnation that Tuan-tuan was soon deserted by her clients. In despair she begged the poet to redress the situation by composing a flattering poem. This he agreed to, provided their relationship was renewed, and then wrote his best verse, likening her to a white peony that never loses its freshness and its fragrance. His 'poetic power' was enough to restore Li Tuan-tuan's fortunes.

Advice to Men Visiting Brothels
Li Shang-Yin

Do not boast of your prowess as a lover.
Do not make excuses for your failures.

Do not perform your toilet in her presence.

Do not spit on the matting.

Do not bore holes in the partition to observe others making love.

Do not make false promises to her.

Do not flatter her with poems unless they are sincere.

Do not believe her flattery or loving words.

Do not make it apparent that you covet her 'foster-sisters'.

Do not steal her possessions on the pretext of borrowing.

Men were not the only ones to receive advice, however, and the ever-flexible and functional novel-form of writing was also used to help and instruct the Fallen Flowers. An eighteenth-century novel, *Sisters of the Green Bowers* by Sung K'ang, features the rise and fall of a wicked 'foster-mother'. But the advice to her debutante 'daughters' was both practical and sensible:

Yours is a demanding profession, and once your youth has passed, your usefulness is over. Therefore do not exhaust yourself unnecessarily, accept all gifts and offerings, always ask for an excessive sum of money. Those clients who are rich will be too proud to quibble, those who feel the price too high will offer less, which can either be accepted or rejected. Old men are the best clients. They demand less, they sleep more and they are more indulgent towards the moods and foibles of young women. The only disadvantage with them is that one may have to work as hard in arousing them as in satisfying a dragon lover. On the other hand they will be prepared to pay extra for aphrodisiacs, and the most expensive rather than the most effective should be used. If aphrodisiacs fail, recommend a long sleep, flattering them with references to the exhausting nature of their important work and affairs. When they waken, offer them a bowl of chrysanthemum tea.

With men who are sensitive about a small Jade Stem, be quick to reassure them, not only with words but with deeds. A client should be made to feel that he is a dragon lover, even when he discharges immediately on entering the Flowery Gates. In this case one should quickly lock the Flowery Gates by contracting the vagina, holding him firm with legs behind his back. If he is normally virile, and if you soon start to move the inner muscles, he will quickly return to the attack. If not, resort to aphrodisiacs or Jade Stem ointments. Great care should be taken with those containing 'telini fly' (*pan mao*), as this can create vomiting or irritation.

A woman will preserve her youth and vigour if she rouses the man to discharge quickly. This is commonsense. If a mason can break a stone with one blow of the hammer, why should he chip away at it with a chisel? The secret of the 'quick blow' is to reach the mind as well as the body. The married man, for example, will be more excited by behaviour that would hardly be displayed by his wife. Reckless words, praise, expressions of terror at his ferocity and at his size — these, with giggles and sighs, should accompany the physical initiative. This initiative should not be obvious and can take the form of the most exciting movement of all, that of moving the hips during intercourse in the circular movement known as 'millstone grind'. This technique, however, should be avoided with men of dragon dimensions, and the art of 'yielding to the tempest' or 'riding the blow' should be practised; and with such men one must first copiously lubricate the Jade Gate with honey and buffalo-fat (*ngiu-fei*) ointment.

The 'foster-mother' is equally sound with the advice to her charges on the subject of acquiring extra gifts and advantages. She goes on to say:

If a man returns to your side four or five times in the same week, and insists on your company rather than that of one of the other girls, the time has come to raise your price. After all, if he wishes to monopolise you, he must pay extra. It is more profitable and more gracious, however, to obtain this extra in the form of presents. The girl should indicate discreetly that she is wearing nothing to indicate his love for her, while the other girls in the establishment are constantly flaunting the jewellery they have received. This is the kindest way of saying that she expects to be taken on a visit to a jeweller's, arrangements already having been made with the jeweller about the pieces that should be recommended to them. When the visit takes place the girl should show no eagerness for expensive pieces since they will be suggested by the craftsman. If the finest pieces do not meet with the approval of the lover, this is because they are too expensive. After criticising the fine pieces, however, he will still buy what he cannot really afford. When he has been persuaded to do this, remove the jewellery you are wearing, and which he knows to be a present from a previous lover, and contemptuously throw it into the craftsman's waste-basket. This discarded piece will later be returned by the jeweller.

As China was a country of many rivers and a long coastline dotted with seaports, the floating brothel (*hua-chuan*) was a feature of most areas with a waterfront population. Junks, sampans and similar oriental craft were traditionally used as homes, workshops and eating establishments, and a constant traffic of small boats supplied and traded in foodstuffs, hardware, clothing and all the various needs of a community that preferred to live afloat. Entertainment was provided by boats of musicians and singers moving along the lines of moored

craft, and diversions of a more venal nature were offered on the stationary 'flower boats'.

These were often floating palaces, containing their own restaurants and bath-houses, and having clients brought from the shore in a flotilla of tenders, the 'flower boats' diminishing in splendour until they were no better than sampans with a canvas screen round them. But whether first category *chingnu* or third category *yieh-chi* (wild-fowl), the prostitutes still qualified as 'Celestial Waterlilies'. High or low, rich or poor, the girls belonged to an honourable profession, which obliged them to greet their clients with a preliminary tea-drinking ceremony, an introduction of politeness and grace, and any references to payment and money would be similarly discreet. And by moonlight, with many of the craft covered with flowers, climbing plants and decorated lanterns, with the breeze cool after the hot day and the current creating a slightly swaying movement, the flower boats must have seemed a most romantic setting for the pleasures of the *Clouds and the Rain*.

In the nineteen-twenties and thirties Shanghai had the reputation of being 'The Sin Capital of the World'. Most of the city was divided into foreign enclaves which were ruled by the western and Japanese occupying powers, and the Chinese population, while tak-

The ladies of the Green Bowers were frequently gifted singers and musicians, qualities which were not necessarily precluded during The Clouds and the Rain. From Yanwo 5 *(Harmony), in the Mitchell Library, Sydney.*

ing every advantage of the wealth brought in by the foreigners, still managed to retain much of their own way of life. An area that was particularly affected by the unavoidable duplicity and 'two-facedness' of such a state of affairs was that of pleasure houses and pleasure girls. There were as many as two hundred dance halls that were regarded as socially respectable, at least on the surface, but which were places where introductions could be made which later took the couples to hotel bedrooms or the girls' apartments; and there were over three thousand brothels. These were divided into categories ranging from the traditional Green Bowers to the low-class establishments in the Fourth Ayenue area (Si-Ma-Lu). In turn, both high and low categories provided separately for Chinese and foreigners, or allowed them to mix. They were open twenty-four hours a day, and since the city was a place of bright lights and constant activity, the brothels were an important and vital element in the life of the metropolis.

In this last gay era, before Communist rule eventually eliminated the brothels and Fallen Flowers within twenty-four hours, one was also conscious of the establishments being a

Kissing and the fondling of breasts, not usual in the older erotic paintings, became more common as Chinese artists were attracted to the 'export' market. From Yanwo 5 *in the Mitchell Library, Sydney.*

meeting place of East and West, the Chinese remaining true to themselves yet adapting the traditional 'Green Bowers' to the tastes and customs of the 'foreign devils'. The following story, *My Night with Miss Ace* by Li-Chung, from *Shanghai Stories* (1928), creates something of the atmosphere of the end of an era; in fact of two thousand years of Willow Lane life. The prostitute in the story, while remaining essentially Chinese, has already absorbed much that was western:

In my small village sixty miles from Shanghai the bright lights of that wicked city, even though they could not be seen at that distance, still blazed each night in the minds of young men like myself. And as soon as I was able, at the age of twenty-two, I had saved up enough money for that greatest of earthly blessings, a few nights of sin. I followed my cousin's advice and walked straight into *The Mists and Dew of Paradise* establishment, which he had recommended as the best in that great city, but instead of being welcomed with friendly informality I might just as well have walked into an office.

Before I had realised what was happening I had paid over one hundred dollars as a booking fee, the balance to be paid on the date of my appointment, and had been told to return on the following Sunday. The price was bad enough, but I had certainly not foreseen a week's delay in meeting the woman of my choice, their Number One *Poule de Luxe,* Miss Ace or White Fragrance.

I had been saving up for two years for this trip to Shanghai and I wanted only the best. One had to pay

for the best, and that elementary law applied as much in my humble village as it did here. So I was intrigued to know what I was paying for. I was also curious to discover what made a woman like Miss Ace Number One rather than Number Two.

'Look,' I said, 'I'll pay a bit more if you can push me in tonight.'

The receptionist did not even trouble to open the gold-edged leather appointments book.

'Your appointment, sir, is at nine next Sunday evening.' She handed me a receipt which she had been completing. 'I've put the time on, so you can't make a mistake.'

She was quite a beauty herself and I wondered how much of her time was spent in secretarial duties. But I said: 'I've come a long way and I can't wait a whole week in Shanghai. Surely Miss Ace can't be completely booked up?'

'Our basis of business is strictly first-come-first-served,' she replied. 'With someone like Miss Ace, no one ever misses an appointment, so a vacancy is hardly likely to occur.'

It was true that there were plenty of foreign devils in Shanghai [1928] and they had introduced all kinds of western style pressures and procedures, but I had hardly expected their presence to affect things like this.

'Look,' I said impatiently. 'I can't believe that Miss Ace is like one of these foreign medical specialists where you have to wait days. This is a pleasure house not a hospital!'

'With doctors it's sometimes a matter of life and death,' she said sharply. 'With us nobody dies if they have to wait a few days. In fact the wait could pep them up.'

'Is there really nothing today?' I asked again.

A second receptionist came out of an adjacent room, holding a similar appointment book and a roll of money that must have been quite five hundred dollars. At least customers were given privacy from the very beginning, I thought.

'To take only today,' went on my receptionist, showing a little sympathy, 'Miss Ace is now with a rich Peking client at the House of Peace and Happiness. She leaves him at four and is with a high-ranking army officer from four-thirty to six-thirty. From seven to nine she'll be at the Great Oriental Hotel with a Cantonese lawyer, and from nine-thirty to eleven-thirty she goes to a regular customer at the House of Fragrance Hotel. So how can I possibly squeeze you in?'

'And she keeps that up every day? She must have the constitution of a champion athlete.'

'She isn't Miss Ace for nothing. Just make sure you don't lose your receipt otherwise you won't be received even next Sunday.'

I placed it in my wallet as if I were taking care of a land-register certificate. And a first-class plot of land at that! When I left the establishment and began to wander back to my lodging room I again reflected on the possible difference between Miss One and Miss Two. Was it her body, her technique, what she gave, what she promised? And for the next seven days, which I decided to spend in Shanghai, it was a question that never quite left my mind.

But days inevitably arrive; and so did that Sunday. In the afternoon I went to a cinema, but did not really see the film, and then called on a cousin, but was so preoccupied I must have left the most awful impression of rudeness. I took a rickshaw to *The Mists and Dew of Paradise* and gave the coolie an extra dollar for being so quick, then discovered I was fifteen minutes early. Would it look as though I were too eager to push between the doors? The hesitation was momentary, and at last I was facing the woman who had received me on the previous Sunday.

'Follow me, please,' she said to once.

I followed her, expecting to be led to a waiting room.

'But this surely can't be a waiting room.' I gasped.

I had never seen such luxury. The carpet was like stepping on to fresh snow, the furniture fit for a millionaire's apartment, the bed covered with a silk lace spread and under the glow of numerous standard and bedside lamps. But what surprised me most were six mirrors forming a screen round the bed and placed so that the reflection went on to infinity. Before the receptionist left me I asked her the purpose of a curiously solid piece of wood dividing the sofa into two sections.

'You'll soon find out,' she said mischievously.

'When is Miss Ace coming?'

'She needs a little rest, you know. Besides, it's still only eight-fifty.'

A serving girl brought in a large tray of tea, cakes, candies and melon seeds, as if the stage was being prepared for the purpose of my visit.

'If I find tonight to my liking, when could I make another appointment?'

'In two weeks. After all, she's the Number One of the metropolis.'

As the receptionist's eyes moved from my face, I was aware that she was smiling at someone who had entered soundlessly. I turned quickly and knew instantly that the magnificent figure standing inside the curtain to the annex must be Miss Ace. How does one describe this kind of overwhelming beauty? By saying that she looked the part? That she was regal, as if we were honoured by her presence? She moved forward — and with what effortless grace. Her dress was western and she was tall, her skin was a creamy-white, and each feature of her face made a dazzling contrast to this lightness of colour.

It was not only love at first sight, it was 'erection at first sight'. Like someone rising from a chair to greet the visitor, within five seconds my Jade Stem was standing upright. When I turned round, the receptionist had disappeared.

'Well, I'm sure you haven't come just to stare at me,' Miss Ace said at last. 'If you'll tell me what pleasure you prefer, we can proceed.'

The question puzzled me. Surely it was obvious what I'd come for.

Then she explained: 'Do you wish to enjoy the excitement of sex or the sensuality of sex?'

'What's the difference?'

She replied by extending a hand, and her touch caused me to tremble.

'Let's get undressed.' she whispered.

I was totally obedient to the command but being a little shy, I was only half-undressed when she was standing in front of me like one of those western statues of naked women. I forgot my shyness in my haste to complete my undressing, and once I had given her body a general survey my eyes stayed on a neat triangle of the silkiest black hair imaginable.

'Since you seem so interested in that part — here!'

She reached into a bedside cupboard and handed me a magnifying glass, then swung round one of the adjustable standard lamps. But in the direction of the sofa, not at the bed. When she lay down she was therefore illuminated by a beam of light, and as I approached she placed one leg on the high wooden bar that had puzzled me. I rested my knees on the edge of the sofa and took up a position that allowed me to stare directly into the lovely Flower Heart. I needed some moments to find the courage to separate the inner pink lips, and since this was a very special experience, I was aware of myself trying to memorise every detail. The Jade Gate is really heart-shaped, I thought, a little like a firmly-curved mouth. The term commonly used among my friends, the 'one-square inch', was not quite accurate, because it was

neither one inch nor square but more like two by one-half inch.

At this point of my inspection I was overwhelmed by a wonderful perfume which became stronger the more I opened the Flower Heart. Did all women smell like this, I wondered. I threw aside the magnifying glass and gave the moist centre a firm kiss, then looked at her with boylike adoration. She winked in return.

'Is your bald-headed "monk" ready to visit the "temple"?' she inquired pleasantly.

'The "monk" is quite ready. Will you receive him now?'

'Except for the goddess Kwan-Ying, who will do battle with your warrior "monk", the "temple" is all yours.'

'Unfortunately this is the first battle for my "monk" so I don't think I can match Kwan-Ying.'

'He may be better than you think.'

With these encouraging words, we moved from the couch to the bed, across which she spread herself like a starfish, then she guided the 'monk' into the 'temple'. It was a slow, even formal introduction into that well-lubricated chamber, but this was deceptive. Once across the threshold, before he had time, really, to become familiar with the surroundings, my poor 'monk' was seized in a stranglehold that was loose and tight at the same time. Suddenly I realised he was fighting for his life and that I had to help him in every possible way. I therefore swung one way then another, pulling him back, shooting him forward. With this Miss Ace, it wasn't sex but a fight to the death!

I looked into her eyes, which had momentarily opened. Her mouth sucked forward into a kiss that was as devouring as the clutch of the Lower Chamber.

'Your "monk" is proving a better fighter than you thought,' she gasped. 'My "goddess" hasn't fought like this for a long time.'

This flattery was worth every cent of the small fortune I had paid for this session, and I was suddenly confident that I could take the initiative. Getting my knees solid in the mattress, I sent the 'monk' into a series of really savage assaults, and my reward was to see the last trace of her smile vanish and become an expression of concentrated passion and fury. She moaned and swore, she whimpered and begged for more, one word contradicting the next. But the message was clear. I was winning and she was enjoying it. When we reached the Ultimate, our bodies had turned so that our feet were on the pillows. We lay sweating for some minutes, and this rest was almost as consuming as the sex had been.

Eventually she led me into a bathroom, douched herself then used perfumed water to wash my Jade Stem. She did this in a leisurely way, turning it and raising it with some curiosity.

'This is really a most powerful and beautiful battle implement. I'm going to tell the receptionist to cancel all my appointments for the night. Would you care to be my guest until daylight?' I decided there must be a catch somewhere, and she added: 'Your "monk" can take a five-minute rest, then I shall expect him to be ready for the next battle.'

When I returned from the bathroom, she was reclining on the bed. My mind was suddenly full of spring thoughts no doubt encouraged by the idea of being in a bower of jasmine, lilac, peonies and lilies-of-the-valley. As I joined her on that wide altar-of-love, she pulled from under the pillows a miniature mushroom-shaped cap.

'This is for that bald-headed warrior of yours,' she said gaily.

I looked inside what appeared a deep pouch, and noticed that it had been dusted with a pepper-like powder and that round the brim there were sprays of stiff bristles. My 'monk' was only half-erect but as soon as I crowned him with the silken bag, he reared forward and up as if inflated with air. Miss Ace lay back and proudly surveyed her achievement.

'You really have a shining knight in armour there,' she exclaimed. 'I think I will light an incense stick to my goddess Kwan-Ying.'

My impatient monk managed to control himself as the object of his desire slipped out of bed and walked naked to a small bead curtain across a recess in the wall. When she pulled the red beads aside, a small gilded goddess on a pedestal was revealed, and when she pressed a switch, a red electric bulb bathed the figure in the rosy light.

Miss Ace lit an incense stick and placed it in a brass urn, knelt before Kwan-Ying, mumbled a plea for divine help, bowed again, then rose to her feet.

'Now I'm ready for battle,' she said firmly, lying instantly on the bed, raising her knees and positioning those exquisite parts in readiness for the assault. 'Why do you hesitate?'

'I will go and close the curtain,' I said. 'It's not fair on me to have Kwan-Ying watching.'

How beautiful are those limbs, I thought, when I was back on the bed and kneeling between her legs. And how luscious the moist Gate seemed, and the silken phoenix hairs flanking it ... But this was not the moment to feel poetical. My 'knight' made an instant rush for the 'pleasure temple', the plumes of his new helmet disappearing through the Gate, and was instantly creating havoc. My beautiful companion reared instantly, and I felt the passion to be genuine rather than a pretence to keep a customer happy. A few wild jerks with the intention of throwing me off yet keeping me there were followed by a vicious biting of the pillow and only a slightly less mad sucking at my neck and ear. Once the battle movements had been established at this explosive level, the pleasure came with the infliction of violence and pain on each other. The kisses turned to biting, the caresses to snatching and thumping, the thrusting into the solid impact of bodies. It could not last long, and it didn't; and once we had *burst the clouds* we collapsed into a silent heap.

The girls on the numerous 'flower boats' of Canton were usually of the Tanka (tan-chia) tribe, did not bind their feet and were not permitted to marry other Chinese. 19th-century erotic album. By kind permission of the British Museum.

Sex Position for the Garden. The male body was usually painted a darker shade than the 'lily' complexion of the woman. 19th-century erotic album. Courtesy private collection, Paris.

But only briefly. She pulled off my plumed 'cap of desire', reached for what looked like a pot of make-up cream, and lavishly greased my now rather sadly-limp 'warrior'. The lifelessness in the soft flesh quickly turned to a tingling sensation, not painful but distinctly burning, and to my astonishment, since this was the third time within the hour, my warrior-knight was again ready for battle. As if satisfied with the miracle she had produced, Miss Ace again crossed to the recess that curtained the goddess Kwan-Ying, and having completed her devotions, returned and said:

'You have clearly conquered the Front Chamber. Now let's see what you can do at the rear. You won't find it quite so easy, I can assure you.'

The sheets of the bed were a peacock green, and as she knelt to receive me, with her forehead pressed on the pillow, I was reminded of a white pony eating the blue-mountain grass of Tai-Shan. When I found her body a little low, I took two of the pillows and made her kneel on them, then aimed for the rear pleasure chamber. Despite my cream-coated 'monk', it was a very difficult entry. Miss Ace had given me to understand that my dimensions were something to be proud of, and so it appeared. She gasped and moaned as I slowly completed possession, lifting her under the stomach and drawing her towards me as I pressed forward. No virgin was ever tighter. It was a curious variation of our previous two battles, and because of this was infinitely more exciting. Particularly as I realised why this love-variation was called 'the strait and the narrow' or 'the slippery and the dry'.

It was a mark of the Number One qualities of Miss Ace that, despite her body being turned away from me, she still managed a number of touches and supporting effects, and it was not long before I clutched her as the spear finally transfixed her for an ecstatic sharing of the 'cloudburst'.

This time we both needed a longer rest, and tea was served by a maid who stared at me with interest; not at my body, which was now between those peacock green sheets but as if I must have special talents to be allowed to stay the whole night. The tea revived me and during the interval Miss Ace told me a little of how, at twenty-two, she had reached the top of her profession. At sixteen she had come to Shanghai from Peking, become the mistress of a French diplomat, been discovered by the man's wife who, instead of showing fury or jealousy, had then instructed the young girl in the finer arts of the courtesan. A trusting friendship had developed between the two women, and the wife eventually confided that each afternoon, unknown to her husband, she spent two or three hours entertaining rich Chinese businessmen prepared to pay excessively for the comparatively rare experience of a beautiful and talented Frenchwoman. When her husband was assassinated by one of these Chinese suitors, who had become jealous of him, both Madame Lucille and the woman now telling me this story had entered the *Mists and Dew of Paradise*. With youth on her side, not to mention all her other qualities, it took Miss Ace exactly two years to become Shanghai's Number One.

'And now, to turn from my past, we shall try one of our imaginative and traditional methods,' Miss Ace concluded.

I had already noticed the surprising number of lights hanging from the ceiling. Now, as she took me by the hand, I realised that four of them were decorative chains and that what appeared to be lampshades were in fact wide leather collars. With the help of a high stool, I fastened the collars round her ankles and wrists and soon she was swinging freely through the air. The chains were so placed that the Jade Gate was wide open for the visitor, and the visitor at the sight of Miss Ace's helplessness, had already begun to rise in anticipation.

'Just the slightest touch will be enough.'

This remark from Miss Ace was true in two senses. She clearly liked being at the mercy of my 'warrior knight', and as soon as I moved between her knees and took a good grip on her swinging buttocks, she closed her eyes and sagged like a corpse. And once I had guided myself into the Flower Heart, it needed only the merest pressure to push her a few inches away from me. Once released, the return of the swing slid her back against my body. Of all the battles we had so far enjoyed, this was the gentlest, the one that required least effort yet the one that gave most pleasure. Miss Ace was completely helpless, a plaything, slave to whatever rhythms and motions I cared to indulge in. And when I finally enjoyed the Ultimate, I collapsed over her and together we hovered in the air like two phoenixes.

'Well, that's enough of this imitation of our illustrious ancestors,' said Miss Ace. 'Now help me into bed.'

To say that I was now exhausted was an understatement, and once in bed I found myself struggling to find my breath. My wonderful hostess, however, was as cheerful and lovely as ever. She called for more tea and cakes, and I was soon sitting up and feeling a little livelier. When I spoke, there was only one thing I could say.

'You richly deserve your title of Number One. When I return to my village, I'll start saving every dollar I can so that I can come back soon.'

For the first time that night, Miss Ace's professional manner changed. Instead of the brightly charming and efficient courtesan who could entertain rich businessmen, highly-placed foreigners and more modest customers like myself, she became the simple and unspoilt girl she must once have been.

'You should look for a girl in your village, someone you can love with your heart and liver as well as with your body. The Yin-Yang pleasures we are having now, and which deceive you because of my expertness and experience, still cannot equal the deepest ecstasy of the Clouds and the Rain, that which comes with the true Yin partner. But you're young. You'll learn.'

I looked at her with disbelief. She was betraying all the wonderful joys we were experiencing. Could any true Yin partner have made me feel better, more triumphant and manly than I now felt? What foreign romantic nonsense had this girl picked up in Shanghai, in this cosmopolitan city? And as for her remarks about my youth — what could be more immature than her talk of love, of thinking that there was more to a woman than the sex-pleasure she could give to a man. As I lay on her bed, surrounded by furnishings that were more western than Chinese, and realised that Miss Ace had somehow crossed a frontier and would never again really belong to her people, the extent of my triumph and my superiority seemed even more apparent. With all her experience, she was the immature one of the two of us. I was still a part of our old and superior civilisation, the Yang expression of it, while Miss Ace was just another female, with a Chinese face, of this modern and deluded society of the West.

'I'd still want to come and see you again,' I said at last. 'But what are we going to do now?'

The question brought the bright professional look back to her face. The sweet peasant girl of a not-so-distant yet infinitely lost earlier life disappeared with a shrug and a twitch of mouth and eyes. Miss Ace began to fondle my Jade Stem as if reflecting on what variation we should try next, and I was glad that she was getting back to business. In life, as our Confucian beliefs teach us, we should know exactly what we are and where we belong in society. Miss Ace was Number One in Shanghai, and in my mind that was something to be proud of, not ashamed of. What was all this western nonsense about finding love in one's village, putting the Yin-Yang Harmony second to some vague spiritual thing called love? But Miss Ace had not lost her expert touch in that moment of romantic weakness. Once again Yang was being prepared for battle. Miss Ace really had that bit extra. And I meant what I had just said to her. The day I got back to my village I'd start saving for my next trip to Shanghai.

Old Chinese Proverb:
The poison of the black scorpion
Or of the green snake
Is less deadly
Than that in a woman's heart.

A young woman wakens from an afternoon rest watched by a neighbour. Gouache. 19th-century album.

Part 3

From Fragrant Silhouettes to the Great Leap Forward

CHAPTER NINE

The Flowery Fiction

If in my heart I love him
Why should I not tell him.
If with my body I want him
Why should I not tell him.
                    From the *Shih-ching* (600 B.C.)

In his preface to *Gems of Chinese Literature,* published in 1884, H.A. Giles deplored the failure of western readers to discover the treasure house of Chinese literature. He stated: 'Dr Legge's colossal labours have indeed placed the canonical books of Confucianism wihin easy reach of the curious but the immense bulk of Chinese authorship is still virgin soil and remains to be efficiently explored.' Almost a century later the position has improved a little but in no way commensurate with a literary tradition older, more varied and versatile, and more prolific in its output, than any of the other ancient and continuing civilisations. H.A. Giles added another pertinent observation which is not without relevance today: 'The sickly praises lavished . . . upon Japan, the odious comparisons drawn by superficial observers to the disparagement of China — these are gall and wormwood to all who know under whose tuition it was that Japan first learned to read, to write, and to think.'

As early as the Chou dynasty (eleventh century B.C.) the importance of stories and poems had been recognised by the court and were commissioned, frequently set to music and distributed throughout the state. A further development of this growing appreciation of their culture was the annual tour by administrators and rulers to discover new works and talent, which were then taken back to the capital, recorded and sent into general circulation. The success of this 'grass roots' culture depended on the popularity of the works, and their being understood when recited by storytellers to illiterate villagers, and they formed an early corpus of folk songs and tales. As such their comprehensibility to the simple and pagan audience was related to the directness and the familiarity of their themes. Love and war, heroes and tyrants, beautiful women and terrifying monsters were therefore the ever-popular subjects.

Among the Five Classics dating from Confucius (551-479 B.C.) or earlier, the *Shih-ching* or 'Book of Odes', a collection of such tales and songs, is regarded as the only one to survive with a minimum of deletions and changes. One of the reasons for its good fortune in resisting censorship and frequent literary purges, which occasionally struck at the most innocuous works, was the fundamental simplicity yet timeless morality of their message.

The river Chen flows sweetly
The knight and his maid lie together
The water is clear in the sunlight
And after love they give peonies to each other.
                    Shih-ching

The delight of simple people in natural pleasures inevitably caused a censorious reaction among the more conservative and moralising of scholars and administrators, and a little after the Early Chou Dynasty, Confucius uttered a warning against vulgarity in poetry and music: 'These "people's odes" composed for the lower classes and sung by both men and women, encourage lewdness and base thoughts, play on the senses rather than on the mind, and cause riotous behaviour at festivals, marriages, and even at funerals.' Five hundred years after the severe strictures of the Master, however the growing influence of Buddhism, together with Taoism, again encouraged that which was most individualistic and pagan in Chinese poetry and literature. The Golden Age of Chinese writing during the T'ang Dynasty that followed, undoubtedly owed much to the naturalism of both of these faiths, if not directly then to a revival of romantic and lyrical simplicity. Among the outstanding poets of this period were Wang Wei (699-759), Li Po (701-762), Tu Fu (712-770), Po Chu-I (771-846); and the glorious era of T'ang dynasty literature at last brought relief from the over-refinement and formalisation of classical writing.

An example of Li Po's romanticism is the nostalgic *She Who Stays Afar:*

> During her days here
> — My enchanted —
> Flowers were everywhere
> With her departure
> — My enchanted —
> Her empty bed remains
> On it the coverlet
> — Three years later —
> That still holds her scent
> The fragrance will stay
> — My enchanted —
> Though she never returns
> As I hold to the memories
> Autumn leaves fall
> And tears of dew
> Lie on the green moss

During the Sung Dynasty (960-1279), the itinerant story-teller was a feature of every tea-house, market place and social occasion, and his repertoire extended to romantic tales, contemporary scandals and other departures from traditional narratives about remarkable ancestors and the supernatural. Emperor Kao-tsung in the twelfth-century found this new genre so exciting that he ordered his eunuchs to entertain him with an original story every day, and for preference recited or sung by the street-entertainer himself.

Such stories now began to be adopted for more sustained narratives, and formed the themes of early novels. The techniques that were so successful in the tea-houses and on street corners, reciting complete episodes yet making them part of a longer and suspenseful tale, were now used in printed fiction. A wide variety of characters could be set in motion, progressing from one exciting episode to another, breaking out of the limitations of both academic writing and the recited story or song. It was an ideal form for pornographic novels; and they soon followed. It was not by coincidence. that some of the masterpieces of the Ming dynasty were set in the Sung period,

The Busy Mother. Another example of Chinese humour. Behind her a child is pacified with a candy as the father is welcomed at the Jade Gate. 19th-century gouache. Private collection, Paris.

and such novels as the *Chin P'ing Mei*, the *Ko-lien-hua-ying* (Flower Shadows on the Curtain Screen or Silhouettes of the sex-act) and the works of Mao Hsiang (1611-1693) and Li Yü have the timeless human qualities — and much humour — that bridge the centuries between those early street-entertainers and the modern Chinese.

Fiction was now committed to entertaining rather than inspiring or instructing, though the novel often contained lengthy dissertations on subjects regarded as too trivial for scholars or too dangerous politically to be presented in a more direct form. The worst pornographic literature, in the eyes of Chinese rulers, was preferable to books questioning their authority, upsetting Confucian ideas and values, or opposing traditional practices such as bound feet or pigtails. But there were times when even pornographic literature was caught in the recurring periods of book-burning. So thorough were these Empire-wide 'puritan' crusades that many of the masterpieces of the past have only survived because, in earlier times, they had found their way to Japan, which always had a high regard for Chinese erotica.

The Chinese erotic novel, despite the boundless flights of fancy in the story itself, conformed to a certain classical style and form. With solemn 'hand-on-heart' propriety, the novel began with an introduction extolling 'right-thinking' and high morals, warning the reader that the story to follow was to be taken seriously, and that the riotous adventures of the characters — or hero — led to their repentance, well-deserved punishment or downfall. Once the sermon was over, however, the hero was let loose among the girls. A second characteristic that paid lip-service to the classics was the habit of breaking off the narrative to insert a poem or verse, the purpose of which was to point the moral of the chapter or situation. But actions — or the adventures of the characters — spoke loudest of all, and the Chinese erotic novel was at all times a gay and pagan affair.

In previous chapters the authors have offered excerpts from a number of novels, usually to illustrate or comment on the subject under scrutiny, but the extracts that follow are situation pieces that can be appreciated for what they are. With excerpts from the two masterpieces, *Jou pu T'uan* and *Chin P'ing Mei*, there are presented more modern examples of erotic fiction and verse, but all seem to share the essential Chinese quality of cheerfully accepting the inescapable forces of time and fate.

The *Jou pu T'uan* by Li Yü was first published in the seventeenth-century, and the following extract is translated from the 1705 edition, printed in Japan. The hero, usually referred to as the Scholar, or the Night-time Scholar to define the period of his most intensive studies, temporarily leaves his wife for a long journey, on which he hopes to improve 'his mind and soul'. In the course of the sex odyssey that this journey becomes, he has acquired the enormous penis described in Chapter Four, and puts it to use at every available opportunity.

The following exploit features a sex-competition, and begins when Auntie Morning Flower, a middle-aged woman, walks into a bedroom where the Scholar is making love to her three young nieces. She at once marches him off to her own room and enjoys a little fun for herself. Her three nieces, however, are not prepared to allow her to be possessive with the Scholar, and they connive to involve their aunt in a game which, though apparently a sex competition, will also punish the older woman for her intrusion. The competition begins with a card-game, each card being illustrated with a position for intercourse; and the wine flows freely.

The rules were agreed and Auntie Morning Flower persuaded to be Chairman-Commander and the Scholar her deputy. She started by drinking a cup of wine herself and ordering Aromatic Cloud to drink two, Precious Jade to drink three and Priceless Pearl to have four. As the Scholar had to match their total consumption, he proceeded to drink ten cups in succession. When he had finished, Auntie Morning Flower ordered Precious Jade to wipe the cards with a damp cloth so that they would not stick, then told her to keep the cloth in her hand to clean away any secretions that would flow during the competition.

They drew lots to decide who would pick the top card, the arrangement being that intercourse would copy the sex position illustrated but that the Scholar would raise his performance from one hundred thrusts with the first partner to four hundred with the last. He was also, with the partner fortunate enough to be last, to nourish her with his Vital Essence. Any failure to join in the spirit of the competition, by refusing to adopt the love position on the card, would be punished by having to drink twenty cups of wine and being disqualified from all further frolics with the Scholar.

Priceless Pearl, however, with the trick they had prepared for her in mind, then asked Auntie Morning Flower: 'And if the Chairman-Commander herself should choose to dishonour her word — surely there should be a specially severe punishment for her?'

The older woman reassured her at once.

'In that case I undertake to drink a triple quantity of wine and I will submit to being forced to go through every position illustrated on all thirty cards.'

The young nieces, all between seventeen and twenty years of age, were satisfied at last, and Priceless Pearl proceeded to take the top card. It showed a splendid picture of a man supported on his hands and feet and arching over a naked woman lying beneath him. His Jade Stem was clearly flicking at the Pavilion Gate and as the position was called *Dragon-fly Skimming the Surface of the Pond,* they all knew what that entailed. The card was replaced in the pack and the Scholar and Priceless Pearl were quickly disrobed by the other women, then helped on to the bed. But if they expected the Scholar to be content with a delicate dance within the Gateway, they were certainly surprised. With remarkable energy he proceeded to thrust into her one hundred times, disregarding the rules but hardly causing Priceless Pearl to complain. In fact, for her part, intent on reassuring her aunt about the genuineness of the competition, she moaned and gasped as if every movement was arousing unendurable pleasure.

Aromatic Cloud was the next to pick a card. It was called *Guiding the Boat by the Current* and showed a woman reclining in an armchair and a man standing between her legs, which had been thrown over his shoulders. The likeness to a boatman was because he was holding on to the arms of the chair as if they were two oars. And when he plunged into the glistening Golden Gulley, the upheaval of bodies was as if they were really being tossed about on a swirling current.

Meanwhile Auntie Morning Flower was becoming greatly excited by what she was witnessing. Although having been married quite twenty years, her own sex battles had always been conducted in the dark. And she had never been able to stand at the feet of others enjoying the Clouds and the Rain and see at close range the thrusting into the Jade Pavilion. She was so affected that she felt her own organs trembling and moistening with anticipation; when it was her turn, she remembered joyfully, the Scholar was to go on until she had gained his Vital Essence. As she watched, however, she could not control her body from copying the up-and-down movements of Aromatic Cloud.

Precious Jade was the next to receive the merciless and apparently tireless Male Peak, and this time, as if now anxious to get at Auntie Morning Flower, the Scholar went through the three hundred thrusts without pause in the position known as *The Lotus Upside Down.* And he had hardly withdrawn his glistening implement when the older woman was reaching to take the top card. Her other hand impatiently loosened the knot of her trousers, and as they dropped round her ankles she eagerly turned over the card.

Her eyes narrowed for a moment as the picture came into focus, then she uttered a gasp of disbelief.

The Bamboo Grove was considered an erotic setting for lovers as well as an inspiration for poets and thinkers. 17th-century blockprint.

The nieces remained silent, pretending to wait patiently to be shown the card. But instead of Auntie Morning Flower speaking, she had gone deathly pale.

'Is something wrong, auntie?' Priceless Pearl asked at last.

'There's been a mistake,' replied her aunt quickly. 'I'll have to take another card.'

The girls, however, had anticipated this reaction, and before Auntie Morning Flower could replace the card, the pack was snatched away and held out of reach.

'Remember the rules!' cried Priceless Pearl. 'After all, you're Chairman-Commander!'

Suddenly Aromatic Cloud pulled the card from the older woman's weakened fingers, studied it, and shouted:

'Why, it's the position known as *Slave Girl Must Accept Anything!* Oh, auntie, auntie . . . '

The three nieces burst into a simultaneous fit of uncontrollable laughter, and the situation was made even funnier by the fact that Auntie Morning Flower clearly suspected nothing. The position on the card revealed a girl being forced over a high couch by two others while the man indulged in the anal variation of 'fire behind the mountain'.

Without troubling to pull up her trousers, which remained round her ankles, the aunt cried: 'This is one thing I never expected. In all my twenty years with your Uncle Wei, not once did I. . . '

The girls at last controlled their laughter and pointed out that if the card was so objectionable, she as the chairman-commander should have removed it before the game had begun. They then turned to the deputy for support, and though the Scholar suspected that the card had purposely been placed fourth, he had no firm proof of the fact.

Holding his enormous implement in one hand, as if its weight required some support, he therefore compromised by suggesting that the aunt should be spared a slave-girl's indignity but that she should submit to four other positions without pause.

The nieces' reply was to shout, 'Fang-pi (dogs' fart)!' But Aromatic Cloud went on to say that at least her aunt should go through the motion of bending over a chair even if the Scholar did not actually press into her.

Three pairs of hands seized the distraught aunt, completed the removal of her trousers then forced her over the back of the chair. The sight of what was exposed to him, and its vulnerability, instead of adding to his earlier concern for the aunt's self-respect, caused the Scholar to go wild with excitement. He approached the exposed posterior with a rush of small steps and instantly tried to insert his hand-tailored implement into what now seemed an impossibly small orifice. At the first pressure Auntie Morning Flower screamed as if she were being murdered, but the three nieces applauded with loud enthusiasm. After five unsuccessful assaults by the Scholar, the girls then showered the target area with spittle, and Priceless Pearl came behind him and began to push with all her strength.

Their efforts coincided with a degree of willingness or surrender from Auntie Morning Flower, because her struggling diminished. Aromatic Cloud instantly seized the opportunity to fetch a jar of couch-pleasure ointment, and after a generous application of this, the position on the card was faithfully imitated. But not without further screams from Auntie Morning Flower. She made a last attempt to escape, but now that the Scholar was as determined as the girls to keep her over the chair, she was completely helpless. And her screams soon suggested delight as well as pain. Priceless Pearl reminded the Scholar that he had to continue until the 'bursting of the clouds', and when eventually this happened, Auntie Morning Flower had apparently lost all consciousness. Her eyes were closed and she draped like a limp cotton garment over the back of the chair.

The maids were then called to carry her to her apartment, and triumphant laughter followed her through the house. As Priceless Pearl said, it would be some time before she again tried to take the Scholar from them. In fact, Auntie Morning Flower remained in bed for four days, three days with a high temperature, and an extra one because she could not sit down in a normal manner.

The *Jou Pu T'uan* was believed to have appeared in 1634, and this date coincided with one of the harshest periods of literary suppression. In 1663 seventy scholars and writers were beheaded by Empeor K'ang Hsi and an Index Expurgatorius was compiled. Most of the banned books were political or revolutionary and Lü Liu-liang (d. 1683) had sixty-eight works listed in the Index. Emperor Ch'ien Lung, who came to power later and was regarded as a patron of the arts, nevertheless upheld the censorship and was, in fact, responsible for extending its severity. Suppressing the interpretations of the Classics by Hsieh Chi-Shih, Ch'ien Lung uttered the terse order of: 'Destroy the lot. Let none be saved.' And banning the books of Ch'ien Ch'ien-i, the Emperor's edict stated: 'Let the governors of every district search the bookshops and the libraries of every town and village, every hamlet hidden in the mountains and the valleys. Not a volume must be left to posterity; and I give the governors two years to carry out these orders.' From time to time the order was reinforced by warnings that despite the encouraging flow of censorable books to the capital, the governors could do still better. They usually did.

The greater proportion of the censored books were published in the late Ming and early Ch'ing periods, and were usually found objectionable because of the topical and contemporary nature of their contents, but those critical of dynasties regarded as ancestral to these were also placed on the *Index*. With regard to novels, the grounds for their suppression were presented as an action to safeguard the highest standards of scholarship and craftsmanship. Without reference to the pornographic contents, they were branded as of inferior quality, badly written, the style unsuited to the contents. A novel by Shu Hung-hsün was burned because it was 'unclear and confused'. A work by Yang Ming-lun was consigned to the flames on the grounds of 'vulgarity of language and a common style'. In some instances the offences of the authors not only brought torture and death to themselves but frequently led to the same punishment for all the males in the family, and the deporting into slavery of the women folk. Ch'ien Lung suppressed approximately three thousand volumes, though the list of writers suffering the same fate was not recorded with the same diligence.

This suppression, as in similar instances in many diverse countries and periods, coincided with, and seemed to encourage, a profusion of the very works that were being banned. It was not by coincidence, therefore, that the Ming period produced many of the most erotic, pornographic and colourful novels of Chinese literature. As well as providing a remarkable catalogue of sexual practices and vignettes of the intimate moments of Chinese lovers of the period, they offer a grand panorama of social and domestic life. The *Chin P'ing Mei*, for example, begins with the conventional warning against worldly sins and the pursuit of material wealth, against fornication and the weaknesses of the flesh. As the hero, however, has to keep his six wives happy, and his intimate relations with them are accompanied by love affairs with numerous other females, his bedchamber battles cover every imaginable manoeuvre and strategy. He finally dies from an overdose of aphrodisiacs, a fitting end for the hero. An example of Hsi-men Ch'ing's non-stop activities, and the quality of the writing, is illustrated in a scene with the beautiful courtesan Moonbeam.

Dressed in his best summer gown and black and white shoes, he is conveyed to the brothel in a sedan chair to spend the afternoon with his new favourite. He is welcomed by the Madame of the establishment who orders Moonbeam's 'foster-sister', Delightful, to summon the beauty and to offer the gentleman tea. Moonbeam's appearance, when she enters, is as softly dazzling as her name. Her gown and skirt are of white and purple and green, her shoes red, and her movements are accompanied by an audible tinkling of embroidery and jewellery. She sips her tea behind a fluttering gilded fan, her glossy dark hair circling her face like the night sky round the moon. When they have all enjoyed the formal ceremony, the two 'sisters' accompany Hsi-men Ch'ing to Moonbeam's room. Here the maid prepares a light meal of scented cakes and sweet dumplings, which are served on gilded plates, and when the food has been cleared away, they play dominoes with ivory pieces. At the end of the game wine and fruit are served, and now in a sensuous mood, Moonbeam picks up her lute, Delightful her guitar, and together they entertain the gentleman with love-songs. At last Delightful, on a pretext of needing to change her clothes, withdraws:

The moment Hsi-men Ch'ing found himself alone with Moonbeam, he pulled from his sleeve a small gold box.

'Is that your fragrant leaves?' asked the young woman.

'No, it's a tonic. I take it every day to keep up my strength. I wouldn't buy a gold box just for my fragrant leaves.'

As he replaced the box, he took out his handkerchief, the design of which caused Moonbeam to exclaim: 'I have only seen two such handkerchiefs before, and they belong to my "sisters" Silver Wu and Cassia.'

'Yes,' admitted Hsi-men. 'But that was before I was introduced to you. Here, take this one.' He swallowed his tonic with a sip of wine. 'Those handkerchiefs are only made in Yan-chow. Here, come and drink wine from my mouth.'

He filled his mouth with wine, and when they kissed, it passed from one to the other without the spilling of a single drop. When the wine was finished, their mouths stayed together and their tongues continued to entwine and play, and soon Hsi-men Ch'ing had his hands inside her clothes and was stroking her breasts. He found them both soft and firm, the nipples like the small pink cherries of Szechuan. Although they were not altogether a novelty to him, he was overwhelmed by the curiosity of someone eager to uncover a hidden secret, and quickly unfastened her jacket. He was not disappointed. Her breasts were mounds of pure jade, white and smooth, and of unbelievable beauty.

As his hands touched them again, he was aware that his Jade Stem was hard and erect, and that he was sitting in such a way that his trousers were causing discomfort. He therefore stood up, removed them and invited Moonbeam to arouse him even more. To his surprise, since they had previously spent a night together, Moonbeam seemed shocked by the suggestion.

'Have I said something wrong?' asked Hsi-men.

'This must be the effect of your tonic,' Moonbeam said, her expression still one of shock. 'It looks so big and red. It makes me pity anyone who is at the receiving end.'

The remark caused Hsi-men Ch'ing to laugh.

'In that case get used to it by playing a tune on it.'

But Moonbeam's neat and pink mouth continued with words rather than action.

'This is only our second meeting. I will play a tune later. Meanwhile let me get the maid to clear away the dishes.' And when this excuse for a delay was over, the beautiful courtesan said: 'The days of the future which we can spend together number more than all the leaves of the trees. Why don't we spend this afternoon in becoming better acquainted?'

The answer to this question seemed only too obvious from the behaviour of the roused Male Peak, and Hsi-men said:

'Well, if you won't suck me, let's get into bed.'

'But you'll half kill me with that. It was a struggle last time, but I swear it's even bigger today,' replied Moonbeam. And when this caused Hsi-men to utter a delighted laugh, she said: 'I'm going to ask the maid to bring more wine. I really need all my courage to give a royal welcome to an ambassador like that.'

'No more drinks. I'm getting into bed.'

And Hsi-men's voice was so determined that there was nothing she could do except remove his shoes and jacket, and loosen her own hair. She then went behind the screen to wash herself, and Hsi-men Ch'ing snuffed out the incense burner, let down the bamboo curtain, fastened the door, and returned to the bed. He was now naked, and when Moonbeam appeared, he made haste to have her in the same state. When her bed-robe had been removed, he enjoyed the first sight of her body, the previous occasion together having been in the darkness. Her skin was as glossy-smooth and white as were her breasts, from her neck to her feet, but he was surprised to notice that no shadow of hair fell over the Pleasure Pavilion.

Greatly intrigued by this discovery, he laid her across the bed and subjected the Precious Flower to a close inspection. The same jade-white skin continued from her stomach and between the legs, and there was not a single hair in evidence. He ran his fingers over the smoothness, then said:

'It reminds me of a freshly steamed dumpling — warm and soft and full of good things.'

He placed his face very close to the object of his fascination and found that it seemed to exhale the natural perfume of a field of spring flowers. And

---

The garden seat was a favourite article of furniture both inside and outside the house. The best were of porcelain, later inferior ones of earthenware. They had many uses and could be warmed. 19th-century erotic album. By kind permission of the British Museum.

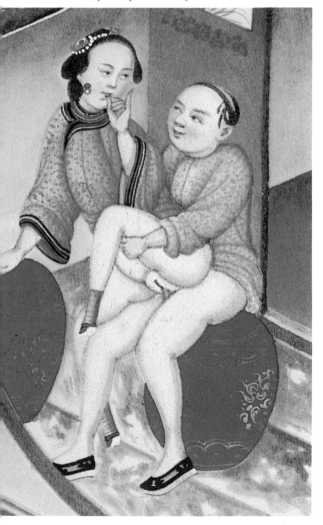

when he parted the Jade Gate to peer into the Pavilion itself, the remarkable perfume made his head spin with dizziness.

'This scent could not be bought for a thousand pieces of silver,' he exclaimed breathlessly. 'But let us enjoy the *Clouds and the Rain.*'

The attack on the Jade Gate was preceded, however, by a preliminary use of the Cap of Eternal Desire, which helped to prepare his entry into the Flower Heart, and once this had been expanded, he was able, despite Moonbeam's pleas, to insert the 'turtle head'. He allowed himself a further sight of the smoothly white lips that were now welcoming him inside, and the excitement of their purity caused him to plunge forward furiously. His pleasure at overcoming this last resistance was accompanied by a cry of pain.

'You've killed me,' gasped Moonbeam.

'Let us begin with seven shallow and two deep.'

Moonbeam took hold of the pillow with both hands.

'Please be considerate.'

Hsi-men Ch'ing relented by raising both her feet and placing them on his shoulders, and began a series of very slow and very shallow movements. The slower the rhythm, the greater the pleasure — he felt that he was casually rowing a boat on a lake. But after a half-hour the waters began to be ruffled by a strong wind, and his slow rhythm changed to livelier movements.

'You are quite different from last time,' said Moonbeam. 'Are your wives pleasing you?'

'It is the afternoon light. Food eaten in the darkness never tastes as nice as it should.'

But in fact the afternoon light was beginning to fade, and as if aware of the advancing day, Hsi-men Ch'ing began a more powerful assault on the Flower Heart, which quickly caused Moonbeam's chatter to change to a series of squeals and gasps. These proved even more exciting than the bare whiteness of the Jade Gate, because in his determination to achieve one thousand thrusts without pause, he completely forgot his private fascination.

Chinese Humour:
Ch'en Ta-lang was woken by his wife who wanted to know why he was panting and jerking in his sleep. When he confessed that he was dreaming of another woman, she jumped out of bed, picked up a broom and gave him a sound beating. He protested, once he had recovered, that a man was hardly responsible for his dreams. She then charged him with not making love to her often enough, and that this was the way to avoid beatings in the future. Ch'en replied by saying that he could show no greater devotion than by advising her to sleep with the broom always by her side of the bed.

Erotic stories and romantic tales were not confined to novels, and verse was a favoured form for much that was most entertaining and popular. The Hwa-tsëen, by two anonymous

Ming poets, is an example of the love epic, and tells of the tyro Liang and Yao Seen, the pure maiden. Although not pornographic either in intent or language, a rich eroticism gives passion to such poems. The work is prefaced, as with the more loosely constructed novels, by an introduction which explains the writer's noble purpose. The following excerpt of the Introduction (and from the poem) is based on the 1824 translation by P.P. Thoms:

When evening after the hot afternoon
Finally brings cool relief
Leave the shelter of walls
And breathe the fresh air.
The autumn breeze carries the fragrance
Of water-lilies, and the new moon
Rises in a sky like a motionless lake.

Tonight the stars of Chih-neu and Këen-nu
Enjoy their conjugal intercourse,
And if love is for the stars
Then it can also be for man.
Let him covet the pearl,
Steal the joys, of Precious Flowers
And exhaust himself in that fair field.

Why should love be for the arranged marriage
When the deepest pledges of adoring lovers
Do not permit the same close union.
So I tell you this, lovers,
You are not forgotten, and with these lines
I shall narrate your story
That posterity may judge your lives.

The poem describes the courtship from the first accidental meeting to a more formal introduction, and then to the moment when Liang, impatient for the joys of marriage, secretly meets Yao-sëen in a field. His responses to her rebuff have a timeless familiarity:

But do you really refuse me, lovely Miss,
Cast doubts on my purest intentions,
Dishonouring our closeness and even,
If I may remind you, your loved one's
parents? If you will not yield for love
What higher consideration can there be?

Yao-sëen, seeing the torment on his face,
Knew well that words of sympathy
Would in his ears sound vexatious,
But said: 'Our marriage is decreed
Let us wait until the chosen day
To be consumed by Clouds and Rain.

'I know the distress men endure,
Scholars and poets forgetting noble thoughts,
Restless nights instead of serene sleep.
But please be patient, dear love,' And Liang
Realising he could not persuade her
Restrained his desire and sat quietly among
the flowers.

Offering to the Male Warrior. Engraving from the 17th-century novel Su Wo P'ien.

Chinese Humour:
The King of Ch'i offered his daughter, together with a large dowry, in marriage to a lowly butcher, T'u. Butcher T'u declined the honour by pleading impotence and sickness of the sex parts. His brother, on hearing such a story, instantly reprimanded him. 'You are the most virile man in town — do you want to spend your whole life in this stinking shop? Why did you refuse a princess?'

'Because she's ugly,' T'u replied. 'I haven't been a butcher all these years without learning something.'

'But how do you know she's ugly, honourable brother? You have never even seen the princess.'

When meat is good, one doesn't have to persuade people to buy it. They come for it freely. On the other hand, most worthy elder brother, when meat is not good I can only sell it by offering twice the quantity for the same price. The princess is like my bad meat — the dowry that goes with her is the same inducement as something at half-price'.

The following week they learned from a Palace eunuch that the princess was as 'thin as a bamboo pole', that her eyes were 'as small as splits in apricots', her mouth 'as large as that of the Giant Carp', and her teeth 'like a row of tiny insect larva'.

The humour of the erotic novel ranged from the boisterous to the subtle and the oblique, but invariably evolved from the unexpected and the unbelievable in sex situations. For someone to behave out-of-character, for the predictable to take a sudden and surprising turn, as with modern farce, was a stock method of raising a laugh at the expense of lovers. In the following passage from an early Ming novel *(Ming-Tai-Yen-shih),* an innocent maiden has been peeping on her mistress while she entertained The Gentleman. The sight has so excited her that when she is asked to lead him from the house at the end of his visit, other ideas pass through her mind:

'Will you follow me, sir,' said the maid.

With one hand she held up the pole to which was hooked the lantern, then placed her other hand on his sleeve.

'It's dark night,' observed the gentleman.

As if this were an invitation to be even more helpful, her hand slipped into his. She was hardly fifteen, and a virgin, and what she had seen through the screen had not only intrigued her mind, it had caused responses within her body that were even more overwhelming. Her legs were both strong and weak at the same time, and between them a moisture of wonderful warmth was spreading over her thighs. Halfway across the courtyard to the gate, at a spot which was particularly dark, she realised that this was an opportunity that could not be missed.

'Sir,' she said, 'can you spare for this humble maiden just a crumb of all the sweet cakes you have been feeding to my mistress?' She held the gentleman's hand more tightly than ever. 'She's had so much and I have yet to taste such delights.'

The gentleman was horrified to realise that he had been waylaid by a sex-starved virgin. Did one listen to the voice of reason or did one consider only the need to please the child?

'Then put down the lamp,' he said, deciding on what seemed the less ungentlemanly course. 'And lie down on this garden bench.'

She seemed to read his thoughts because she was already removing her lower garments before he had finished speaking. When she lay on the stone slab only the upper part of her body was clothed.

The gentleman now found himself faced by a second problem of gallantry. If he made love to this lowly maid, surely her mistress would regard it as an insult to the hours of delight they had just enjoyed together. But a solution immediately presented itself. He would give this impatient maiden a quick taste of what she had so far missed, then chase her back to the house before her mistress had noticed her absence. He therefore placed himself between the girl's legs, opened the narrow lips of her virgin vagina and tried, without any preliminaries, to introduce his battle-worn yet ever-eager Male Peak.

'No!' she gasped. Then, in an even more tortured voice, she cried: 'Stop!'

As her plea had been accompanied by a jerk of the body that caused it to draw away as if the seat was of softest down, he found that he had momentarily lost contact.

'Please make up your mind,' requested the

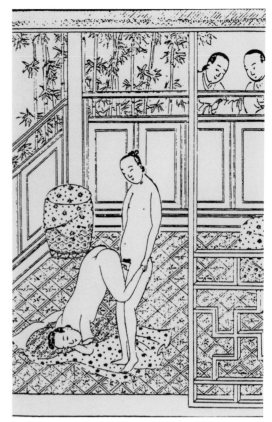

The maiden Wu San-ssû is introduced to the Mists and the Rain. Engraving from the 17th-century novel Su Wo P'ien.

gentleman. 'Either you want the pleasure or you don't.'

'How is it that it gave so much delight to my mistress yet gives me such a pain? Are you sure you are using the same implement?'

'It's exactly the way it was when it gave your mistress such delights,' he assured her.

'Then perhaps you should try again — but more gently.'

Again he aimed for the Flower Heart, and though the maid suppressed her screams, he found himself lodged with only the 'turtle-head' beyond the Jade Gate.

'Dear child,' said the gentleman, again troubled by his conscience, 'this is something that cannot be managed with this haste. For a virgin to enjoy it, it requires at least ten encounters of the Clouds and the Rain.'

The girl, still transfixed by the tip of his instrument, and apparently lifeless, replied at once.

'Then let us enjoy the Clouds and the Rain ten times, honourable sir.'

'No, this is neither the time nor the place,' the gentleman went on firmly. 'Besides, I am much too big for you, which is neither your fault nor mine but the way nature made me. Tomorrow I will send one of my young servants to you and you can taste all the honey you like with him.'

With which words the lodged implement was freed from the painfully tight Flower Heart, and he stepped to the ground. When the maid had pulled on her trousers, she picked up the lantern and continued guiding the way across the courtyard. And being a gentleman, he repeated his promise to send one of his young servants the following night.

The writers of such novels were not insignificant literary figures, nor men seeking quick fortunes or notoriety by offering to the public stories likely to titillate their basest instincts. As sex was remarkably free of moralising and social strictures, apart from the necessary lip-service to Confucian beliefs, the erotica of the time was a subject worthy of the scholar and the writer. Some of them, in the variety of their talents and in the vast sweep of their imaginative work, matched the creative geniuses of the West, and Li Yü, with his fame as a dramatist as well as poet and producer, could fairly be compared with Shakespeare.

Who were these writers of such books as the *Jou Pu T'uan* and the *Chin P'ing Mei*? They were men who had brought together the three necessary virtues of writers appreciated by, and reaching, a universal public — those of wisdom, intimate experience with all kinds of people, and a personal humility. The creative expression of such human qualities therefore gave to their work a benevolence and humour that reached the hearts of high and low and of many different societies, and enabled such writers to indulge in an irreverent and quite uninhibited approach to the subject of sex.

Wang Shih-cheng, the reputed author of the *Chin P'ing Mei,* was a distinguished Confucian scholar of the Ming dynasty and one of the leaders of the traditionalist forces in the country. The authorship as well as the date of the first publication have, however, been matters of controversy, and the name of Hsü Wei (1520-1593) is favoured by such authorities as Arthur Waley. To add to the conflicting claims of authors and sources and dates, there are some remarkable legends, the favourite being that Wang was asked one day about his literary activities by Yen Shih-fan, the son of the man responsible for his father's execution. The enquiry was posed as the two men stood by a metal vase of plum-blossom, and Wang impulsively replied: 'I'm finishing a novel called *Chin P'ing Mei* (Metal Vase and Plum-blossom).' Wang was then under a compulsion to write such a novel, and in the short period of a few weeks completed a work of 1,600 pages. It was a work devoted to a bitter satirization of the Yen family, the central character of Hsi-men Ch'ing being the hated Yen Shih-fan.

The legend does not, however, concern only the creation of the novel. In those days the paper of Chinese books was so thin that the reader had to lick his finger before turning the page, and the copy that Yen received from Wang had a little powdered poison rubbed into the corners. As Yen finished the book, the legend claims, and had been made to realize that the finally poisoned hero was himself, he collapsed and died. Whether the author of the work was Wang or Hsü or even a certain Feng Meng-lung of the 'Crazy-ink School', they were all major writers respected for their learning and literary style.

The most prolific of such authors in fact blended the erotic and pornographic, drawn from a life rich in travel and adventure.

Li Yü (1611-80) was born in Kiangsu, and his early life was affected by two traumatic events. One was his repeated failure to pass the provincial examinations, the other the upheaval of the civil war and the invasion by the Manchus that preceded the end of the Ming dynasty. Even in his early years he revealed the mature sense of humour of someone accepting human society for what it was, making the best of it and being philosophical about his own misfortunes. His home in Nanking, which was a not inconsiderable estate, was called Mustard Seed Villa, a reference to smallness and the fact that the *Great Mountain* itself could, figuratively, be placed in such a seed. At the age of thirty-five he began to write as a means of supporting himself and his forty wives, concubines and children, and he had soon added a troupe of singing girls to his household. He then had the idea of writing for the girls, and such was his talent that he was persuaded to form them into a travelling company.

He toured the country, producing and directing his dramas, adding to his reputation and increasing his household of concubines. During the fifteen-year period of his travels, he wrote numerous novels, essays and poems, as well as the plays, and his fortunes constantly varied between success and failure, wealth and poverty. The range of his essays illustrates Li Yü's versatility and they cover architecture and travel, human and social affairs, feminine beauty, drama and acting, diet and hygiene *(Hsien-ch'ing-ou-chi)*. Towards the end of his life his health troubled him and in 1677 he rejoined his sons in Chekiang, dying approximately three years later. His humour and playfulness, and his benevolence towards human failings are nowhere better revealed than in the seduction scene from his novel

Chueh-hou-ch'an (Enlightenment higher than knowledge):

That afternoon Scented Jade decided to take a bath. The tub was brought into her bedchamber and she was soon happily splashing about, the windows closed but her activities audible to anyone who passed by. At the same time Honest Chuan, the gardener, chose to return to the house, and on hearing the sound inside the bedroom of his employer's beautiful wife, hopefully emitted a loud cough.

Scented Jade could have ignored the sound but instead chose to shout: 'I'm having a bath. Don't you dare come in!'

Honest Chuan's reputation of having an implement the size of a sea-cucumber had briefly stirred his mistress, and this thought had caused her warning shout to sound both coquettish and inviting. For his part, he could hardly disregard the warning, and as all thought of returning to his work had disappeared, he walked past the door, out of the building and began to inspect the windows in the courtyard. Soon he reached one through which could be heard

the unmistakable sound of splashing, but as there were no cracks in the wooden frames, and the parchment through which the daylight passed was almost new, there was no way of peeping at the incomparable body of his jealous employer's lovely wife.

Although only a gardener, Honest Chuan was not without cunning, and with a great deal of stealth he wet his finger and began to rub at the opaque paper. Soon there was a hole big enough for one eye, and to this he instantly pressed his face. In the room itself, Scented Jade was not unaware of what was happening, and of the identity of the watcher. But her indignation was muted by the flattering thought that his tremendous Jade Stem must now be reacting excitedly to her beauty.

The idea made her stand in the tub, which came to just below her waist, and as she sponged her breasts, she casually turned her body towards the black dot that had appeared on the window paper. She prolonged the teasing for a few moments, then lifted herself a little so that she could sit on the wide rim of the tub. As usual, this had been next to the bed, and once she had made herself comfortable on the rim, she placed her feet on the opposite edge of the tub and leaned back so that her shoulders lay on the bed.

The Embrace. In this beautiful 19th-century painting the artist creates a 'chain' impression of arms and legs binding the lovers. Courtesy private collection, Paris.

For a full minute she kept her feet and knees together, then suddenly allowed them to fall apart.

The sight of the Flower Heart now revealed to him instantly caused Honest Chuan to become so excited that he rubbed a second hole in the parchment and set his other eye to feast on the scene. The second black dot, in turn, added to Scented Jade's delight, and in an abandoned upheaval, she flung feet and legs into the air and began to kick about playfully. To Honest Chuan, the message was clear. This was an invitation, and if he rushed into her bedroom she was hardly likely to chase him out.

Scented Jade slipped back into the water when the two eyes disappeared, and she was not surprised, despite her pretence at indignation, when the door was flung open and Honest Chuan immediately dropped to his knees.

'Most noble young mistress, forgive this coarse brute. I know this is a crime for which I can be beheaded, but I will gladly suffer that fate.'

His mixture of terror and pleading was interrupted by a sharp: 'How dare you burst in when I'm in my bath!'

'But most noble beautiful mistress, ever since I was first employed here, I've waited to see you like this. It's an opportunity I couldn't miss. What am I to do!'

The man looked so terrified that Scented Jade was now afraid he was going to run off. Her reply was worthy of the honesty of Honest Chuan himself.

'Well, we can't do it right here. I'm in the bath and all kinds of people are about.' The man's pleading and panting had paused, and she added: 'There's a right time and place for everything.'

The gardener became a little more coherent at last.

'I realise that the afternoon is hardly the time, and a bathtub overflowing with water hardly the place for it. But your lowly slave is ever-willing to attend you anywhere and at any time — just tell this insect, this maggot, when he should come.'

'At night you're in bed with your wife As-You-Please. She's hardly likely to let you come.'

'She can't stop me,' replied Honest Chuan. 'Besides, once we have enjoyed the Clouds and the Rain she falls asleep instantly and there's no waking her.'

'Then come tonight,' Scented Jade said. 'But make sure you're not too exhausted.'

Before leaving, the gardener found enough courage to plunge his arms into the tub, enjoy the first touch of the Golden Pleasure Palace which that night would be welcoming him, and then rushed happily from the room. By nature Scented Jade was a very methodical woman and, once alone, she prepared herself for her appointment with all the care of an actress or a musician about to take the stage. First she dried and scented herself, and lay down to rest and relax. Then she ordered chrysanthemum tea for her breath, lychees, pomegranates and peaches to freshen her spirits, and Moon Festival cakes for her pleasure. She then argued with her guil-

Hsi-mên Ch'ing picks up a plum and aims it at the Flower Heart. From the game of Flying Darts *in the illustrated 17th-century edition of the* Chin P'ing Mei.

ty conscience and convinced it that her husband's neglect was an excellent reason for her imminent infidelity. Finally, she ordered sprays of jasmine to be placed around the room.

At the second watch of the night, two hours after she had retired to bed, the door creaked as it was opened, then creaked as it was closed.

'My heart-chasing pursuer — is it you?' she whispered.

'This is your slave,' he replied.

In case he stumbled on his way across the unfamiliar room, and so made too much noise, she left the bed and guided him back to it. But once they were naked and lying next to each other, Scented Jade said:

'This mighty club of yours is the subject of gossip among all the women of the household. I must ask you to respect this favour I'm granting you by being very gentle. At least until I get used to it.'

'This coarse creature could hardly bring himself to cause the least discomfort to my mistress's delicate and aromatic body. You can rely on me to be as gentle as the wafting of willows in a light breeze.'

But as soon as he had covered her body and she had carefully guided him to the very step of the Jade Gate, he decided that her timidity was part of her coquettish behaviour and that she really wanted him to be brutal. Once she had removed her restraining hand, he therefore made a tentative and gentle push or two, then hurled himself forward. The effect on the lovely woman underneath him was instantaneous, but it was hardly the passion he had expected.

'You brute! Have you gone mad!' The exclamation was followed by a gasp and a cry. 'What do you think you are — a bull in a field of cows!'

The protest was too genuine to doubt, and as Honest Chuan hesitated before making further movements in that Jade Pavilion of apparently limited dimensions, he realised that he had behaved like an animal.

'Please forgive me, precious mistress,' he exclaimed. 'I have never before been with a lady of such perfection — how could I be other than like the man who has drunk five jars of Kwangtung wine! I promise to proceed with double gentleness and triple care.'

'My husband is a man of very small dimensions, but even he has difficulty.'

'Have no fears, precious lady. It is only three months since I lay with my virgin bride, and I will behave as I did with her.'

He kept faithfully to his promise, and once the giant Male Peak had been freed from captivity, he lightly played up and down the Pleasure Valley, occasionally knocking at the Gate but making no attempt to invade the Inner Chamber. Soon a flow of pleasure essence from numerous deep spring began to flood the valley, magically transforming it. The inundations of the Yellow and the Yangtze rivers could hardly have equalled it, and he quickly found himself swirled along by the current.

But it was Scented Jade who showed her impatience first.

'When is your "envoy" going to present his credentials at the palace?'

'My "ambassador" is like a ship waiting for the right tide, precious lady.'

'Make sail at once, I beg you.'

'Perhaps you would like to push me into midstream.'

His suggestion caused her to seize the slippery eel and unceremoniously plunge its head into the Flower Heart. It was at once apparent to Honest Chuan that any difficulties she might have had with her diminutive husband could hardly have been her fault. In a moment his full ten-inch Jade Stem had been accommodated even more comfortably than in the spacious chamber of his wife As-You-Please.

'Oh my heart-and-liver,' gasped Scented Jade. 'But are you sure you have nothing more for me!'

Honest Chuan had never before received such an insult and he was now determined to make her suffer for the hint of inadequacy. Placing both her feet on his shoulders, he took hold of the sides of the Golden Valley, and by pulling them apart, gained an extra inch. Then he pressed forward as deeply as possible and created a rhythm of movements that were both strong and steady. It was apparently exactly what Scented Jade desired.

Inside Scented Jade's mind she was convinced that she was no longer either a body or a life but part of a movement. For half an hour not a coherent word passed her lips, then for the next half hour the expressions of her feelings came as a series of explosions and climaxes, paroxysms and outpourings of vital essence inside and outside the Pleasure Pavilion.

When Honest Chuan had exhausted himself, and she was in the same state herself, her first words were:

'I'm very pleased with myself. For a woman built as delicately as myself, I think I did very well.'

'Oh, precious lady, not even the Emperor has found such a wonderful Treasure Pavilion for his dragon implement.'

Scented Jade, as has already been said, had a very calculating and careful mind, and she was already considering the future.

'We must think of a way for you to come often to this bedchamber,' she said. 'I am not worried about my husband, because he is often travelling abroad, but I am worried about your wife. The best way to stop her from being jealous would be to persuade her to join us. Do you think she'll agree?'

'Precious lady, when I have beaten her enough, she will certainly agree. And she will consider it an honour to share the bed of so considerate a mistress.'

But it was now the hour of the third watch. As the night-watchman, beating lightly on his bamboo drum, passed by the window dotted with the two holes made earlier that day, Scented Jade decided that she would not trouble to have the parchment repaired. If this was what happened when a man peeped on a woman, who could say it was better for her to take offence.

She had to wait on him (her husband) day and night. When he went to sleep she had to take off his shoes and clothing; in the morning, she had to put them on again. She had to light his cigarettes, pour his water, hand him the cup with both hands and with a subservient smile on her face. He struck her daily as a matter of course and beat her unmercifully if she did not obey his commands on the instant.

Golden Flower's Story
(Early 20th-century)*

CHAPTER TEN

The Great Leap Forward

The Great Leap Forward, to conclude a study of the long history of sex in China with its colourful practices and strange beliefs, to the modern Communist state, is like a jump of centuries rather than decades. But it has happened. It is a fact. The Dragon Emperors and

eunuchs, with bewildering swiftness, have given way to Party leaders and cadres, Confucian disciplines have been exchanged for Communist principles, and Bound Feet and Fallen Flowers have become the steady march and the unpainted faces of liberated women. A quarter of the world's population, its civilization and traditions the oldest and most idiosyncratic in history, has set itself on a new course.

No society, however, completely buries its past. Along this new course with its different

---

Traditional pillow books are now regarded in China as pornography. In their place is the plain instruction book Information on Sex. *The remedies for the sexual urge are abstinence and correct political thinking. 19th-century erotic album. By kind permission of the British Museum.*

political system and morality, people still carry their natural instincts. Whatever the new circumstances that inhibit free sexual practices, place constraints on marriage, regard romanticism as a bourgeois sickness, the changes have been imposed in the manner of adopting a new style of dress. Those wearing it remain Chinese.

The People's Republic is considered to be a puritanical and 'anti-erotic' society but the constant factors are its heritage and its men and women. The catalogue of recent changes, that is during the last forty or fifty years, do not contradict this. 'Anything may happen in China,' wrote Lin Yutang, citing a Shanghai court case of 1934 when a nun sued a monk for infidelity. He was expressing his belief not only in the unpredictability of his people but in its unchanging nature, and the same can be said of sexual patterns following the *Great Leap Forward*.

Sex practices during the early years of the Communist Party were very different from today. In Yenan in the nineteen-thirties, where the surviving comrades of the Long March had established themselves, a system of free love was adopted. This was in keeping with the pragmatism of the Chinese who, in the mountains of Shensi and with men outnumbering women by eight to one, encouraged promiscuity under the revolutionary pretext of furthering sexual liberation. If a man and woman desired intercourse, then it concerned no one else. The 'political correctness' of the Yenan period demanded that love-making be regarded in the same way as having 'a drink of water', which became the popular term. One's sexual desires, like one's thirst, were too personal to regulate.

When the Party came to power, however, and had responsibility for a population in 1949 of seven hundred million, 'drink of water' sex seemed not to be the right policy for the tasks ahead. The old feudal system had to be abolished, the flourishing sex commerce in such major ports as Shanghai and Canton had to be stopped, women granted equality and liberated from concubinage and male tyranny, and orderly marriage laws introduced. Most important, however, was the need to control the growth in population and to change the traditional belief that large families gave protection to parents in their old age.

Any study of the sex practices and attitudes of modern China must accept that the principal influence since 1949 has been the policy to control population growth. It may be true that the need to work single-mindedly for a new and better society has diverted the normal sex drive into more productive channels, similarly with the conscription of youthful libido for more important exertions than Yin-Yang battles, but the major reason for the 'less-sex' campaigns has been to reduce the birth rate.

These campaigns have been conducted with a zeal not unlike the moral exhortations of Western churches. A Party song has the following lines: *I am a propagandist / For family planning. / Insist on delayed marriage / And do not waver.* A Party slogan is, simply: *Practice birth control for the Revolution.* In such an atmosphere, the consequences of unwanted pregnancies or of having more than the recommended norm of one child, create even more inhibitions than the usual fear of pregnancy. The mistakes, the carelessness, of the parents incur both the disapproval and penalties of the state.

This contemplative Lotus Position evokes the spirit of Taoist tranquillity. 17th-century pillow book. By kind permission of the British Museum.

'Planned Parenthood' is a programme conducted by labour unions and political organisations, women's federations and student groups. Special committees function at all levels to advise on birth control, sterilization and abortion, to exert pressure for late marriages or even total sexual abstinence, and to fix communal 'targets'. The keeping to target figures is the responsibility of special advisers, usually women, who visit homes to give personal guidance to parents. The importance of the adviser's role is such that her location may be as small as twenty mothers.

Modern China is therefore a society in which the sexual side of marriage, extramarital relations and romantic feelings between Yin and Yang are either ignored, discouraged or prohibited. If there has been a degree of relaxation in the post-Mao society, it is only apparent among those small groups most likely to come into contact with the foreign influences of Western and Japanese visitors. For the great majority, sex remains a relatively joyless function, socially acceptable only between those legally married, the practice of which is best illustrated in such handbooks as *Information on Sex.*

The traditional manuals are no longer published, the illustrated pillow books are regarded as bourgeois pornography, and in their place is the plain instruction book. *Information on Sex* was reissued in a revised publication in 1980 and explicitly states that one should not, ideally, have intercourse before the age of 25, and that one should avoid masturbation because it caused 'physical weakness and nervousness.' The ideal of abstinence for the celibate would be helped if one renounced alcohol and cigarettes, books and entertainment that provoked sexual desire, and if one dressed sensibly. Such dress, in the case of men, meant the wearing of loose underpants since tight briefs 'heated' the genitals. There are no references to *Heaven and Earth Postures* or *Glorious Passion-rousers.*

The old manuals believed in repeated enjoyment of *The Clouds and the Rain* but the new one states: 'After marriage, couples will indulge in intercourse perhaps once or twice a week for the first few months. Later, with increasing familiarity and age, sexual desire declines and it is customary to have intercourse two or three times a month.' The complaints of the Yellow Emperor to his First Minister that the Yin-Yang essences were not flowing through the land as they should, and that this lack of virility meant that the *Laws of Nature* were being flouted, seem even more pertinent five thousand years later. And the greatest of the dragon emperors would be mortified by the advice of modern Party rulers: 'If, after making love during the night, the couple find they are worn out and short of breath, suffer from weak legs and headache, then they are over-indulging. The remedies include abstinence and correct political thinking.'

The remarkable contradictions of a system that seeks to liberate men and women while at the same time imposing such constraints on the most natural of their feelings is summarized in a recent work by Ruth Sidel. She writes: 'In China ... liberation is not interpreted in any way to mean sexual freedom. It is interpreted to mean economic freedom and political freedom, freedom from physical harm, freedom from working like a slave, freedom from one's mother-in-law, and freedom from having ten children, but distinctly not sexual freedom.'

The *Great Leap Forward* is therefore an uneven advance. Social revolution will permit only so much, and nothing that will divert energies and purpose from the main task. Like traditional parents, the rulers believe, correctly, that sexual freedom creates an independence of spirit that will not be so subservient to authority. This is not the only instance of Party thinking coinciding with the old Confucian beliefs. Some of the current puritanism is also based on the ancient concept of Yang suffering at the hands of Yin in the nightly *Flowery Battles*. Feuerwerker, in a study of earlier Chinese novels, writes: 'A man done in by lust, for which the woman is to blame, was a common theme in popular fiction.' Today it is Party policy to discourage men from being

'Variations in love-making distinguish men from animals, the educated man from the ignorant.' Sex Methods by Yeh Tê-hui. Illustration from a 19th-century album. Courtesy of the W.H. & Elizabeth M. Deane collection, University of Sydney Library.

'done in' by lusting wives and concubines and, concurrently, to induce women to come from under the embroidered silk coverlet and direct their passions elsewhere.

A woman factory worker, Shu Ting, in a poem written in 1979, expresses the feelings of the liberated woman:

I am one of your thousand million hearts,
Country of ten million square kilometres.
With your breasts, despite your wounds,
You suckled me, this girl comrade
Who grew up faithfully and fervently.
Now, in my maturity,
I offer my body and passions
For your prosperity and your glory ....
My motherland,
Dear motherland!

Anticipation. Late 18th-century painting. Courtesy private collection, Paris.

The legal framework for the great changes was the formulation of the *Marriage Articles* of 1950. This not only provided the basis for lawful marriage but pronounced the equality of women. The *Marriage Articles* were therefore a powerful instrument of revolution. They began: 'The feudal system of marriage, based on the superiority of man over woman, is abolished. Bigamy, concubinage, child betrothal, interference with the remarriage of widows, and the exaction of money or gifts in arranged marriages, are all prohibited. A marriage can only be contracted when the man has reached 20 years and the woman 18 years.'

The success of the new law, and the remarkable achievement of the equality of the sexes after thousands of years of male superiority, must be related to the puritan nature of the new regime. Old customs and beliefs, from Yin the subservient to Confucian ideas on the misfortune of having a girl child, were more easily swept away when men might suffer penalties for indulging in promiscuity or trying to insist on their traditional authority.

The feudal system is therefore seen as being abolished with the introduction of the *Marriage Articles*. The transition occurred with spectacular suddenness and completeness. After a certain date, a woman's life was no longer restricted to the home or, in rural communities, to labouring in the fields. She had a role in the political cadres, in the administration and the armed forces, and in the 'leap forward' to modernization and industrialization. The 're-education' of Fallen Flowers and other unfortunate females was also her responsibility, and it was claimed that prostitution disappeared 'overnight'.

Occasionally the prosecution of recidivists was over-zealous and a Shanghai newspaper of 1953 reported a case of ten women, two of them pregnant, being punished for soliciting in neighbouring villages. A local 'mass struggle' meeting was held to try the women and, when found guilty, they were bound and exposed to the sun, had needles inserted under their nails and were subjected to other brutal punishments.

Inevitably, there were violations of the laws on marriage, usually for what the *Articles* regarded as 'feudalism', which included such male misdemeanours as 'contempt for women', driving an unhappy wife to suicide and expecting certain traditional privileges for himself. Although arranged marriages were illegal, 'semi-free' marriages, as they were called, between a willing boy and girl introduced by parents, were permitted. Traditional arranged marriages however, were legally regarded as rape, the girl being seen as 'unwilling', and for this the courts inflicted severe sentences. Two such cases were reported in *Chungking Ta Kung-pao* (1951-52). In the first, a widow, Mrs Chung, invited a man, Hung, to lodge at her home with a view to eventually marrying her daughter. The device was so transparent that neighbouring 'women's groups' managed to catch Hung making love to the daughter and reported the matter to the police. Whether the daughter was a consenting partner was unimportant, and Hung received a three-year sentence. Mrs Chung was regarded as more culpable because not only had she been a party to the 'rape' but, in the opinion of the court, she had wanted her daughter to find a husband to insure herself against old age. She received a five-year sentence.

The second case concerned an adopted daughter, Ho Ch'un-yü, who went to live with old school friends, the Wang family. They soon introduced her to Mr Wen. When he proposed marriage, she refused. The Wens and the Wangs then devised a plan to get round legal problems and, unknown to Ch'in-yü, she was registered as Wen's wife. Once this had been done, and in face of persistent persuasion by the families, she felt obliged to resign herself to the situation. A little later, however, she was visited by her father, to whom she told the story, and he angrily called on the local Women's Association to take up the case. The court subsequently sentenced Wen and his daughter to two years for 'arrangement' and 'coercion', Mrs Wang to one year, and one of Chun-yü's old classmates to two months for encouraging her to live with Wen.

The success of the 'instant' equality of women has been accompanied by campaigns to minimize the physical distinctions of the sexes. If people can be seen as comrade workers rather than men and women, their service to the community will be greater. In her work on women in China, Sidel has written: 'The Chinese have eliminated most forms of sexual differentiation. Although there have been variations over the years, currently women's clothing is purely functional, designed to cover and protect, not to delineate or arouse.' But Bernal, on the same subject, suggests that while the outward differences might have been eliminated, a deeper reality is concealed. 'In China, with its unisex clothing, sexual passions run hidden and deep.'

With the more relaxed regime that has followed the Mao period, that is from 1976, evidence is accumulating of the extent to which these passions were hidden. Such manifestations are currently limited to elitist circles and those most exposed to the Western influences that have recently begun to infiltrate into the closed society of the People's Republic. An example of this has been the rehabilitation of the poet Feng Xuefeng (1903-76). Feng was expelled from the Party in 1957 for his 'Rightest' views but some of his poems have now been printed. One, in particular, captures the atmosphere of repression. *Even Though You Can't Stop Work For Me* was published in *Chinese Literature* in March, 1980:

When I stroll by the brook where you are
  washing clothes
Even though you can't stop work for me,
Please raise your stick higher
And pound more vigorously,
For this is a secret sign
That I shall understand.
When I pass under your window,
Please light your lamp.
Though you cannot allow me to stay for
  the night,
Please signal with the lamp;
For this is a secret sign
No others will understand.
When we meet in a crowd,
Though you can hardly greet me,
Please knit your brows
And cast me a tender glance,
For as I am very observant
I can receive your love without others
  noticing it.

If the picturesque wooden bridge to the Bamboo Grove has been demolished by the new political order, the steel and concrete construction that has taken its place is beginning to lose a little of its rigidity. At this early stage, following the uncompromising years of the Mao period, such changes are apparent only in the large cities where women are again being tempted by more feminine dress, fashionable hair styles and cosmetics, and where new hotels filled with foreign businessmen and tourists are creating a fresh variation of the old imperial enclaves. These concentrations of 'foreign devils', with their economic advantages, are now welcomed as friends.

In 1980 certain changes were made to the 1950 *Marriage Articles,* and these provide further evidence of a slight liberalization even if some of the details are contradictory. For example, the need for strict control of the birth rate is as great as ever and, to this end, the permissible marriage age has been raised to 22 for men and 20 for women yet the penalties for exceeding the one-child family are less rigorous. Other inconsistencies are apparent. Marriage between cousins is forbidden and those looking for partners 'of good class background', a still desirable distinction, are accused of 'feudalism'. On the other hand, bourgeois marriage bureaux are now permitted and run by student and Party cadres, an evolution of

the despised old matchmakers and professional go-betweens. Yang and Yin, the Party seems to be admitting, need to complement each other after all. Love for the abstraction of a new social order is not enough.

As the system slowly submits to the human factor, further proof is evident in divorce cases. In the civil courts of Peking in 1980, 40% of cases were concerned with divorce. Of these, half were granted, and Judge Li Cheng said: 'Since marriage is based on mutual affection and freedom, then that freedom must also cover divorce.' This enlightened opinion reflects the greater willingness of people to risk bringing their problems to the courts. Grounds for divorce divided into 15% for infidelity, 12% for maltreatment and 30% for 'constant quarrelling over in-laws and money.'

An anomaly is a stricter law to protect soldiers on duty from being divorced during their absence from the marital home. Too many wives, deciding to make use of their newly liberated status, seized opportunities

Hsueh T'ao, T'ang dynasty courtesan, one of the Hundred Beauties of the period (618-907). 19-century collection.

previously denied them. Military morale suffered as husbands found themselves divorced or feared for their domestic arrangements, and the *Marriage Articles* were accordingly adjusted. Such promiscuous behaviour, however, is untypical and the appraisal by Delia Davin of the Mao period continues to be valid: 'Social attitudes remained extremely puritanical so that for a couple to hold hands in public would be considered ill-mannered. Pre-marital sex, though not theoretically illegal, met with strong social disapproval, and when classed as seduction has occasionally joined adultery in being treated as a crime punishable in the courts.'

The Shanghai Court of the 1950's, perhaps because that region had been the 'Sin City' of China before the liberation, was particularly severe on fornicators and adulterers. Prison sentences and periods in reform camps were common punishments, a severity apparently supported by the public. There was little comradely understanding on the part of a divorced wife who 'expressed her satisfaction that her husband's girl friend (and future wife) must serve eight months.' Adultery was, and is, regarded as a social offence as well as being an example of bourgeois selfishness. The implications of 'undermining another person's family' *(fang-hai chia-t'ing)* are serious matters. There have been public debates on the extent of a women's guilt when she does not know that her lover is married, and a Peking newspaper posed the rhetorical question: 'Should we marry?' This referred to the private torment of a salesman who wanted to marry someone else's wife. 'In asking her to marry me, will not a divorce mean undermining another person's family?' The newspaper *(Kung-jen-jih-pao)* was uncompromising in its verdict. 'To fall in love with a married woman is immoral because her knowledge of that fact can turn her against her husband. This is an example of putting selfish bourgeois happiness before Communist morality and will result in undermining another person's family.'

After the present, comes the future; and the future is already becoming evident. The long history of China has seen a succession of natural disasters, political turmoil and social changes unparalleled elsewhere, but the outcome has always been a return to the traditional character of the people. Past invaders have departed or been absorbed by their subjects, disasters have been accepted stoically, change has been moderated by pragmatism. Does it really suit the people? Is it of them and

for them? These are the questions that must be applied within the present context of the first moderating shifts from revolutionary puritanism.

The morality of the People's Republic in sexual matters is the very opposite of much that is happening today within The Golden Triangle. Large Chinese communities in Taiwan, Hong Kong and Bangkok, following their traditional life patterns, have created societies in which Confucianism, Taoism and Western commercialism, continue to flourish and to permit the existence of 'sex playgrounds' unrivalled in other countries. Lin Yutang has written: 'For the Chinese are a hard-boiled lot. There is no nonsense about them; they do not live in order to die, as the Christians pretend to do, nor do they seek for a Utopia on earth, as many of the seers of the West do. They just want to order this life on earth, which they know to be full of pain and sorrow, so that they may work peaceably, endure nobly, and live happily.'

Love Games. From the novel Su Wo P'ien. *Courtesy of the Library of the University of Indiana, Indiana.*

155

This fatalistic philosophy, though it may seem a somewhat lofty concept when related to the commercialization of sex in the Golden Triangle, is not specious. If the profitable ordering of 'this life on earth' is conducted with the consent of all parties involved, it will hardly seem a reason for guilt. As the continuous traffic of Japanese men to Taiwan and Hong Kong, and of Chinese from Hong Kong to Bangkok and Taiwan, enjoy their 'package tours' or slip through the 'escape hatches' to *Hot Springs,* they are not only indulging in modern permissiveness but returning to a time when man was master. Money, as it has throughout history, can buy almost anything. Even a little of past society.

The style of sex-commerce in this Chinese-dominated region of the world is very different from the red-light districts of Western cities. In place of the brash and the sordid, much of the presentation continues a tradition of subtlety and complexity. Among those who fled from Shanghai when it came under Communist rule were the leading figures of the film and theatre communities, fashion models and aristocratic beauties, as well as the local sex 'barons' and entrepreneurs. The women, with little opportunity to follow their careers, made the most of their one instantly saleable asset, while men, particularly in Hong Kong, quickly prospered at a time when Overseas Chinese communities were enjoying the beginning of the industrial boom.

Precious Moments in the Fair Field. K'ang-hsi (1662-1722). A painting on silk from the C.T. Loo collection.

From the modest dance halls of Hong Kong and Taiwan, with their exotic sense of occasion and hostesses trained in oriental social graces as well as in the bed arts, to luxury palaces for the wealthy, the need to satisfy traditional male fantasies is paramount. To be obedient and submissive, bowing to male superiority, is as profitable for the Fallen Flowers of today as it was in the past. To protect the male from 'losing face' is also improtant. The 'escape hatch' tours describe the hostesses as 'guides' or 'interpreters', visits to temples and museums give the occasions respectability, while the description 'business trip' covers everthing. The expensive game of make-believe includes 'temporary wives' with luxurious domestic arrangements, and a variety of massage parlours where a good masseuse treats every customer as her Lord Yang.

There is also a demand for western women, the traditional contempt for foreign females giving way not only to curiosity but, in this modern age, to a greater self-confidence with the alien. Nevertheless, the opinion in *The Diary of Tseng Kuo-Ting* (Peking, 1932) is still shared by many Chinese men: 'For us the western woman is extremely voluptuous. She has large limbs and large breasts, her eyes are of many colours and round, and her laughter is uninhibited and free. Every time a western female laughs, I imagine it is an invitation to the bedchamber. But the most obvious difference from our own women is the well-covered body. One does not have to treat her too gently, one does not have in one's arms a fragile, delicate-boned doll. When the European female beckons with those large eyes, when her face lights up with a brazenness that a Chinese woman's face simply cannot match, then which of us men can remain indifferent to such blatant sexuality? There is also the glory of her hair, the range of colours, the different textures, straight and curly, wavy and fluffy. This, too, is a most exciting characteristic.

'But there are two features of western women that can hardly gain favour with the Chinese male. The rawness of her odours are exactly as one would expect from 'raw' barbarians, and no amount of soap or scent can change this. Secondly, the pubic hair of many western women — how coarse it seems after the Chinese female. It reminds one of riding camels and donkeys bareback, rough and wiry, and sometimes extending in a fuzz towards navel or knees.'

The two extremes of sexual behaviour, that practiced in the People's Republic and by the sex trade of the Golden Triangle, now co-exist, though in different societies. One has been imposed by the Party and the state while the other is a reflection of the transient capitalist market conditions of supply and demand. Has nothing, then, from the past endured? One must return, again, to the human factor and what is essentially Chinese, the character that has evolved over thousands of years. Confucius proclaimed: 'Truth does not depart from human nature. If what is regarded as truth departs from human nature, it may not be regarded as truth.' Sex is an aspect of that truth. In neither one society nor the other is it being true to itself.

And yet, having stated that, truth is not totally isolated from circumstances and change, and one must consider the form that sexual behaviour will take when the people of China can again exercise freedom in their personal lives. There can be no going back to the colourful, and frequently cruel, excesses of the past, while the sex commerce thriving among the Overseas Chinese is part of the frenetic pursuit of material wealth among people becoming increasingly remote from their heritage and

Lovers. Their bewildered expressions suggest that they have seen a future society that no longer enjoys the Bedchamber Arts. 19th-century. Courtesy of the Mitchell Library, Sydney.

their culture. But the Taoist side of the old dualism and which, through the ages, encouraged the joyful bedchamber arts, still unobtrusively survives. The 'truth' of which Confucius wrote, ironically for such a disciplinarian, implies natural desires, erotic playfulness and self-expression.

One of the characters of a Li Yü novel wrote the following quatrain. From the Bamboo Grove of Lord Yang and Lady Yin to the new society of the People's Republic, the meaning will be understood:

So be it, throw aside the rough-sack matting
Of self-denial in this world,
And for your prayer mat take flesh
As the place for your devotions.

BIBLIOGRAPHY   ANCILLON-SAMBER: *Eunuchism,* ed.1718.

ANDERSON, A.: *Lord Macartney's Embassy to China,* London, 1795.

Asia Major (New Series) Vol.7, 1959.

BAUDIER, M.: *History of the Court of the King of China* (translated from the French), 1682.

BACKHOUSE, Sir E.T. & BLAND, John O.P.: *China Under the Empress Dowager,* 1910.

BERNAL, M.: *North Vietnam and China: Reflection of a visit.* 1971.

BEWICKE, Alicia E. Nevia: *Li Hung-Chang — His Life and Times,* Cassell, 1903. *Intimate China,* Hutchinson, 1899. *A Marriage in China,* White, 1896. *Guide to Peking,* Tientsin Pr. 1904. *The Land of Blue Gowns,* Unwin, 1902

BLOODWORTH, D.: *Chinese Looking Glass,* Penguin, 1969.

BOXER, C.R.: *South China in the Sixteenth Century,* London, 1953.

CHANG, Ching-Sheng: *Sex Histories,* Peking, 1927.

DAVIN, D.: *Woman-Work,* Clarendon Press, 1976.

DAVIS, Sir John.: *The Shadows in the Water, Twin Sisters, The Three Dedicated Chambers,* 1822. *The Sorrow of Han, Fortunate Union,* 1829, (translations of originals by Li Yü).

DOOLITTLE, J.: *Social Life of the Chinese,* Sampson Low, 1868.

EDWARD, E.D.: *Dragon Book,* Hodge, 1936. *T'ang Tai Ts'ung Shu* (prose literature of the Tang period), Hodge, 1948.

FITZGERALD, G.P.: *China, a short cultural history,* Cresset Press, 1950. *Empress Wu,* Cresset Press, 1956. *Barbarian Beds,* Cresset Press, 1956.

GILLES, H.A.: *Gems of Chinese Literature,* London, 1884. *Chinese Bibliographical Dictionary,* 1898, *Strange Stories from a Chinese Studio,* 1909. *Quips from a Chinese Jest Book,* 1925.

DE GROOT, J.J.M.: *Religious Systems of China,* Leyden, 1892

VAN GULIK, R.H.: *Sexual Life in Ancient China,* E.J. Brill, 1961.

HALLIDAY, M.A.K.: *Secret History of the Mongols,* 1959.

HUA, Chien Chi: *Chinese Courtship,* P.P. Thoms, London, 1824. *The Flowery Scroll,* P.P. Thoms, London, 1868.

HUMANA, C.: *The Keeper of the Bed,* London, 1973.

HUMMEL, A.W.: *Eminent Chinese of the Ch'ing Period,* 1943.

IMBERT, H.: *La Sardanopale Chinois,* Paris, 1875.

KU, Hung-Ming.: *Discourses and Sayings of Confucius,* 1898.

LEVY, Howard S.: *Harem Favourites,* 1958. *Biography of Huang Ch'ao Sinologia,* 1955.

LIN, Yutang: *My Country and My People,* Heinemann, 1936.

LLEWELLYN, Bernard: *Friends of China Road,* London 1946. *China's Courts and Concubines,* London, 1956.

LOCKHART, J.H.S.: *Chinese Quotes,* Hong Kong, 1893. *Chiu Chun,* 1903.

MURRAY, H.: *Travels of Marco Polo,* New York, 1845.

MOGRIDGE, G.: *Points and Pickings of Information about China,* London.

MARCO POLO: *Viaggi di Marco Polo,* Venezia, 1847.

PAYNE, Robert: *White Pony,* Unwin, 1949.

Marriage Law of Communist China, Peking, 1950.

MACGOWAN: *Chinese Folklore,* North China Daily News & Herald, 1910.

MALONE, C.B.: *History of the Peking Summer Palace,* 1934.

NEEDHAM, Joseph: *Science and Civilization in China,* Cambridge University Press, 1954.

NORDENSKIOLD, N.A.E.: *Le Livre de Marco Polo,* Stockholm, 1882.

SCHLEGAL, Gustave: *Histoire de la Prostitution en Chine,* 1886.

SIDEL, R.: *Women and Child Care in China,* New York, 1972.

SMEDLEY, A.: *Portraits of Chinese Women in Revolution,* New York, 1976.

STAUNTON, G.L.: *Embassy to the Emperor of China,* London, 1797.

STEELE, J.: *I-Li* (Book of Etiquette and Ceremonial), translated from the Chinese, New York, 1917.

STENT, Carter G.: *Fanning the Grave,* Shanghai, 1873. *Chinesische Eunuchen,* Leipzig, 1879.

VARE, Daniele: *The Last of the Empresses,* John Murray, 1936. *The Gate of Happy Sparrows,* Methuen, 1937.

WALEY, Arthur: *Preface to Dream of the Red Chamber.*

WANG, Chi-Chen: *Traditional Chinese Tales,* Columbia Univ. Press, 1944.

WANG, Hsiang-Chen: *Famous Chinese Stories* (retold by Lin Yutang), Heinemann, 1953.

WANG, Shih Fu: *The Romance of the Western Chamber,* Methuen, 1935.

WANG, Tzu-Hsin: *Le Divorce en Chine,* Paris, 1932.

WIEGER, Leon: *Folklore Chinois,* Hsien-Hsien Press, 1909.

WOLF and WITKE: *Women in Chinese Society,* California, 1975.

WOLF, M.: *Women and the Family in Rural Taiwan,* California, 1972.

WU, Francis: *Classical Chinese Beauties,* Hong Kong, 1951.

YANG, Ping Yu: *Love Story of a Maiden of Cathay,* New York, 1911.

YANG, Chu: *Garden of Pleasure,* Wisdom of the East Series, 1912.

Chinese Sources
(consulted in the original)

Chang-Shen-Tien (Palace of Eternal Youth), Peking, 1955.

Ch'a-Hsiang-Shih Szu-Ch'ao by Hsu Ta-Ch'o (Yuan Dynasty).

Chu-Ling-Yeh-Shih (Unedited History from the Bamboo Garden) Anon, Ming Dynasty.

Hsiu-T'a-Yeh-Shih, by Lu T'ien-Cheng (1580-1620).

Chao-Yang-Ch'u-Shih, published 1621.

Ch'ien Chin-Fang, by Sun Szu-Mo (Tang Dynasty).

Ch'ing-Lou-chi (Records of the Green Bowers), by Huang (Yuan Dynasty).

Ch'in-Huai-Shih-Nu-Piao (Survey of the Ladies and Young Gentlemen of Chin-Huai) by Ts'ao Ta-Chang (Ming Dynasty).

Unedited Panorama of the History of the Ch'ing Dynasty, Shanghai, 1921.

Chin-P'ing-Mei, by Wang Shih-cheng, (Ming Dynasty).

Chin-Ku-Ch'i-Kuan (Strange Happenings, Ancient & Modern) Ming Dynasty.

Cho-Keng-Lu (Miscellaneous Records) by T'ao Tsung (Yuan Dynasty).

Chien-Ching-Yao-Fang (Recipes Worth a Thousand Pieces of Gold).

Fang-Nei-Pu-Yi (Nourishments for the Bedchamber), by Sun Szu-Mo (60I-682).

Fou-Sheng-Liu-Chi (Jottings of a Floating Life), by Shen Fu (1763-1820).

Han-Wu-Ti-Nei-Chuan (Private Biography of Emperor Wu of the Han Dynasty), ascribed to Pan-Ku (A.D. 32-92).

Jou-Pu T'uan, novel by Li Yü (1611-80).

Ou-Chi, Essays by Li Yü.

Ko-Lien-Hua-Ying (Shadows behind the Curtains) Ming Dynasty novel.

Pao-P'u Tzu, by Ko Hung (A.D.300).

Shen-Nu-Chuan (Biography of Fairies and Goddesses), by Sun Wei.

Pan-Ch'iao-Tsa-Chi (Reminiscences of Beautiful and Accomplished Girls), by Yu Huai (1616-96).

Yen-Tu-Chi- P'in (High Class Prostitutes of the Capital) by Ts'ao Ta-Ching (circa. 1570).

Ching-An-Ts'ung-Shu (Collection of the works of Yeh-Te'-Hui, 1864-1927), Shanghai, 1914. Including: *Su-Nu-Ching, Su-Nu-Fang, Yu-Fang-Pi-Chueh, Tung-Hsuan-Tzu.*

Shih-ching (Book of Odes), edited by Confucius (Chou Dynasty).

Ta-yeh-Shih-i-chih, by Li Ta-t'ien (631-725).

Mi-lou-chi, Anonymous Tang author.

Chao-hou-I-shih (Sung Dynasty).

Yeh-ho-yuan-chi (Summer Palace Tales), Shanghai, 1915.

Shan-Ku-shih, by Ssu-ma Ts'ien (140-80).

Chih-pin-chung-shu, by Wu Khiu (twelfth-century.).

I-hsueh-ching, by Li Shi-Chen (Fourteenth-century).

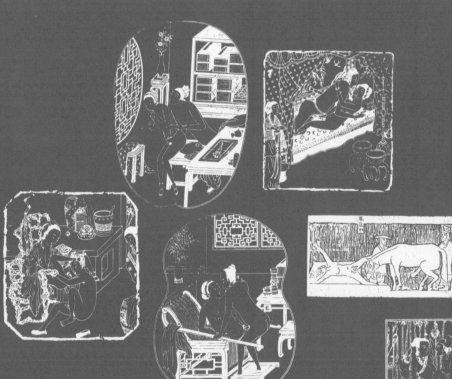